Stay Ahead of the Game

GENERATION LOSER

Stay Ahead of the Game

GENERATION LOSER

Arlindo Fernandes

STAY AHEAD OF THE GAME
GENERATION LOSER

iUniverse books may be ordered through booksellers or by contacting:

iUniverse
1663 Liberty Drive
Bloomington, IN 47403
www.iuniverse.com
1-800-Authors (1-800-288-4677)

Because of the dynamic nature of the Internet, any web addresses or links contained in this book may have changed since publication and may no longer be valid. The views expressed in this work are solely those of the author and do not necessarily reflect the views of the publisher, and the publisher hereby disclaims any responsibility for them.

Any people depicted in stock imagery provided by Getty Images are models, and such images are being used for illustrative purposes only.
Certain stock imagery © Getty Images.

ISBN: 978-1-5320-5645-1 (sc)
ISBN: 978-1-5320-5644-4 (e)

Library of Congress Control Number: 2018909947

Print information available on the last page.

iUniverse rev. date: 09/11/2018

Contents

Introduction

As we find ourselves consumed by the mysterious process of turning ourselves into something extraordinarily amazing, we have no time to reflect on our responsibilities or to devote time to the tasks that await us. This process brings complicated internal chaos, strange to our innocence, as well as lots of enjoyment, in which we indulge without reserve or prejudice, leaving little time for something else. The little we know is more than enough for us to understand that we are very special. We are not certain why we are special, but that doesn't matter, because it only increases the excitement. We realize that as we grow older, the fun decreases—it's reduced in duration and pleasure. For that reason, we don't want to grow up. On the other hand, we see endless possibilities pushing our desires forward. For that, we can't wait to become grown-ups so that we can experiment with the new areas of excitement.

Then we look back and don't believe how quickly we got here. We feel like we not only evolved fast and developed in a rush but also grew overnight to young men and women, ready to embrace the journey. We understand now that the journey can be challenging and that our development hides bitterness behind the excitement, killing some of the enthusiasm and throwing us into undesirable turns and spins that may leave us frustrated and disoriented. Somehow, the developmental phenomenon of life is confusing and increases our carelessness, which, unfortunately, has the power to turn us into something we are not—losers—unless our determination puts up a fight. In the end, however, we are still young and beautiful, life is fun and interesting, and we aren't concerned about worries and distractions. There's no need to spoil the fun with drama and the anticipation of calamities, which could be nothing more than a simple product of our imaginations.

It is good to engage in, worship, and celebrate life to the fullest. In the meantime, it's mandatory to pay attention to the responsibilities attached to the fun, joy, and amusement, without which life would be a boring passage from one dull moment to another. Fortunately, that tiny, thick, whitish liquid that has shown how extraordinary life can be still shines brighter in each new generation. And for that, we are so grateful. At the same time, we cannot hide the pain, anguish, and suffering anymore. We have run out of inspiration, strength, and endurance to go on strong. We go to bed with worries, concerns, and fears; we float through nightmares and wake up to face the monsters that make our lives more daunting that they were in our dreams.

Some days we feel threatened by our own existence, and other days we can't figure out the unwinding of events under our feet that extends to all of humanity and beyond. The mystery of the mysteries is simply too hard for our imaginations. Many who have seen what's to see—both for the young and powerful and the older generation—say that this current generation is the generation of losers, and there's a clear sign of the beginning of the decline of power and distinction in a steep dive to gloom and doom. The young are our saviors, except our hopes could slip into the deeper darkness of the abyss.

Whether or not this conclusion is fact, it is discouraging, insulting to hear, and hard to digest. Losers belong to the past that was dominated by plagues, diseases, and world wars and other barbaric acts and devilish behaviors. The twenty-first century is not a saint or a purified soul, spreading its wings of love, care, and benevolence to humanity, nor is it disease-free. Indeed, it's much the opposite, carrying hereditary stains that are worsened not only by shadows of the devil blocking our intelligence but also by our bad behaviors, neglect, and mistakes and the natural degradation of things and creations. Yet we come out of all fights and tragedies as the heroes that we are. We believe that the young and powerful have not forgotten that they are winners at birth for their continuity and difference and that they have not forgotten that, as Voltaire said, "With great power comes great responsibility."

We continue our journey with faith that they'll catch and investigate our adversaries and take the necessary measures to ensure that such power, instead of hypnotizing them into losers, will boost their drive to become outstanding winners who continuously stay ahead of the game. They will find the poisoned roots and the contaminated branches that cause trouble and then restore the beauty to the tree. We also want to remind them that the challenges are great but they fear nothing. Even though they aren't veterans of life, they should fear nothing. We will play together, and together we'll make the game even more interesting. They are, after all, the greater power.

With greater power comes greater responsibility.

1

The Game Continues

THE END OF A GAME is the opportunity to start another. Scientists believe that after we are no more, we embark on a new journey. Whether six feet under, at the bottom of an ocean, laid in a sarcophagus, sitting in a museum, or resting in a jar in the living room, we are in a different game but still playing. At six feet under, or at the bottom of an ocean, we decompose to give way to new lives and serve the world in different ways. On the opposite aisle, organized religion, in general, believes that when we are no more, our souls leave our bodies to begin the infinite journey in hell or heaven, the eternal places for the condemned and blessed souls, respectively. Some souls will make a temporary stay in paradise and then proceed to heaven. Regardless of the philosophy by which you live, the end of the game is something over which we don't have much control; therefore, it deserves less of our attention. Yet it should serve as an inspiration to do well and to continue to win the games of life, over which we can have the total control.

During our three most important phases of life—childhood, adulthood, and old age—we'll face different kinds of games. Some of them are completely new; others are an extension of the games we have been playing. Luckily, for each phase we have better cards, and our knowledge is wiser and broader. The downside is that the games become more complicated, the players are the worst of the jerks, and consequences for losing are more devastating.

While some games of life are easy to dominate, others are not. Our odds of winning any game are decided by how well we master it and how determined we are to dominate. By staying ahead of the game, we make the odds look good, but then the game goes through unforeseen changes, leaving us stunning and scratching our heads. Even the experts—the senior citizens, who thought they had seen it all before—cannot understand the rapid (and not always good) changes. The millennials, while the main drivers of such changes, are themselves caught up in a reality of life that is not forgiving; nothing is clear-cut. It is hard enough to dominate in a game that's simple, friendly, and transparent; never mind sitting at a table where the players look at one another with hidden anger and disdain. The scary part is that as the game goes on, it brings familiar yet distorted faces, as well as ugly new faces covered by scary masks. The ugly new faces are slick cheaters who pull all kinds of tricks to distort the game and confuse the players. The game, facing headwinds from three fronts—greed, nature, and technology—is no longer the fair-and-square game where everybody's a winner. The game now is all about winner takes all. And the dealer wants to give out just enough coins to keep the players hypnotized and engaged.

It shouldn't be a surprise that the big companies want to make as many millions as possible in profit as fast as possible and done as inexpensively as possible. The employees, who are treated as money generators, are given just enough fuel to keep the motor going. What they take home from one job is not enough to cover the basic expenses, never mind attending to wish intruders. A second job becomes mandatory, yet it's under the same conditions and causes almost the same misery. There's no time left for anything else. When you dodge death and get a community college diploma while you're holding full-time and part-time jobs, you may find yourself stuck with what you have because your employer has no room for you to climb the company's ladder. Unless you can make an extraordinary amount of money for the company, your diploma means nothing to them.

Nature has been harsh on us for a variety of reasons. One reason is global warming. Whether or not you believe it, this phenomenon is real and is happening. Agriculture—the main supplier of food—has been hit with devastating and more frequent droughts; harsh, freezing temperatures; and excessive rain.

Technology has flipped social norms and blanketed it globally with the new standard—social media. The little time that our crazy, busy lives leave for us is snatched by the powerful, hypnotizing forces of the online world, where we must read, post, and show selfies, or we don't count. Before we know it, it's too late to cook, so we order pizza, a delicious killer meal, for dinner. We check out a couple of stupid videos on YouTube that are supposed to be funny, and then "Damn it; two in the morning!" As a consequence, we wake up late and face a frustrating day that begins with traffic jams on our commute. It continues in a hectic day at work, where we blame all the coworkers, supervisors, and managers for suddenly becoming such assholes, while in reality, we are the ones who need more sleep. And while we're driving back home, we fight the temptation to post online, "OMG! You cannot believe how fucked up my day was!" Once back home, we have the temptation of doing the same thing we did the night before.

It wouldn't be fair to let the government—the major players onstage and behind the scenes—go free. Every little country wants to be a nuclear power, and the big countries on top want to stay on top, crushing the ones climbing the steps. Fallen empires that came back from the dead shout that the world better listen—or else. Politicians, dazed and confused, act ever so stupid, encouraging people to vote for the eccentrics out of desperation. Greed, human nature, and technology, coupled with government's idiocy, by no means make the lives of ordinary people smooth sailing from one port to another. On the contrary, they cause anger and frustration, as the captain lands us in jail for shaking off a frustration or leaves us at a hospital as victims of a drug overdoses when we tried to forget an unbearable traumatic situation. Either scenario is an ugly, low card in our hands.

On top of these powerful headwinds, we must deal with the side winds blowing us off course. Friendships are untrustworthy, relationships are troublesome, brotherhood is cursed, and homes are a miniature battlefield. Wherever we are, wherever we go, there's something to disgust us. Indeed, all the games of the past were full of surprises and disappointment. Such surprises sometimes might have been the fault of the players, most of the times due to circumstances out of their control, and a few times the combination of both. It's a shame that the millennial generation is cursed by all three. In the same way that the players of the past beat the odds and had outstanding victories, which we still cherish, and paved the way for our success, we can take certain measures and continue to win—to stop being losers. Determination and perseverance are powerful cards, and you bet we are going to use them. We are going to not only stay ahead of the game but also make sure the game continues—and with better characters.

Millennials, we would like it very much if you would stand up for what you believe in and make us proud.

Millennials and all, there's not much we can do to change the way the world behaves, nor can we stop it from spinning crazily, but we can change our philosophy and adapt to what surrounds us. We have goals to achieve and dreams to turn into reality. The game continues and so does our power to dominate the games.

2

Who Are You Now?

SOMETHING MYSTERIOUSLY COMPLEX BEGINS VERY small and evolves into something extraordinarily amazing. Life is a complex journey that begins with insemination and ends with death. Three critical ingredients are part of this complex process and exciting journey: heredity, a socioeconomic factor, and the environment.

Unfortunately, many of us don't have the best of human genetics. This is not to say that we aren't still big winners, which indeed we'll forever be, but that deficiency makes our journey harder. Our bad temperaments interfere with our ability to deal with hostile situations, and more often than not, we are the cause, not the consequence, of hostility. We could find ourselves on many troublesome roads simply because we became less tolerant of situations that require a cold-blooded reaction. Or we could've inherited a variety of cancerous cells, some of which are active and others that are on our radar. This should be a reminder that it's our obligation to constantly analyze the happenings within our close and distant relatives so we can predict our odds of something unpleasant coming our way and prepare for it or stop its first move, so who we are now is not worsened by heredity.

If your parents were very poor, you lacked a wealthy childhood experience. You possibly were hurt in your learning ability and many other skills. You could have had a bad temperament, a criminal record a mile long, social integration difficulties, and so on. You could have quit school at age sixteen to become a mom, or maybe at age forty-three you are living in your mom's basement—all as a result of your growing up in poverty.

If you are living in a refugee camp because your country is torn apart by senseless wars and dictatorship, or you are battling illnesses caused by air pollution and water contamination, then reminding you of human greatness is probably an insult to your intelligence. You see yourself now as a cursed loser, boxed in and without any possibility for any prosperity or greatness. And that's understandable.

On the other side of the river, where the grass is green year-round, your family has paved the way for your success. You are now an upgrade of something distinctive. The garden turned out to be rosier and prettier than you imagined. You are an invincible beast, a king of all jungles. You are empowered to make miracles. That's so desirable!

Regardless of how frail or strong our genetics are, how poor or wealthy our families are, or how sickening or sanitized our surroundings are, we have elevated our chances of success astronomically. We have reached outstanding achievements individually and collectively. And the millennials are the truly gifted ones. We are the lucky ones, but they are the ones who got the jackpot. As a millennial, whoever you are, you have all it takes to transform yourself into your desire. One of the greatest tools for that is education, of which there is easy access, twenty-four/seven. We have yet to value and respect the power of education in transforming our power into outstanding potential, as well as in molding our personalities to the best they can be, regardless of what our family trees gifted us during our insemination marathon.

Education accessibility, combined with other empowering factors, has changed our lives immensely and played an important role in making us who we are now—the greatest of all. Always remind yourself that whoever you are, you are who you are, anywhere you are. You might see yourself as a loser. People may never stop calling you a loser who does not deserve any piece of the pie. You may be despicable and destitute, but you are a winner from the very beginning—in your house, at your friend's house, at the mall, in the United States, Russia, Ethiopia, or Kenya. You are destined to reach greater heights and take many first-place trophies. You just need to fight the negative forces that turn you into a loser, even when you win.

On a hot summer day in Lisbon, Portugal, a dark-blue pickup truck pulled into the TJ Auto Sales lot. Antonio got up from his chair and walked out to greet the customer. As he approached him, he concluded that both the driver and his truck were in rough shape. The man's Chevy was beat up and consumed by rust. The man, about six foot three and with a strong build, hadn't shaved in months and didn't seem to care. His arms—uncovered, as his sleeves were rolled to the elbow, showed signs of many days of sun exposure. His worn-out faded jeans, ripped at the knee, and his dirty work boots indicated almost certainly that he was a farmer. And his hunched back and his insecure, short strides was an indication of a back injury or wear and tear on his body due to hard labor in the fields.

Antonio extended his arm, offering a handshake, to which the customer responded in kind.

"How are you today my friend?" Antonio asked.

"I have seen better days," the farmer responded.

"I hear you! How can I help you today?"

"I came here to take a look at the Tundra."

"The pickup?" Antonio knew it was the Tundra; he just wanted to keep the conversation going to put the customer at ease. "For you?"

"Yes, for me. My old vehicle has already paid her dues. Time for a long vacation." The customer used a funny metaphor for his pickup truck but showed no humor.

"Yeah, I believe you're right. Well, you've come to the right place."

"I hope so."

The previous Sunday, this customer had taken a detailed look at a few dealerships and concluded that the Tundra at TJ Auto Sales was the best deal. As he was looking around, as if he'd never seen the 2006 Tundra before, and pretended not to notice the price tag of $6,795. He asked Antonio, "How much is she?"

Antonio couldn't believe the customer's question—the price was clearly displayed—but he played along without answering the question. "Why don't you take her for a ride? We can talk when you come back."

Despite the fact that this customer was acting unusual, Antonio, in his heart, had already sold the car to this customer, whom he had judged as a hardworking farmer. In fact, the more he looked at the man, the more his heart broke for him. This customer reminded Antonio of his old man, who was a hard worker who never complained a day in his life as he supported a family of seven. Antonio also understood the sacrifice, as he was raising three teenage daughters. He was going to surprise this customer.

Ten minutes passed, and the customer returned with the hope of sealing the deal.

"So how do you like her?" Antonio asked as he led the man into the office. "Take a seat." Antonio pointed to a chair in front of his desk.

"I like her a lot," the customer answered without enthusiasm.

Antonio had a hard time reading this customer. "Would you like to take her home with you?" he asked, looking straight into the customer's eyes.

"I would. The price is the problem."

"How good is your credit?"

"I don't believe in that nonsense. It is all bullshit. I am a cash man. No gimmicks. All clean."

"I respect that! Well," he said, adjusting himself on the chair, "I ran some numbers, but I couldn't find much room to play. Still, I think you'll like my offer. I'll let you have her for sixty-five hundred. And I'll fix everything to make sure this truck lasts forever."

Antonio was counting on the customer's satisfaction. Instead, he got a question.

"Is that the best you can do?" the customer asked with his eyes glued to Antonio's eyes.

"Sorry to say, yes. After I fix everything, I might lose money on this deal. But I think I'll live. I want to help you."

After a brief pause, the farmer accepted the offer. "It's a deal."

"That's a good deal! For you, of course! Not for me."

"I appreciate it."

Antonio was waiting for a smile or any sign of happiness, but there wasn't any.

A couple of days later, the customer returned to TJ Auto Sales to seal the deal. On that day his personality was even more saggy, and he seemed concerned. He sat down in a chair in front of Antonio's desk.

"You look worried. Is everything alright?" Antonio asked.

"I have a small problem. I thought I had enough in my bank account, but I came out five hundred dollars short. Do you think you can drop the price to six grand?"

Antonio leaned back in the chair. Then he sat up straight, pushed himself closer to the desk, and looked the customer in the eyes. He couldn't see any sign of lies. He tapped on the table with a pen he was holding loosely between his two fingers, hoping for a quick solution to this dilemma. To sell the Tundra for $6,000 would be a bad deal. On the other hand, he would feel bad letting the frail man go somewhere else to look for a truck.

"Tell you what," Antonio said. "You look like a decent, hardworking man. I am making no profit on this deal, but I'll let you have it for six grand."

And for the first time, he saw a bright smile—at least as much as was visible behind the customer's full beard. Antonio was counting on some sign of happiness but not to that extent, especially from this customer. And he was about to be shocked when he found out why.

The customer handed over a check in the amount of $6,500, the smile still shining, and said, "You owe me money."

Antonio grabbed the check and looked at it in disbelief. He stared at the man for a few seconds, saying nothing at all. Then he broke the silence. "Son of a bitch! You're right. I owe you five hundred dollars!" Fighting hard to keep his professional composure and to show he was still in control, despite that this had made his blood boil and his looking for an escape, he said, "I could refuse to finalize this deal. I can have my mechanic screw up your truck and give you headaches after the warranty expires. I can make your life a living hell in many ways. But I am not like you. Honestly, you broke my heart. But this deal is just another loss, except in a fucked-up way!" Antonio laughed. "I am not even mad at you. You are an old man of apparently no integrity. I am still going to fix whatever needs to be fixed on the truck. And I wish you good luck."

Where I come from, it would be taboo to say that this customer wouldn't enjoy his Tundra. I believe that this man was a sick person who clearly needed help. Whether he was born sick or became sick, he was despicable in his dealing with Antonio.

When we allow the demons to take over our souls, we become despicable human beings whose worthless personalities are empty of integrity—complete losers. When this occurs, we should seek help.

A broader look at who we are now gives us a beautiful picture. We are the bridge by which human greatness crosses over into a new dimension. This transitional process of human only to human machine and robot cooperation is a task almost entirely for the millennials. Interplanetary exploration and colonization are our big dreams set forth, and it's their obligation to turn them into reality. The success or failure of this mission lies on the millennials' shoulders, arms, and legs. And the light for all beacons must come from their sight.

Millennials, you are now the North Star. It is your time to shine. Make us proud!

3

Friends

"CAN'T LIVE WITH THEM; CAN'T live without them." This seems to fit very well with regard to friends. The passing of time makes this philosophy stand out even more. Some reasons for that are blamed on stupidity and circumstances out of our control. And a small part—or the biggest part—of the blame is our lack of understanding of what a friend is supposed to be. It's not as easy as it sounds, so let's talk about some of the bad guys of friendships, starting with the feeling of being left out—the chill of silence.

The Chill of Silence

We are taught from a very young age to share with our brothers and sisters, to be polite, to be respectful of our elders, and to always help those in need. These principles, instilled in our minds and souls, go everywhere we go, and they evolve with us too. As we grow, we develop an appreciation for our good deeds—when we help Dad wash and vacuum the car, we want a dollar or two; when we help our neighbor mow the lawn and clean the yard, we want some cash or a show of appreciation. And if we allow a driver to pull ahead of us, he or she had better wave at us, honk the horn, or flash high beam at us.

My son Carlos was cold to his brother Claudio because Claudio almost never called him and didn't return Carlos's calls. I waited until both were home visiting to bring the issue back to life so I could hear both sides of the story. My findings were that both were simultaneously right and wrong. I explained the basis of my findings, and Carlos left the "courtroom" angry about the whole ordeal, unsatisfied with the verdict, and (probably) silently cursing the judge. But I know I was impartial and fair.

Even in old age, we hear about brothers and sisters complaining, such as, "I am the one who calls all the time. If I don't call, she doesn't call, so forget it." When our friends give us their phone numbers, we call once or twice and wait for them to call us too. If they don't, we call no more.

This instinct-driven human behavior is alive and well in friendships. No one can escape it. The chill of silence spreads its wings even farther up to the area of bragging. When our friends aren't as warm as we think they should be, we brag about the favors we have done and the sacrifices we have made for them. We mention things they wouldn't have gotten without our help, dreams they turned into reality thanks to us, and on and on. We simply cannot understand their lack of appreciation.

While this is all true and well deserved, it's not a wise attitude for the following reasons:

Hypocrisy. We think of ourselves as perfectly flawless human beings. If someone has chosen us or accepted our "friend request," it must be that we are awesome, special, and exceptional, but we could be equally flawed or even greatly more imperfect than those we are accusing of being bad friends.

Bragger's corner syndrome. Every time you make remarks about what your friends have, and you mention yourself as the main actor, you exhibit bragger's corner syndrome. People don't like to hear about favors done for them. It sounds like a reminder of failures and desperation. Once your friend hears your comments, the friendship between the two of you might begin to cool off. When your friends chose to accept your friendship and favors, they lost the opportunity to accept friendship and favors of other friends who might have been better friends than you. By their accepting your friendship, you could have robbed them of the opportunity to reach many great achievements. Almost everybody suffers from bragger's corner syndrome. The symptoms begin with the chill of silence, and it progresses to hatred.

Misconception. You should never expect your friends to be there for you, day and night, rain or shine. Friends are for spiritual and emotional support, as much as their situations allow, not to be your partner in crime. In fact, the less you expect from your friends, the more friends will come to your rescue. And to better serve yourself, be a friend who *is* there for his friends, day and night, rain or shine, unconditionally.

Opportunists and Two-Faced Friends

Opportunists are the worst kind of friends. Every time we trust them, a nasty surprise is on the way. They never get tired of taking advantages of our friendship and loyalty. And their two-faced behavior, sooner or later, will crush our loyalty to death. Let's read a couple of stories.

Alfonso, a long-time friend of mine, is wise, caring, and unbelievably supportive. One day we were talking about old friends we hadn't seen for a long time, and he took the opportunity to lay out his new approach to friends, especially the opportunistic ones.

"You know me, Arlindo. I am always happy to help people, but I don't care about friends like I did before. I can't do it anymore! My back cannot take it! Some friends are bad and have no shame. They'd borrow money from me and then come up with thousands of excuses not to pay me back. When they needed to go somewhere, I'd be the first one they'd call. But when I needed help with something, they wouldn't have time. Look, I'll always help you because you are a real friend. But believe me, man, these days you need to put yourself first and be tough with dogs who pretend to be your friends."

"I know what you mean and couldn't agree more."

A friend and coworker once borrowed my car to pick up his girlfriend at work because his car wouldn't start. Three weeks later, a better friend told me that my friend's car was fine.

In the early '90s, I was determined to form a band. I had taken enough guitar lessons and had practiced more than enough. A friend introduced me to his friend, who also wanted to form a band. About three months after our first acquaintance, we did just that. We had agreed, unanimously, on the band members' responsibilities, according to their individual skills and grit. Any issues would be resolved in our monthly meetings. We were serious, determined, and moving fast. Then an internal conflict sparked. Some members talked trash behind others' backs. The two-faced character drove our band to extinction before it had hatched.

These stories are not strong examples where opportunists and two-faced friends' actions brought drastic consequences, but I am sure you know of cases where a friendship ended in ugliness. I don't know which is worse—two-faced friends or opportunistic friends—but I know that both are bad and can bruise or kill friendships. And to avoid drama, once you discover the true colors of your friends, be prepared for their sucker punches and their swinging behind your back so you're not shocked when they hit you. If it results on your living without friends, so be it.

Rather Alone Than in Bad Company

I was raised by wise, conservative grandparents, and philosophical phrases like "Rather alone than in a bad company; be the best friend of all your friends" frequently rang in my ears. Had I been raised by my mom and dad, I would have heard the same songs. You likely have been warned about the bad crowds. The consequences are about the same everywhere for everybody ...

My roommate and I went home after dodging trouble at a nightclub, but I was kind of upset because I had warned him about the possible consequences of his bad behavior. He understood and apologized. About six months later, one of our friends brought a couple of drunk girls home for a fun night. He felt sorry for me because I was without a girl, but he apologized and promised to bring three girls the next time. To be polite, I said I understood and that I appreciated the promise. The girls weren't my type anyway; I judged them to be troublesome. They all had fun that night and woke up sober. But a while later, I heard loud knocks on the door, and when I answered, four guys almost forced their way in. The first one in said, "Wassup?"

I was angry at myself for naively opening the door, yet I interpreted his "Wassup?" as a greeting. I responded, "Not much."

"We heard that some shit's going on here."

With that, I understood the reason why they were there. At this point, the girls came out of the bedrooms to greet their friends—although I thought of them as their pimps. One of the guys asked the girls if they were all right. And one of the girls answered for both, "Yeah, we're fine."

"You sure?"

"Yeah. He was bothering me"—she pointed to my troublemaker friend—"but he stopped. Everything is fine."

"We good, my man?" the guy asked my friend.

"Yeah. I was playing with her. That's all it was."

The guys hugged the girls and said goodbye, adding "Catch you later" and "Peace" to us.

Luckily, nothing bad happened, but it was enough for me to realize that it was time to take a new approach to our friendship. We stayed friends, but I kept my distance and turned down all invitations to go to the clubs and house parties. I even turned down family events. And I explained my reasons, which he understood. Better alone than in bad company, right? We stayed friends, though, and still laugh at the things he has done. But my point is that if your friends are dragging you along troublesome roads—bullying, vandalism, drugs, guns, gangs, robbery, and so on—you'll soon earn yourself many nights in jail, a mile-long criminal record, or a death certificate. Be smart and walk alone.

Still, we are meant to belong to a community. In fact, the world has plenty of good friends. Until you find some of them, though, you need to walk alone. While you do that, turn yourself into a super-friend. As a matter of fact, turn yourself into a super-friend regardless. Step beyond friends—the ones with whom you work or go to the same gym or church. Jump beyond good friends—the ones with whom you go to the gym as partners, ride with to work, or club together. Fly beyond best friends—the ones with whom you share intimate secrets, or who are your business partners. They are the ones you borrow from and to whom you lend money without hesitation; they are the ones you choose to take care of your spouse and kids if you die young. Then you land in the best-friend field yourself and become a super-friend. You are a super-friend when you are always there for your friends with unconditional love, care, and a helping hand. You don't bite off more than you can chew for your friends, but you don't hold back. You empower yourself to never rely on friends for a rescue, yet you are open with a helping hand.

Friendships are full of joy and enthusiasm and are very interesting. Then, as time passes, one friend begins to neglect small things, such as returning a borrowed object or cash, or causes big, ugly disappointments, such as sleeping with our friend's lover. What a betrayal! On the other hand, we are wired to seek interaction with people outside our family circle. We even turned wild animals into man's best friend and a companion. Friends are, in a way, indispensable in our lives. Do your homework, learn from experience, be conscious of betrayal and disloyalty, and then live among friends, whoever they are, regardless of what they can throw in your face.

4

Society

IN THE BEGINNING, THERE WERE only small families. There were not enough people to form a large community. We would've returned to our cave with the family's safety as our main concern. And because continuity of the species is in our DNA, we formed large families. Then curiosity inspired some brothers and sisters to move beyond the horizon in search of new places, new faces, and new adventures, hoping that their troubles were worthwhile. And they were!

They gave birth to families of their own and blended with other families. This trend continued in a progressive way to give us races, culture, tradition, ethnicity, population, continental nations and global nations—the society. Unsatisfied with the size, we continued on the quest of finding new lands beyond the horizon. We brought people from our homeland to colonize our new lands. We also turned indigenous people into second-class citizens. We turned blacks into slaves. Tribes fought each other. Nations went to war and brought devastating consequences to humanity. There was massive loss of human lives (soldiers, men, women, children), vast destruction of property and the ecosystem, and chaos and economic calamities during and after wars. Suddenly, we faced problems from what we wished for—a large society—at seven billion and counting to about ten billion, when, hopefully, the numbers will stagnate and then decline. Until then, we find ourselves fighting for a means to survive.

Our founding fathers in the caves of Africa didn't see this coming. We simply screwed up the blueprint badly and implemented the plan in the worst possible way. In our hands lies a society ever so complicated, chaotic, and divisive, which is walking toward the deepness of a truly ugly abyss. The problems of the past, as well as the ones we create daily, tag along. Dear millennials, would you please change this course?

Prosperity Mishap

In a chaotic and complex society, prosperity to all can't find a home. The people with money are pushed by greed to look for ways to increase their wealth. Their focus is on business opportunities. They explore all their options in their own countries and then expand abroad. They take their businesses with them, or they move into something completely different. It's not a big deal because when they venture into something new, they are almost certain they'll succeed. The consequences will be absorbed by the employees, who will have to look for other employment and endure the hassle and frustration that comes with that, and by the government which will have to deal with rising unemployment. Clearly, those who are empowered will continue to grow, while the rest will continue to suffer, face setbacks, and see possibilities dwindle.

If the many elements of life, especially finances, weren't so harsh on us, we wouldn't raise our voices about social issues, such as inequality, immigration, racial discrimination, but life takes ugly turns that leave our assembly lines messed up, and as we see others indulging in luxury, we have to speak up. It's not fair that the "1 percent club" keeps getting richer while the rest becomes poorer. Sure, we know that all the way from the jungle, the circumstances of life were that we lived with social classes. Some of us were better fit for hunting and others were skilled in skinning the prey we caught. The individuals' natural-born skills became the driving force in the formation of groups within the community, which is a smart move, as we are equal but not the same; we have different skills. (And luckily, we have applied those skills where they fit the best.) Then the theory of "like attracts like" steps in to increase the number of individuals with identical skills, and they gather together to create something special. If we are attractive, rich, and intelligent, we join an attractive, rich, and intelligent circle. If we are in the park shooting hoops, we join the guys making the most points.

Way back then, people with extensive land holdings grouped to find ways to benefit from the leverage they had. They realized that they could compensate people for working on their lands for a fair amount of money or harvest. This paved the way for sharecropping. From there, things began to take the journey that continued to increase the odds of success for some, while narrowing the doors of opportunity for many. How bad will this get?

Opportunity Windows

Opportunity is one of the main keys to success, and the lack of it is the main reason for social dysfunction. Lack of employment, for example, keeps people locked in stress and frustration. In looking for relief, people sometimes take stupid actions, such as vandalism, riots, drug use, and alcohol. Even in peaceful protest, violence erupts, people die, looting and vandalism take place, and people are arrested. (While you are looking for a stress relief, you actually could increase your problems. Be aware of that!)

The prosperity of a nation, low taxes, and flexible regulation are some of the greatest opportunities for riches. In a bad economy, poor people suffer a lot because unemployment rises and the rich refuse to hire, pay more taxes, and increase employee benefits, a move that governments don't like because doing so will not improve any economy. The rich have a different view when it comes to improving an economy. They blame the poor for dragging down the economic recovery and draining the government's coffers by abusing social services.

Regardless of who is right or wrong, the hope is that everybody stays afloat and ahead of the game. This reality does not stand with poverty claiming more people, while the rich keep smiling, even when they cause us sadness. We know that the windows of opportunity are wider at the small clubs, where the grass is greener, and the members rub the American-dream pie in each other's faces every day. They live in a society apart from the society to which they belong. That's so unfair because on the other side of the river, the 99 percent are scrambling to get a slice of the pie for survival but are in a continuous struggle to make the ends meet. Ironically, this struggle sometimes gives way to actions that land us behind bars.

Crime

Sometimes crime comes to us, and at other times, we walk into it. In the struggle to survive, crime walks to us. The situation can be so devastating that desperate measures become the only means of survival. As a man must do what a man must do, home invasion, robbery, and shoplifting become acts of survival. Natural-born criminals commit crimes, from vandalism to trespassing, up to felonies and gruesome murders.

Society takes measures to stop criminal actions from happening again. Crime-prevention departments and strategies are created. The government steps up public safety and security measures. One of the measures is to crack down on criminals, monitoring their activities and collecting information that helps determine the crime patterns. And the growth of this phenomenon gives birth to spying.

Government Spying

Society accepted spying as an extension of the government's means of ensuring order, peace, and tranquility. Therefore, it should be supported unconditionally.

When it was clear that Santa Claus was a Grinch, someone woke up the fight against privacy invasion. Some of us cared, others didn't, and the rest stayed indifferent.

The pros: The pros are individuals who go on with their lives, hoping that their actions and everybody else's actions are monitored twenty-four/seven. They believe that the government has a right to know what the population is up to, worldwide, and that doing so enables the government to find out who its enemies are, what they are doing, and what their plans are. Then they can take the necessary measures to keep the nation safe and continue providing prosperity to its citizens. In fact, the pros think that there's never enough spying because every day humans act in barbaric ways, killing people and destroying the means of our survival.

The pros could be right because nations don't trust each other. Even with treaties, agreements, and compromises, nations have to ensure compliance through spying. In some cases, watchdog teams must be created for this purpose. Then there are groups and individuals lurking around, ready to strike at the first opportunity.

The cons: The people who stand with their fists clenched against the government's spying programs do so because they don't trust the government. They believe that the data the government collects will be used against them and that it violates their privacy rights. They also believe that the pretext that governments must spy on everybody for security reasons is bogus because crime and terrorist attacks continue to happen every day. They welcome spying on a few, and full spying on criminals and terrorists but not spying on everybody.

I think they too have a point.

The neutral: The third crowd, which seems to be the smartest one, is formed by the people who believe in spying on everybody for peace and security. They believe that the government could unfairly use the information it collects to incriminate, blackmail, conspire, or destroy the reputation of some individuals. They know that it wouldn't matter how much spying there is because there will always be crimes and terrorist attacks—because humans are idiots with big brains—and that nations will always spy on and lie to one another. The neutral faction also understands people's right to privacy is fragile.

Historically, when it comes to the government vs. people, people rarely, if ever, win. The government wins almost all the time, even when it loses! When the courts find government's invasion of people's privacy unconstitutional and order the government to stop such action, the government uses other means to get what it needs. On the other hand, people must stand up to avoid government's abuse of power. Sounds like a dilemma, doesn't it? It is! Those who couldn't care less about the government's spying programs won't let the dilemma be an obstacle on the road.

I am with the neutral faction, but I know that whether you are pro, con, or neutral, the best stance for you with regard to government spying is to know your priorities, defend your beliefs, and understand the outcome of your stance. As long as it empowers you and brings happiness and resolve, voice your concern. Otherwise, ignore it, and move on with your dreams. And keep in mind that regardless of how angry you are or how loudly you scream at the government, you still might be ignored, even when you are given some attention.

Monkey See, Monkey Do

Some things don't go away, no matter what. The expression "Monkey see, monkey do" fits right in with this philosophy. And it gets better when we jump on the bandwagon of science and technology, which have given us the opportunity to see what other people are eating, driving, drinking, playing with, and spending money on; how they socialize; how they are entertained; with whom they go to bed; and what they do under the sheets.

This is somewhat empowering because it forces us to upgrade ourselves to that which is clearly better. On the other hand, we have suffered from predatory social behavior as a result of "monkey see, monkey do." It's all good to protest police brutality, government corruption, and social injustice, but massive murders or any atrocities inspired by the monkey-see–monkey-do philosophy empowers no one. Rather, it creates fear and social chaos, just like any other stupid act of humankind. Sadly, the curse of the generation is that it has made us suffer. The number of people who have joined criminal organizations due to inspiration from online stories and brainwashing is astonishing.

The Games You Win Only When You Don't Play

LGBT (lesbian, gay, bisexual, and transgender): Despite the wide range of social evolution, including improving human rights and the freedom of speech and expression, we still have nations where people oppose the social integration and rights of the LGBT community. In Russia, India, South Arabia, Iran, Nigeria, and many other countries, homosexuality is still a crime. In some of these countries, the punishment for this crime can extend to death. With so many countries legalizing same-sex marriage and putting equal rights for the LGBT community on the books, I believe that the few countries that impose resistance eventually will follow the crowd. Let's look, however, at the cliffs and flatlands of the LGBT community.

Unnatural: We reproduce for the continuity of the species. Since Adam and Eve, we have continued multiplying to fill the world. With a small exception to the rule, it takes the sex act—the party of male and female genitals—to reproduce the same species. In this sense, LGBT will drive the human race to extinction.

A family killer: For the longest time, we have shared a society in which a man marries a woman to have children and raise a family. The two will have children of their own. The children will grow to have a family of their own too. LGBT kills that tradition.

A hell for the kids: We are blended in the traditional family structure with a dad (man), a mom (woman), and brothers and sisters at home. When a couple is formed by two females or two males, who's the mom and who's the dad? How will this play out for kids who are not gay but are raised by gay couples?

A major social disintegration: Kids of gay families could have a hard time socializing with straight kids, which would force them to socialize with gay friends only to avoid being mocked or facing the trauma of stigmatization. Some parents restrict interaction between their kids and gay kids; this is out of fear that gay kids will be a bad influence and because of the stigma that nonstraight people are a derogatory, disgusting class.

My take is this: We are living in the twenty-first century. Faster than ever, we embrace change and innovation. We have seen changes that we like, changes that we hate and despise, and changes that have frightened us. Usually, we resist most of the changes because it is in us to hold dearly to the familiar and to push the unfamiliar aside. Fortunately, the changes we may have most resisted brought innovation that made our lives easier and spread happiness. We're learning to accept that we are better persons and thriving because curiosity forced us to break what we have to find something new and different—and that's definitely stronger than the genes that want us to stay in our comfort zones. The LGBT community fits within change territory. We need to make room for them to sit, and here's why:

Thanks to evolution, natural reproduction is the best way to maintain human beings' continuity, but there are other ways. We no longer need a woman to have sexual intercourse with a man to have a child. A man donates or sells his sperm for artificial insemination. It is also true that the LGBT community tampers with the core family values we have cherished for thousands of years, and they could kill such values—except they won't. Traditional and social taboos aren't growing; they are shrinking and struggling to survive. Family tradition has lost its meaning. The divorce rate is astonishingly high and continues to increase. Single parenting has become the norm in affairs of the family; the uncompromising relationship also is the norm—just to mention a few of what we considered as drastic changes in the family tradition and philosophy, which now bother no one.

The definition of marriage and its philosophical bond between a man and a woman is a fortress that has been in decay for a long time by many other factors, not only the LGBT community. LGBT is nothing more than a small society that had kept itself in the closet, waiting for the right moment to claim its territory. Now, the light has been lit, the doors are open, and the right moment has arrived. Relax! The LGBT community is not here to force us to follow in their footsteps, as many fear. Rather, as we accept our brothers and sisters for what they are, we'll all live as the brothers and sisters that we are—always complaining and quarreling with each other, but unable to live without one another, regardless of color, gender, belief, or philosophy.

As to social disintegration, we have nothing to fear—at least not from the LGBT community. Technology, media, advertisers, and the government are the real threats. They are the ones who make us independent and antisocial every day, thanks to smart toys and the flood of commercial drones and robots on the way; thanks to the total control of what we must listen to, watch, and buy and who we must have as friends; and thanks to the animosity unleashed by wars, racism, bigotry, and hatred. So fear nothing! LGBT is like a dog that doesn't bite even after you've stepped on its tail. Furthermore, any orphan or refugee would prefer to be raised by a gay couple instead of dying of trauma, cold, and starvation. Yet the bottom line is that any time you engage ferociously in arguments about LGBT, chances are you will lose. I suggest support without persuading.

Racial discrimination: We cannot go anywhere without finding racial discrimination alive and well, whether or not it's visible. There are no law, rules, regulations, or policies to stop it. We have it in our blood. Driven by ignorance and other factors, so many of us suffer the consequences.

Politics: Politics is never as easy or as clear-cut as it looks. It's only well intended. And we, the people, are never served as we wish. In the meantime, there always will be one large group that approves of government's behavior but a larger number that disapproves of it. The arguments between the two can go on forever without even agreeing to disagree.

Conspiracy theory: In almost every country around the world, freedom of speech stands strong. This gives us the right to praise, curse, talk trash, and protest against governments and their actions with the hope that they will change their behavior. In general, we praise them a little and curse them a lot. (They know about it, but apparently they don't care much.) We get very mad and frustrated when they screw up and don't listen, but they move on with their business, ignoring our madness and frustration. Very often, they engage in murky activities that raise suspicion, and their explanation is always buttered with white lies. On top of that, so many activities that seem legitimate, full of integrity, and transparency have come out of the clouds to surprise us and leave us as mad as hell. Still, stamping "conspiracy theory" to every catastrophic event on earth is foolish. This is a very bad attitude, one that paralyzes our powers and erases our dreams.

Sports: The usual dispute in sports is about which sports, teams, and players are the best. Usually, we stick to the sports that we (or our family and friends) can play and dislike the rest. Once we dislike some teams or players, it will be very difficult for us to give them the credit they deserve. By contrast, a team that sucks, based on statistics and other objective means, could be the one to which we give credit, simply because they come in line with our desires and satisfaction. That's what makes us fans.

Society is made of different people with different tastes and desires, so stand by your sports, teams, and players, but avoid engaging in arguments about which ones are the best.

Abortion: Our beliefs, culture, tradition, and philosophical principles make up a set of values that guide our course of thoughts and actions. Each ingredient in this set of values plays a distinct role in our approach to specific issues. A Catholic person who lives by the Bible, for example, will be against one of the most sensitive and controversial issues of all—abortion. To our surprise, some churchgoers wouldn't think twice about having an abortion. And rumors are whispered that someone in the church has had an abortion, helped someone to have an abortion, or supported the idea. An atheist might not care.

Here's what makes this issue the one that no one should poke: Should a fetus get cut off from his or her right to evolve and become what he or she should be? Should an infant be punished by hunger, starvation, and disease and die in pain and suffering before he or she celebrates his or her second birthday? If a fetus knew that his or her birth would kill his or her mother, what choice would the fetus prefer? Should a mother be allowed to die for the sake of the rights of the unborn?

You lose when you support abortion, but you lose when you don't.

Religion: Almost all religions have one common and basic fundamental: the gathering of people in brotherhood to worship a god, along with becoming a better person and asking forgiveness for sins. No single religion, therefore, is better than another. Unfortunately, ever since there was society, people from different faiths have killed each other.

These are some examples of the hundreds of social issues that cut you short of your potential when you engage in arguments of supremacy, instead of understanding and respecting the views of other members of society. Any of these social issues come with deep complexity on both sides of the argument. Each side has a face that looks prettier to me but uglier to you and to others; wrong to me and right to you. And then there's the truth—both sides are equally beautiful and equally ugly.

We understand what these social issues represent only when we don't pick sides. So when you feel the urge to play a narcissist, get up and leave the table, and take your cards with you. They are valuable to you but not to the game of society. Society is a team. A team requires the effort of one for all and all for one. It means not agreeing with every point of view but respecting the view of other players and giving room for them to play. Sensitive social issues demand that you hold your beliefs and philosophical principles for your well-being and advancement, instead of imposing them on others and insisting they are the beacons of all beacons. Otherwise, you'll be a loser for playing an endless game. Sadly, this seemingly unseen losing attitude is spreading in society and leaving the millennials as the biggest losers.

The Countdown

So far we've defeated all the purposes of society. Society is, after all, an extension of a friendship we made millions of years ago, and it was rooted in brotherhood, helping hands, and well-being for all. And what did we turn it into? We turned it into hell, with nations bombing each other, causing an exorbitant loss of life and massive destruction, particularly during World Wars I and II. Nations killed their own people—genocide; the Mafia and terrorists killed people. Lunatics caused the massacre of young, bright minds. Police killed people; people killed police; individuals killed each other. People ran slavery rings and forced hard labor of children. The mentally ill massacred children. Priests sexually abused children. Parents killed their own children; fathers assaulted and raped their daughters; sons and daughters killed their parents; brothers and sisters killed each other. Whites hated blacks; blacks hated whites. Cyber wars spread viruses fast and everywhere. One percent of the population owned everything and controlled everything. Food went to waste while children died from hunger. There was fear of nuclear and chemical attacks by sea, land, and air. Artificial intelligence became smarter than its creator, and humans tampered with God's creation. It all make us want to rush to the bunker and press the button.

No! Hold your horses. Let's have a conversation. This is the only society we ever will have. We can't reduce it to ashes and build a new one. A good way to keep it in good standing is by remembering that despite our differences, we can unite our individual and collective forces to keep peace and brotherhood strong. There are many ways to repair the broken social chains, especially with regard to racial discrimination, inequality, and lack of opportunity. We are all in this together. We can heal this world and its society.

Remedies

Live and let live: Society is complex and has so many ways of shaking up things that can make us lose our cool and get ourselves in trouble. It starts with our children disrespecting us; our wife or husband treating us like a piece of crap; frustrated idiots on the road dumping their loads on us; kids bullying our kids for the color of their skin or for fun; up to the madness of a slow internet connection. That's life. That's how society rolls. If somehow you're a victim of any of such phenomena, play it smart. If you are the perpetrator, learn to live without interrupting the flow of oxygen to others. Take your seat, and leave the rest alone. Be humble and compassionate, not a creep carrying guns and machetes. Don't only listen to what is pleasant to your ears; listen to everything, and then select your favorite tunes. Create room for others to play the game they like, with the cards they have. Allow people to exercise their philosophical rights, and don't impose your way of life on theirs. On your journey, you must digest foods you dislike, live with people you despise, and accept values with which you don't fully agree. That's the only way. We only have one society for seven billion people, and we are equal but not the same. So find your way around and make sure that your life is going well and headed to prosperity.

Respect the world of others: You don't have to believe in superstition, black magic, witchcraft, or tarot cards, nor do you have to follow taboo traditions, rituals, and norms of other people, but you should respect them.

Open your mind: Try to understand people's behavior under different circumstances. This allows you be less aggressive when you encounter situations of rage. There's always a reason why we act like irrational animals. Poverty, stress, and frustration from, say, lack of money to pay rent, credit cards, or the car loan, as well as relationship hardships or PTSD are some of contributing factors to people's madness. If you respond in kind, things can get very ugly and leave you with weak cards and a losing hand.

The clues: Experts use individual clues to predict behaviors. Hitting the nail on the head repeatedly creates a pattern. A pattern becomes an accurate prediction of behavior. Sure, you can find yourself stereotyping, but if you see clues and pick up the vibe of a criminal, or you smell something bad about to go down, be smart and walk away.

The call for success: As long as you have a purpose, a plan, and determination, nothing can stop you from achieving your goals. Any social problems on your path simply will be crushed by your determination of taking nothing but the victory. Stay connected to the call of success in front of you. As a matter of fact, your success is a contributing factor in reducing social problems. Society needs your success, not the rage of your misfortune. Some of the strategies you can use to be successful in any situation or society are to avoid engaging in games you win only when you don't play, and focus your energy on things that push you closer to your main goals.

The beacons: Lately things have been so chaotic that we see only a screwed-up society with terrorists and oppressive political leaders, who cause all kinds of trouble and calamities by imposing their philosophical social principles on everyone. That certainly shadows the beacons of society's greatness. But if you look hard enough, you'll find the beacons of greatness even in the oddest places. Luckily, we have a large society that's rich and full of complexity! It allows us to walk among the best and socialize with the best en route to the beacons of greatness. And so, find that beacon, raise its towers, and pave the ways for others to see it clearer from a greater distance. Stay determined to worship nothing but happiness in whatever crowd you find yourself.

Friends: Friends are the support beams, the first building blocks, the cornerstones, and the foundation of the society. Make as many friends as you can. If you are on the other side of the river, you're an antisocial, and that's bad. Leave isolation and join the crowd. Make friends from different walks of life; different races, ethnicities, and backgrounds. You will double-down. First, you'll have many helping hands when you find yourself in stormy waters. Second, you'll have a rich knowledge and understanding of society's complexity and dynamic. Just be aware of the tricks of friendships.

We wish for a society full of security, peace, and prosperity, with intellect and brotherhood shining brightly day to day, forever and ever. Unfortunately, this wish cannot be granted because it would go against the core of the society—the diversity, complexity, and unpredictability. It's also unfortunate that there is no such thing as one society that fits all. The true reality is that all must fit in. And that includes people who disrespect social norms and morality. It doesn't surprise me that some people wish they could smack those who talk loud and use foul language on public transportation, at the gym, or at other public venues. They want to get out of their cars and whip idiots on the road. They won't do that, however, because there would be drastic consequences from such actions but most importantly, it's because such individuals still are part of the whole. Besides, they might accuse others of behaviors of which they themselves are guilty.

Understand human behavior. It helps you manage social misbehavior and go through social chaos without losing your cool. You are right if you think people are stupid. Then expect social stupidity. At the same time, empower yourself to be the best member of society that you possibly can be. Get yourself a higher education, and engage in social activities that aim for your empowerment and the good of many.

5

The Government

WITH THE EXCEPTION OF FEW countries, the people elect the government. This means that people and the government share a strong, inseparable bond. Unfortunately, this bond is bipolar—in one minute there's love, and in the next, there's enough hateful sentiment to cover the world. This bipolar bond is triggered by the responsibility for each other. People have their dreams, projects and goals to turn into reality. The government has the responsibility to protect and hold the values of the nation for which it stands, which include running itself efficiently and attending to people's demands, such as peace, security, and prosperity, among tons of other responsibilities. Attending to these responsibilities could force the government to take measures that could violate people's constitutional rights and hurt their wishes and desires. This makes people think that the government grew to become abusive and too powerful. And the government thinks that people are ignorant and incapable of running their lives and that they interfere in government's affairs, instead of obeying the laws and living their lives accordingly. This heated bond seems to be in an eternal furnace, where rubbish and fuel are constantly added to the fire by big, little, and insignificant things.

Fresh in our memory is Edward Snowden's revelation of the United States' spying program. For all that it was worthwhile or stupid, people were very angry about the spying program. There were those who believed that all major catastrophic events in the United States and around the world, no matter how tragic and bewildering, were the work of a government conspiracy, and they felt a boost to their shadowy belief. Clearly, instead of love, care, trust, and happiness, we have mistrust, hate, and madness as the main driving forces of the people/government bond. Other than spying, many other government acts and actions keep this bond going from sour to bitter and from bitter to outrageous. Here are some of them:

Corruption: It doesn't matter how impressive a plan is; if it's implemented and controlled by corrupt minds, the outcome will be a disaster. History has taught us that corruption has been inseparable from all government. Politicians can't break free from it, and people can't stand it. We have been complaining and asking for a restraining order in the House since day one, but we haven't seen any significant results. When things look normal and loyal, somehow someone trips and break the cookie jar, leaving us furious because the cookie jar was full of lies and betrayals.

For the longest time we have been walking this endless path of corruption and carrying hope of change, but unfortunately, with so many things destroying the politicians' integrity, there won't be signs of light at the end of the tunnel any time soon. And this is becoming increasingly discouraging to voters. But politicians aren't stupid. They hypnotize us with their rhetoric. And sadly, even when they speak in true words, their sincerity evaporates once they take the elected seat. We know that nothing destroys or impedes a country from advancement more than corruption.

Government spending: The people understand that governments must have a spending budget. That budget is increased by so many factors and that's fine with the taxpayers. What gets us heated is the unnecessary spending, such as on new furniture and office redecoration, simply because a new mayor, governor, or president is coming to office. I too see that as a waste of the taxpayers' money and a motive for rage.

The wars: Despite science and technology advancement and better combat skills, the principles of war stay the same—destroy the enemies, or bring them to their knees, and then force them to suck it. The devastation is more catastrophic, and the consequences are much greater. We continue destroying great minds, shattering the lives of children and innocent people and creatures, and bringing nightmares to humanity. We bring misery to soldiers and other war participants through post-traumatic stress disorder, one of the worst consequences of war. This is taking a more devastating turn with each war, as soldiers face more advanced war tactics and expose themselves to more potentially harmful weaponry. And then there's the war cost, a hard blow to the economy, that is felt years afterward. We still fall short on estimates of the duration and cost of all wars, the number of casualties, and the long-term consequences, such as political instability and social chaos. In some cases, decades pass before the cost of a war delivers its poisonous bite through failing miserably to take care of the veterans.

Even the most insignificant wars continue to cause horror and devastation worldwide. Yet we continue going to war. We continue spending trillions of dollars developing new war weaponry and creating more destructive war strategies. Nations continue to spy, lie, and threaten each other. When peace and agreement are reached, very seldom do they endure, if they're even enforced. When they do endure, it's on shaky ground almost certain to become a sinkhole.

It almost never occurs that one nation decides to attack another nation and start a war for no particular reason. We know that. In fact, as unfortunate as it can be, war is usually the last and the worst resort for solving disputes between nations, tribes, or ethnic groups (because humans are stupid!), but we seem to look for reasons for wars. It has become so bad that big nations are using war as a means to call for attention, and they disrespect international treaties and human rights. Every nation wants to be the sole superpower. Every nation wants to own the most powerful nuclear bomb, and those facing the United Nations' pushback threaten to blow up enemy countries. Yet until we colonize space, there's only one planet and one universe for us to share.

We felt safer and more optimistic about world peace and prosperity as the cold war ended (1947–1991), but here we are, back at it again, except now we have scalding temperatures and freezing weather conditions, with cyber war putting on a very ugly mask—and terrorism tags along. Definitely not a pretty picture! Sure, war seems to be an evil we can't live with and can't live without, but how is it that this trend points to a prosperous generation on its way to greater greatness? And how can we not be angry at the government?

Environment: The universe could be playing tricks on us, planet Earth could be messing with us, and scientists could be missing important details about global warming, but there's no doubt that Mother Nature is talking. Whether or not we understand her, she's speaking to us much more frequently and in a harsher tone each time she opens her mouth.

From torrential rains to the extremely powerful tornadoes and hurricanes; from a winter deep freeze with snowstorms and blizzards to scalding summer temperature; from ice melting (causing sea rise) to drastic droughts and wildfires, who dares to deny the drastic weather changes that brush our faces every day, everywhere, as the sign of something unusual going on? These changes are not just weather doing its thing. They are, individually or collectively, clear signs of nature's anger for our bad behavior. And who or what is to blame?

Decades ago, the United States was the main culprit in the massive pollution of nature. Manufacturing, military activities, and space exploration took the blame. Now the blame is on China, India, and Brazil, but almost every country is polluting Mother

Nature on a much larger scale. Worse is that now the pollutants are more harmful and diversified by all kinds of waste. Our current way of life makes it impossible not to harm Mother Nature head to toe, side to side, and standing up or lying down flat. In fact, we have been stripping Mother Nature as we pollute the air, land, and water. Carbon dioxide, which continues to be the main culprit in global warming, has even nastier surprises as the world rushes to live larger. A car is the first proof of living large, especially in developing countries. Despite strong efforts to find alternative fuel, we are far from coming up with a clear-cut solution. First, we are still split on global warming. Second, even if we all agreed today on global warming, developing countries and poor countries will lag behind when it comes to alternative fuel. Fossil fuel will be their choices for a long time. Third, the Environmental Protection Agency (EPA) has little power to fight the big money—the oil industry. So while greed pushes us to devour the apple pie, we are also eating dust, breathing toxins, and drinking poison to the grave (a slow self-destruct), leaving future generation to battle for humanity's continuity. The marketers hypnotizing us into consuming more—and trashing more as a result—deserve the blame for that, but it's hard not to give government the biggest share of the blame.

Social services: A variety of factors separates big, rich countries from small, poor ones. After the Gross Domestic Product (GDP) comes the greatness of social services as the first indicators of a nation's prosperity. But social service is a global nightmare that shadows the rainbows of any country. The reasons for that are due to the inefficiency of the social services administration and human bad behavior, among other things. The inefficiency begins with the qualification process, and it never ends. Due to the complexity of social services, some inefficiencies are understandable, but most are stunning. (When thousands of deceased persons are active in the system, and millions of dollars are wasted, we are left in disbelief.) Human beings are selfish and greedy. Even when we don't need assistance, we apply for it, especially when we find a loophole. Then we stay alert to the next loophole that can give us better service and more cash. People who receive assistance don't fully benefit from it because they have poor financing skills, and they don't have the intellect to help them do better. On top of that, they have cigarette, alcohol, and drug problems, among other bad habits.

Combine the inefficiency of social services with human bad nature, and the government doesn't have enough money to assist people who are truly in need. The result is an increase in starvation and homelessness. I am sure when people say, "Social services sucks," they mean, "This government is a joke."

Too Cold to Handle

Immigration: We are what we are—lucky primates who possess superior brain power over all other creatures on earth since millions of years ago. That brain power gave us the ability to think, coordinate thoughts and actions, invent, innovate, build, speak, read, write, plan, organize, implement, and control, among infinite other things we're capable of doing that other animals aren't.

About two million years ago, the first of our ancestors moved out of Africa, either because the habitat became unbearable or because the genes of curiosity pushed them to discover the mystery beyond the horizon, and they decided to stay at one of the paradises they found; their descendants migrated to the entire globe. Immigration, then, is not a contemporary phenomenon. It is, say, an Ice Age phenomenon. But if ancient history doesn't refresh our memories, recent centuries should, and modern society definitely keeps us fresh on exodus.

Fortunately, immigration was welcomed everywhere it went. As a matter of fact, when big countries noticed the benefits of immigration, they began inviting foreigners to come in on a visa. The ones who could not come in on a visa still came, and no one cared that they did. There was enough happiness to go around.

There was prosperity, abundance, and more to come. Immigration was some of the diversified prosperity wagons. It was responsible for the richness of the United States culture, with more diversity and mixes than in any other country in the world.

Any beginning comes full of goodies and simplicity and with the potential to bring great benefits. It also carries the dormant malicious power that can evolve into big problems that will bite us like a vicious dog. Necessary measures ought to be taken to either keep malicious power dormant or create a means to tackle it when it wakes up.

After an economic downturn hit in recent decades, nationals started shouting that illegal immigrants were taking jobs away from them, causing low wages and wage stagnation in nonskilled jobs. They claimed that immigrants were destroying the country with drugs, crime, and abuse of social benefits. The government then had a problem that was a problem in itself. And the real problem was that any issue for which the government needs to find a solution is dragged down by senseless fights and political games, leaving people frustrated and pissed off. And since moving around is part of what defines us, and wherever we settle we leave distinct footprints, why is immigration an unsolvable problem? Isn't the government equipped with the best heads, powers, and resources?

Furthermore, how did immigration become too cold to handle? Probably because instead of pouring all available resources into finding a solution for immigration problems, each administration did its best to smooth out the noticeable rough edges, softly clip off the thorns, and then kick the can, hoping that the next guys would catch it and score a touchdown. So far, they all have missed the catch or fumbled miserably. Even though the genes of curiosity still play an interesting role in immigration, the harsh living conditions triggered by war, politics, bad economy, and natural disasters have become the main reasons for an exodus. These reasons will drive immigration way into the future—not a good sign for this generation and the generations to come.

Gun control: We have lost friends, close family members, and soul mates when they were intended victims or innocent bystanders of gun violence. We've lost powerful young minds in domestic homicides and suicides and in gang wars. Massacres of children have given us lifetime emotional scars and lasting tearful memories. We've mourned our loved ones and cried for gun control. We continue to mourn. We continue to cry and sob for gun control. It all indicates that we might run out of tears way before the government delivers what it must deliver in gun control. Too much is at stake, and not even the massacre of children has moved the needle toward the gun control solution.

The police: The police brutality that resulted in the killings of many black individuals, which consequently caused the killing of cops in retaliation, has erased the "serve and protect, without discrimination, bias, or prejudice" policy and philosophy. Jails are filled with inmates who are predominantly black, Hispanic, and other minorities.

As for crime, the public believes and studies have concluded that whites are as guilty as other ethnic groups but are let go more frequently or get light sentences. (Too many incidents make it impossible for coincidence to stand.) Coincidence or not, the feeling is that society has been victimized around the world by protectionism and unfair games, with damaging ramifications for freedom, liberty, justice, and prosperity for all. The police play a big role. Crooked policemen engage in discriminatory behavior, and dirty work has driven the hatred toward the police worldwide at an unprecedented level, especially in the USA. And when the courts must get involved, they appear to be idiots in the eyes of the public, enraging us even more. There are examples of numerous sensitive issues from ancient times that the government has done its best to avoid; they are too cold to hold. And the brothers and sisters—the too hot to touch—get just about the same Easter basket.

Too Hot to Touch

Obesity: You can be sure that the government understands that an obese individual produces less than the average and has a higher risk of diabetes and heart diseases. The government also knows that if obese individuals become victims of any illness, their health costs will be exorbitant. Multiply that by millions, and you have the perfect recipe to bankrupt a country's health care. With the already lazy lifestyle we cherish, big companies responsible for furnishing foods and beverages to humanity have found how to have it their way—by pumping millions of dollars into politics. When the government steps in to do its job, it faces resistance and a dilemma. On one hand, there are voters' demands, and on the other, there's the big money. Ignoring voters' demands is a betrayal. Biting the hands that feed you is not a good idea. More often than not, the voters lose. Who or what can stop Coca-Cola, McDonald's, or Dunkin' Donuts? As they gain more territory worldwide, so does obesity. And the government seems to keep its hands crossed out of fear or compromises. It sounds like the government is a judge sleeping with two ladies after hours, and now he's to give the verdict to their dispute in court. It's impossible to be impartial or to keep business as usual. He too is about to get his verdict tonight.

Health care: We elect the governments to take care of the problems bigger than us. Health care is one of them. The first blow to health care came from people in free care. They don't have the resources or skills to take good care of themselves through fitness and balanced nutrition. They get sick easier and more frequently than other people, and it takes longer for them to recover.

The second blow comes from Medicare. We live longer, and the current environmental condition sickens us more often and more easily. The government has been trying to fix health care, only to see the problems grow bigger and more complicated. Time is running out, and the odds haven't looked good yet. Frustration and madness mount; pharmaceutical games and gimmicks are no longer a mystery ... and the government seems to only be able to crawl behind the speeding train. Sad and sickening!

Drugs: The crisis now is the overdose. Other problems have not gone away, but death due to overdose has become an epidemic. Why is the government so behind in this game? The government is doing its best to keep a distance from these issues; they are too hot to touch (and not get burned).

Let's not ignore the important work and the responsibilities of the government. I am sure that we, the people, are thankful for all that the government has made available for us to cherish. We extend this appreciation and gratitude to say that by no means do we want a world without government. At the same time, we can't hide our anger at and frustration with the government. There's no better feeling than when politicians keep fighting for the survival of their parties, instead of attending to people's demands. That creates waves that rock all boats, treating all as one and one as all and preserving national security, sovereignty, and superpower, regardless of time and circumstances. I don't think that we are ungrateful or greedy when we demand that the government do better. In fact, we should peacefully voice our concerns, frustration, and madness more ferociously.

The government needs our input for a variety of reasons, and we want to see better progress. Yet the best way for us to stay ahead of the game is by empowering ourselves with what the government has available for our success, combined with our powers and determination to accept nothing but success as answers for all our questions.

When you encounter obstacles imposed by government, don't spend your time cursing both the obstacles and government; there are enough people doing that. Go around the obstacles, find a new road, rearrange your journey, and move on. You are in charge of your destiny, wishes, and desires, and you are a winner. Forget the government. Turn the losing cards it's given you into the ace of hearts. Win the game, and then go get your trophy, loser generation. You can do this because ... you can!

6

Poverty

IT WASN'T LIKE THIS IN the beginning. We were wandering around in the jungle as one, picking low-hanging fruits and whatever else we wanted for nutrition from an endless variety of foods. In fact, there was natural food waste. As humanity evolved and the population increased, harsh conditions occurred. The land, which had been everybody's mother, went through rough times. Nature wasn't as friendly or as giving as before. Friends with possibilities grabbed the opportunity to cover their insufficiency and looked for ways to stand strong and apart from the others. The owners of large properties opened doors for sharecroppers, a truly complicated reality. In the end, it was hard to say if it was a helping hand to the brothers in need or a trap to push them deeper into their misery. But the economy still was supported by the low price of goods, as every family produced most of their basic needs.

Agriculture was still the man! Money wasn't that important. I remember childhood stories and fairy tales of flamboyant guys who filled their shirt pockets with money to show off; it was a strategy for picking up girls. No one really cared, and the girls didn't fall for it. Farmers who performed like machines were the ones getting all the girls.

With the arrival of manufacturing and the decline of farmlands—among so many other declining factors—the ability to maintain basic needs became increasingly harder worldwide. Those who had done well and were ahead of the game could use technology to boost their economic means, while the rest kept struggling through harder and harder times. The number of poor rose steadily, while the wealth of the rich continued to grow. Nations around the world were divided into three categories:

The developed countries, where manufacturing drove the economy and brought the possibility for their population to thrive and become rich

The developing countries, where agriculture was the main economy, with the support of small industries

The poor countries, where the national economy could not support the population and therefore had to rely on international assistance for their survival.

The devil (money) saw an open window and stuck its head out to spice things up. And how did it spice things up? From here, the train of opportunity kicked into another gear, rocket-boosted the rich, and left numerous low cards on the table, making the game of poverty an impossible hand. If that wasn't enough, the shackles of poverty started to tighten.

The Shackles

Humble philosophy: It is dismissive to say that people in poverty face a daily struggle to make ends meet, and their poorly humble philosophy—or lack of it—worsens the struggle. They seem to believe the life they have is the life meant for them—for life. If there is pain or suffering, then so be it. They fall flat into the hands of destiny. In fact, a great number of poor believe that poverty is God's design and that pain and suffering are the gates to heaven. And humankind should not mess with them.

Flamboyance: Flamboyance is one of the measures we use to show off our success. This is usually associated with unnecessary and/or excessive spending. Poverty takes the biggest blow from it because poverty has no reason to show off. The poor, however, try to escape the psychological effects of living in poverty, by making flamboyance their painkiller. This only makes the beatings of poverty worse for them and their families. The kids will not have strong support for higher education. As a matter of fact, flamboyant parents may have no concern about their children's education. Higher education—a card that gives you an edge at the table—can be impossible for many high school graduates without the financial help of their parents. Without a higher education, the chances of moving out of poverty are very slim, let alone when parents worship flamboyance.

Laid-back personality: Millions of individuals simply choose the easy path of life. They want to live one day at a time, hassle-free. They lack the drive to jump on the wagon of adventure, unless the ride is free and the seats are cushioned. Any sacrifice made to excel is out of the question. Chances are that the little cash they earn will be spent on weed, cigarettes, and liquor. And no one can change their minds.

Low integrity: You might be surprised by the number of people, especially the poor, who have lost great opportunities to better their lives, simply because their low integrity stood in the way.

Jonathan was an auto mechanic who earned the trust of his manager and supervisors at the A-Z Garage. He was making good money and was on his way to earning significant raises and bonuses—until someone noticed that Jonathan was ordering parts for his personal use without the approval of the garage. He was fired.

Larry worked for a furniture store. He made a decent salary and monthly bonuses. He was confronted about the sale of a few items not included in the tally. He confessed (or lied) that his actions were motivated by a personal financial hardship. Whether or not the owner believed him, Larry was fired shortly afterward.

Crime: For so many reasons, crime hits the poor unmercifully.

Illiteracy: Illiteracy is the King Kong in the room. It reduces our chances of escaping poverty to zero. It robs us of the basic ingredients of delicious meals. It doesn't matter how great our power and skills are; illiteracy locks us up and then blocks all the exits. It's like we're surrounded by a great variety of foods yet dying of starvation because our mouths are stitched closed.

Stress: Stress has a mansion in poverty, and it enslaves the poor. In poverty, stress can see its contagious virus spread nonstop. The reason is that people in poverty have fewer and weaker weapons to fight stress.

War: Every time a war—civil or military, national or world war—breaks out, poor people are the ones to suffer the most, as they lose homes and belongings and flee the country or are displaced. A supply of clean water, electricity, goods, and services become insufficient and very expensive. Meeting basic needs becomes an impossible burden, and prosperity is just a dream for them or a reality they see other people cherish. In some countries, people haven't seen peace in decades. In these modern times, there is globalization—one nation coughs and the rest of the world catches a cold.

Corruption: International assistance to poor countries doesn't do much because when too many hands handle the pie, by the time it reaches the table, there isn't much left.

Cash only: There is so much leeway out there to give people an uphill ride, and credit is one of them. The poor have a slim chance of qualifying for that ride. A good-paying job is the first of the requirements to qualify for a credit card or loan. Without it, you have no way to build your credit score or buy a very important item for which you have no cash.

Let's look into the benefits of your credit score because we usually don't see them. When you need to buy a car, a kitchen set, or a bedroom or living room set using credit, your credit score determines how much you'll save. A credit score of seven hundred or higher can save you up to thousands of dollars. The car, an indispensable commodity in industrialized countries, where the USA takes the center stage, is a good example of getting great savings if you have a high credit score. On the other side of this coin, a low credit score can stop you short from getting the car, house, or furniture of your dreams. There's more; a bad credit score can stop you from getting a job offer or the keys to a rental apartment. I think this is unfair, but unfortunately, this is what "it is what it is" has become. And this is not the only arena where the poor are left out for just being poor.

The science and technology whip: It sounds unfair to include science and technology in shackles-of-poverty list, as both have given us a greatest boost in achieving outstanding greatness in all sectors of life. Unfortunately, in order to better take full advantage of technology's potential that throws people ahead of the game, there must be a lot of what poor don't have—money. The big brains make it that each discovery or innovation is beneficial to everyone, but some discoveries or innovations replace the existing reality, which in turn hurts the poor. For example, just as poor people are getting comfortable with a twenty-seven-inch analog TV, they will be forced to buy a digital flat screen and a cable service package, or there won't be any television at home. (Good luck if you have young children at home.) In the end, the side effects of science and technology shackle poor people in many ways.

Malnutrition and lack of exercise: Poor people lack the means to have balanced nutrition. Junk food and sugary drinks make up the gross part of the grocery. As a result, health complications are always lurking, striking, and returning for more. Going through hardship financially, socially, or in the family means enduring physical, mental, and spiritual pain with lots of suffering paving the road for frustration, stress, and depression. Exercise, one of the best tools to fight off frustration, stress, and depression, is out of reach. While finances shouldn't be a problem, as a gym fee nowadays is as low as ten dollars per month, transportation, time, and the inability to understand exercise benefits make it impossible for the poor to go to a gym or exercise at home.

Family size: As hard as it is to raise children, the poor have large families with many children.

The shackles of poverty alone have the power to keep us in gloom and doom. On top of that, many more aspects of life, such as political games, natural disasters, intruders in life, and so on, are huge contributors to keeping us stuck and boxed in, with no light at the end of the tunnel. Every generation seems to come with inherited resolve to tighten the belt one more notch as a strategy to fight poverty, but the millennials appear to lack this natural gift. They embrace poverty as part of a game they cannot win. That is a shameful attitude and is disrespectful to the ancestors. They must change their approach and leave poverty.

Moving Out

Former president Lyndon B. Johnson declared a war on poverty by signing the Economic Opportunity Act in 1964. Fifty years later (2014), poverty was still standing strong, and it continues standing strong currently. This means that we have been doing our best to turn this quicksand into firm ground and avoid a catastrophe, but we're still sinking miserably. Each new step we take, each new strategy we implement, or each new philosophical principle we adopt turns out as a failure. That explains how difficult the war on poverty is.

On the other hand, it shows how badly prepared we were and how ineffective we have been in this war. A great part of the blame goes to our reliance on government to take the wheel of the poverty wagon. The wagon has been going in circles and in the wrong direction for five decades. It's time to replace the driver and change direction. For that, we must make ourselves stronger before we take on the moving-out-of-poverty challenges. The reason is that the forces against us are much more powerful than our resources. Among such forces are the powers of the wealthy people and smart minds driving our lives. (Others claim that even the government is an enemy soldier. I know the gimmicks, but I am not sure about "enemy soldier.") Defeating them takes serious work, determination, and the commitment to endure. Even though each poor person has a different challenge to face and different means to meet goals, some steps, such as the following, can be applied to all of us.

Investment in your future—your kids: Raise your kids to be great thinkers, not street warriors. Higher education, which you should have (and if don't, it makes it imperative that your kids should have it), is the way to go. It could be that the fight to leave poverty is too much of a challenge for you to face alone. Investing in your kids' education empowers them and you to finish the fight against poverty. It could take many generations to lift your family out of poverty. Someone must make the first move. Why not you, through seriously investing in your kids' education?

Savings: Saving is one of the hardest things for poor people to do. Poor people don't have enough money to cover the basic needs. How can they save? They can't! But they must. Once we understand the game, we adjust ourselves to it. Don't worry about how much you save; worry about a steady saving. The principle can be more powerful than the action itself. The stronger your attitude about this, the better the chance of success.

Financial watchdog: This is not about what you have, which is not much, but about managing to get more from less. In order for this to happen, you need to pay close attention to the intruders of want, and seriously stick to the budget and the principles of your philosophy. Nine months of financial stability is your first priority. This is part of your foundation. It requires a lot of financial sacrifices, but you have to do whatever it takes. If you lose your job, you have the means to sustain your expenses without interruption. That will keep you free from worry about paying your bills and focused on fixing your situation.

The sacrifices: Life in poverty is a sacrifice in itself. Adding more sacrifices to the sacrifice doesn't seem like a smart move. But it is. You'd rather make sacrifices to be out of poverty than to stay in poverty for an eternity. Instead of working two jobs for the rest of your life, work three for a decade or two and then only one for the rest of your life.

Always be growing: Use "always be growing" to lift yourself out of poverty—it's smart and empowering. What it means is this: Find the number that works for your annual expenses—say, $29,000. Then make sure you make more than that to cover for inflation and your living upgrade. Once you have this principle under reasonable control, work on having a surplus every year. The surplus has the power to lift you out of poverty. Make sure that every year you double or triple the surplus. You must be very careful not to fall into the trap of luxury and flamboyance. You want to improve your life, but your surplus is what you want to grow fast and tall, every year. Ten years of this sacrifice can put you in a position to start a small business or buy a house or land. And if you stick with this principle, in a couple of decades or less, you'll be ready to claim yourself out of poverty.

The goal of all goals: Define what "out of poverty" means to you and take nothing short of it.

I believe that every poor child vows to be rich or at least not to be bruised by the whips of poverty, as his or her ancestors. Unfortunately, only a few children see their dreams come true. Children of the loser generations like this one, who lifted themselves out of poverty, faced pain, anguish, and disillusionment. They cried wet tears of enduring pain and sacrifice; they cried dry tears of disgust, but there's no doubt that they loved their accomplishments. Whether you, the millennials, accept this generation as a loser generation, you must embrace the challenges and collect even greater rewards, such as lifting yourself out of poverty quicker and indulge in a larger lifestyle. Pour all your efforts into reaching that goal. If you come up short, you can be sure that you've reached greatness.

You simply can't go wrong by fighting poverty. If you're not sure about this, please allow me to remind you that the whips of poverty inflict worse pain than those of any challenge you take to lift yourself out of poverty. Besides, you're invincible. There's not a dream you can't turn into reality! You can start your journey of lifting yourself and your family out of poverty now. Why wait?

7

The Middle Class

THERE'S NO NEED TO BRING up the millions of good reasons why—
unless you're crazy—you should want to belong to the middle class.
What's important is to know how you can get to middle class and/
or stay there. The strategy and work to get you there are pretty much
the same as for keeping you there. Without delay, let's get to work.

A head start: If you're a child of the middle class, you're one of
the lucky ones on the road to success. The visibility is good, with
fewer stop signs and traffic lights and no moose, deer, ducks, or wild
turkeys or wolves, lions, or hyenas on your path. Most, if not all, of
the obstacles have been removed all the way to your destination. If
you have trouble with your car, road assistance is just a call away.
And if you ever get lost, help is right next door to put you back on
track. You're simply blessed with a head start—a winner itself. We
all should have had a head start as a birthday gift. Unfortunately,
we didn't. It's becoming increasingly harder to receive such a great
gift, especially if our parents didn't have it.

From many years, the middle class has been an upper-poverty class, fighting a steep descent to poverty. In fact, it does look like it's headed to the death chamber. That means you won't be gifted with a head start, but you also won't belong to a middle class without hassle. Many of you have realized this reality, and as a result, you've embraced the possibility of living with your parents forever or paying rent until you die. Oh yes, you're doomed!

But you don't have to be. You can give yourself a head start and be ahead of the game in no time. Other people have done it; so can you. A good time to start the process is when you're in high school. Doing so means that you give yourself enough time to move at a reasonable speed toward a head start, which eventually will make you a great middle-class member. You'll safely clear obstacles, take a break to catch a breath or two, take a look at your speed and the safety of your progress, and make the necessary adjustments without rushing. While others will be stumbling, falling, and ready to give up, you will thank yourself for the head start. This means you simply will be ahead of the game.

A head start is a great move, but it comes with a lot of sacrifices, particularly for the millennials in high school. If, however, you understand the demands of life, are seriously committed to your project and dreams, and feed your mind with determination to take nothing except victory, the means for success will come. And the challenge will no longer be so daunting. You don't have to take leaps or bite off more than you can chew. Move slow and steadily. Pick up the pace as the opportunities come. You are young and powerful. The best of you truly lies ahead. If destiny keeps you in disarray, and lack of maturity laughs at you, don't worry. You can give yourself a head start at any age. It's better if it's early, but late is better than never.

What It Means to You

Any reality comes with two definitions. Whether we're talking about happiness, sadness, wealth, poverty, intelligence, ignorance, or the middle class, there's one definition accepted by the majority of the people—the objective definition. The definition based on an individual's experiences, taboos, and philosophy is the subjective definition. It's always a very good idea to incorporate both into your philosophy and then lean on individual definitions for support. As long as it doesn't clash with the viewpoints of other people, your definition is what matters the most, especially when it comes to your pursuit of happiness. The middle class could mean a family consisting of a husband and a wife with seven kids and no dogs and a house big enough for the family, a garage, and a big yard with green grass. Or it could be a husband and wife with three kids, one dog, and three cats and a one-car garage and a small yard with a couple of tall trees.

Although keeping your competitiveness up and running is a good idea, don't follow on the roads of others. Anyone who lets his or her moves be driven by the moves of other players shouldn't be playing. Define the ingredients that make your dish, and then hit the kitchen. Add items to enrich the life you have chosen, not because you must match your friends and neighbors but because you're a free mind, focused on growing your empire according to your blueprint of the middle class. Dream big! Don't be afraid of including things that seem unrealistic. If, later on, you must let go of something, crossing off what's no longer important is trouble-free. It could be that three kids and a dog no longer fit your middle-class dream, or a duplex has become a better choice than a large house. The middle class is what brings you happiness, not what people think. Then, focused on the best, lay one brick after another until your castle is complete. Being part of the loser generation doesn't mean you have to be a loser or stay that way.

The Recovery

The 2008 US presidential race was strongly focused on the middle class, with their heads barely above water and their being exhausted, hungry, and thirsty. "Hope and Change" was a slogan that seemed to give Barack Obama the ticket to a smooth ride to the White House. Eight years later, despite a considerable drop in unemployment, "Make America Great Again" was the slogan that, pushed by the angry and frustrated middle class and other factors, became the red carpet on which Donald Trump did "insult his way to the White House," leaving the world in disbelief. Apparently, Americans elected Trump to forget the "hope" that never came and the "change" that never happened. Taking into consideration what we know about government, politics, and politicians, holding our breath until we "Make America Great Again" (whatever it means) could be a mistake.

It all points to the fact that the middle class has been hopeless. But you can't give up. It is not over until is over. If you haven't seen the light at the end of the tunnel, you need to use your navigation skills to sail your way to your destination and become a middle-class member in charge of your destiny, no matter what the false promises of politicians are or any bad weather on your route.

If you haven't previously gone through rough waters, you are about to face a bitter swimming challenge in cold water for the first time. You will come out as a winner. Sit down in a quiet place, and think things through. Be realistic about your situation, and make a fair assessment of it. Weigh your strength and weakness, and then pack the determination to cross over to the green land. If you have gone through rough waters, apply what you've learned from the strategy that saved you before. Either measure is a good recovery procedure. And you can double-down by pretending that you've never belonged to the middle class, and that regardless of the weather conditions, you're going to get to the dry land—strong and safe and sound. You have what it takes to get there and move ahead. If you are already a middle-class member, these principles will keep you there and help you to improve.

Staying Ahead of the Game

If you are young and smiling at life and the future, you might not have noticed the failures of your schoolmates for whom you had great admiration and respect. Such failures have not come yet, but we, the grown-ups, have. We have not only seen the failures of our schoolmates but also experienced failures ourselves. We didn't like it; it was painful. You won't like it either.

Staying ahead of the game is like having a full stomach, with food reserved for months; having a full tank of gas and a reserve of five gallons in the trunk; wearing running shoes and carrying water and energy drinks for crossing a desert, while people are starving to death, running low on gas, or wearing slippers for crossing a desert. Staying ahead of the game is the best birthday present you can give yourself. It takes you to the middle class and keeps you shining like the North Star. Staying ahead of the game is the unbreakable umbrella of life, protecting you from the rain, sun, or storms. You must get that umbrella. The process of getting it starts with the understanding of the reality that the middle class supports the lower and upper classes:

The government collects taxes from the middle class to help the poor through social-services benefits. As the world spins crazily, the inequality of opportunity, for example, makes more people seek the support of the government. Obviously, the middle class's support bag becomes heavier, and the struggle is much harder. On the other hand, the rich class relies on the power of the middle class for the booming of their companies, as the middle class has a greater purchasing power. If the poor class is doing okay, and the rich class is booming, the middle class will sail through smooth water under clear skies. By contrast, when the poor and the rich classes see only bad cards on the table, the chain reaction of the middle class will spin out of control. And so it is very important that you understand this phenomenon in order for you to avoid nasty surprises. It is very important also to keep in mind that the government will always ask the middle class for extra support for the poor through a tax increase. And the rich class will always look for ways to suck up more money from the middle class in good and bad economies. Once you have a clear understanding of that, you're ready to start building your castle.

Your journey of fulfilling your desires and making your dreams come true can take off now. And be realistic. You'll face turbulence, course deviation, crew mismanagement, stress and fatigue, disorientation, and missed ground references because the trip to staying ahead of the game is complicated and has many surprises, both human and natural. But you can only keep going. Proceed with caution, optimism, and the certainty of landing at your destination, safe and sound.

Don't believe that every detail of your blueprint is engraved on the walls of your brain because they are not. To stay ahead of the game, you have to play like businesses do. They hire the best of the best to create a blueprint. Then they hire the best of the best to implement the blueprint. Some workplaces display, in detail, the daily, weekly, monthly, quarterly, and annual goals in plain sight. Then they sit in their offices to monitor the performance of each employee. This is to ensure that what is expected of them has been met, or someone will be called into the office to justify the consistent underperformance or get fired.

There's no reason why you shouldn't treat your life as the big corporation that it is. You don't need to hire a life coach, unless you've tried your best to stay ahead of the game but are going nowhere. You do not need to have a plan as detailed as a company's, even though having it wouldn't hurt. Have a visible chart that you talk to at least once a month. You'd be surprised how better organized you become and how much control you have over your life. Print many copies of that plan, put them in plain sight, and get your life going. Not even the luck of the Irish will stop you from enduring the thrills of the middle class. If you stay truthful to the middle class that fits you, and you stay vigilant for things that can erode the foundation of your lifestyle, you will be protected from all intruders and shadows of death. And you'll rock in the middle class ahead of the game.

Is It Worth It?

The greatest greatness of life resides in the middle class—a true paradise, from where we can look down to where we have been (poor), commend ourselves for our achievements, and look up toward what we can be (wealthy) to get inspiration for the continuation of our growth. Or it can be a Disneyland, where we celebrate our achievements, indulge in the goodies of life, and go home inspired to do better.

But if the middle class is so full of joy and happiness, how is it that not everybody is in it? Because being in the middle class doesn't happen by wish and desire, by an overnight miracle, or by selling your soul to the devil. It happens through blood, sweat, and tears and with a little bit of luck. Not all of us are cut out for such a challenge and sacrifice. Some of us are simply lazy or want to sit at the tables of the easy games only (we found the millennials are guilty as charged). And the majority of us are so blinded by poverty that we can't see the light at the end of the tunnel, no matter how bright it is. Or we are so fed up with stress, frustration, and disappointment that we don't care if we live large in the middle class or die of cold and starvation.

Well, the reality is that we must do better. First, we are to serve a purpose and leave inspiration before we are no more. Second, life, while so enjoyable, comes in a full package. The package includes the mix of good and bad, easy and difficult, happiness and sadness.

If you ever feel tempted to doubt the worthiness of the fight for the middle class, don't think twice. Its worth is more than you can imagine. Therefore, if you don't belong to the middle class yet—the place where we find the true meaning of life—roll up your sleeves, pack your bags, and go to work. Don't be discouraged, even if you feel powerless. There are many ways to make this journey a success, and there are three invincible musketeers—education, finances, and relationships—ready to give you a hand.

Education: It doesn't matter how much you hate school, education is the main instrument for excellence in all areas of life. It makes you as tall and wide as you want to be; the more education you obtain, the greater your possibility to live large. Education opens the door to outstanding achievements. It's your obligation to learn continuously throughout life. You cannot let obstacles of any kind get in the way.

You can have the brain of a genius and all the money and treasure in the world, yet find yourself unable to stand on the land of the middle class, unless you have a higher education. Education is the cornerstone for your middle class and all the other castles you wish to build. A castle built on sandy ground will be washed away by even the weakest wave, and that definitely stands no chance in a powerful storm.

Finances: A good financial system, synchronized with your ideas and higher education, allows you to shine in the middle class and propel yourself to rich class. In fact, under normal circumstances, your financial success is directly proportional to your ideas and level of education. A strong financial principle paired with education keeps you financially stable, with room to breathe. This has become urgent for all classes and is a must for the middle class.

Relationships: This one is very complicated, but, like education and finances, it lives in our genes. Although we can manage to live an okay life without a relationship, there's no way we can harvest the best of the middle class without one. We can hide the pain and cover the shame, but we know that the importance of relationships to humankind has no match. Similar to a rhythm guitar, which is noticed only when it's missing, the importance of a relationship is noticed only when we are lonely. And so you must be in a relationship and take care of it as a precious treasure of the middle class. So far, a relationship is a doubly powerful card that deals the strongest hands for any game. And it's definitely the best you can wish for in the middle class.

Getting these three musketeers to join the battle to become a middle-class member is to ensure that you will enjoy the thrills of life throughout your entire life. Keep reminding yourself that enduring the sacrifices of becoming a middle-class member is, by all measures, worth it.

8

The Rich Class

BEHIND EVERY GOOD LIES POWERFUL evil. The rich class carries a variety of evils that will land our souls in the furnace of hell, but I won't suggest we should stay away from it. Rather, we'll focus on how to belong to the rich class—the class with the financial ability to live the way we wish, to excel, and to fulfill our desires with ease.

No one says, "I need to be poorer." Even the wealthiest individual says, "I need to make more money." It seems like the desire for better and more is in engraved in our DNA. Almost everyone wants to be rich. Many of us could be rich, but we either didn't play our cards right, or we didn't take the game seriously. Don't make that mistake.

You have two approaches from which to choose. The first is to pocket every single dime. If your parents are rich or have the means to put you on that road, you have to take life seriously. Save what you have, and make it grow as tall as it can be. The second approach is to believe that destiny is not written in stone. If it is, you will need to rewrite it. Just because you were born poor, with a broken wooden spoon in your mouth, doesn't mean you have to die in poverty, without knowing the taste of a silver spoon. We humans have the strength and endurance to make any dream come true, accomplish any task, and build a legacy. It's important, though, that we act smart and choose the roads we know best. That doesn't mean you should see yourself as limited; just be realistic. You can't be a football star if you have disabilities, and you can't be a hip-hop star if you can't sing. If you suffer from a chronic respiratory disease, professional boxing is not a career for you. Pursuing wealth in areas where you are the weakest link will prove to be a mistake. So find your strength and endurance before you embark on the journey toward wealth. Real estate, professional business, sports, acting, and modeling are some examples of venues with the potential to turn you from destitute to filthy rich. Be warned that the pursuit of any happiness is a journey of sacrifices, yet you should go for a short, intense burning rather than an eternal slow fire. Forget the pain and sacrifice and focus on rewards at the finish line. Once you understand and accept the challenges of becoming rich, you can count on success from day one. You might not be a champion at the finish line, but you'll be a distinct winner because you tried.

This journey to become rich consists of two different roads. Road A is paved and has a guardrail, with real estate, retailers and wholesalers, music, and sports. It takes you to the land of wealth. Road B is paved and has a guard rail, with doctors, professors, rangers, SEAL teams, and special forces. It takes you to the land of the rich, where there's no wealth but enough cash and plenty of joy and happiness pouring from the enjoyment of what you do. (This road is, by the way, an indispensable contribution to the extension of the human existence and greatness.)

It is worth honoring the fact that both roads will serve you well and give you purpose, but it is very important to step with your strong foot first and into the territories you feel confident. Millennials are driven too easily into the hip-hop world, especially rap because it seems to be a freeway to wealth land, which is not to say it isn't. Sean "P. Diddy" Combs, Dr. Dre (Andre Romelle

Young), and Jay-Z (Shawn Corey Carter) were the top three richest rappers in 2017. At the bottom of the list of Top 100 Wealthiest Rappers is Yung Joc (Jasiel Robinson), with a net worth of $10 million, up to $770 million for P. Diddy. These are the perfect examples of what rap can deliver, but hundreds of other individuals also chose rap and didn't get far at all—and it was at the expense of their natural, untouched gifts. Many more—those who had the right package—didn't take the game seriously, and the consequences were not pretty. This is one of the reasons the millennials belong to Generation Loser. Whatever road you choose, make sure you're fully certain of your choice and prepared for the storms you'll encounter. Take your game seriously, and ensure the success of your journey as the only ultimate reward—period.

Pursuing wealth is an almost impossible journey, or a journey almost doomed to failure. But *almost* doesn't count. Forget obstacles and current calamities; they should be the main motivators for your moving to happy land. Everybody who had determination, commitment, and perseverance turned their dreams into reality and reached their destinations with glory. Nothing says that you can't do the same. If you, the millennials, can't make it big, no one can. Don't take on this task, however, just because it's so cool and distinguished to have a mansion with a runway for your private jet, vacation houses everywhere, own a couple of islands overseas, or be able to throw a million-dollar party for the models and beauty queens on your daughter's sixteenth birthday. Take this task because *you can do it*.

If you really can't find the inspiration or confidence, join the rally anyway to see how far you can go. Remember that if you aim for the stars and miss, you can be sure you'll hit the moon. And for that, I hope to see you—millennials and the rest—on the other side, where the grass is greener year-round.

9

Leverage

HAVE YOU EVER WONDERED WHY some people live better than you do, achieve goals greater than yours, finish projects faster than you, and sleep with more people than you do? They do because they have something you don't. It is called leverage.

Leverage is a great element. It's a sturdy trampoline that leapfrogs us onto the road of success; the greatest wheels to move the wagon of our destiny; the special tools that help us fix any broken section of our assembly line; and the aces that give us a winning hand. Leverage comes in many ways, shapes, and forms. And in whatever way it comes to you, embrace it, respect it, protect it, and indulge in its benefits.

If you are cursed with zero leverage, it's urgent that you earn some. The earlier you can start building it, the sooner you'll see its benefits and the sooner you'll begin to stay ahead of other players. In fact, as we swim in a large pool of leverages, it's such a shame that the young and powerful allow themselves to be losers.

The good times don't last forever. You should stock up in abundance, so you can relax when there's scarcity. Even the most disregarded leverage, such as spiritual leverage, can be so powerful, especially in this crazy world, where we create reasons to tear each other apart. A mind filled with spiritual leverage will defuse any hostile situation. If the least is great, imagine what the best can be! Wouldn't it be great to have as much leverage as you can?

Let's look into different types of leverage and get enough courage to earn some of it.

Natural-born leverage: We all are equal but not the same; that means we are born with different takes on the same task. A fighter pilot once said he had a huge advantage over his enemies because his vision was much sharper than the standard twenty-twenty. While the enemy pilots were looking for him, he'd already seen them, miles out. We know about people with super strength in their legs, arms, and teeth. Most of us who live an ordinary life are conditioned to believe that we are simple, ordinary individuals. In reality, it's the lack of opportunity or other misfortune that stops us from cashing in our natural-born leverage. We're all special. Every day we listen to girls singing tunes with their golden voices, and we watch people with perfect figures walking down the street who aren't professional pop stars or models.

On the other hand, some of us are born with poor leverage or no leverage at all. This means that staying ahead of the game may be harder for some people; that's all. And in case your natural-born leverage is dormant, wake it up. The natural leverage is not to be taken to the grave.

Surrounding leverage: This type of leverage is the one given to you by your surroundings, such family, friends, schools, government, society, and so on. Each one of them is able to give you an edge. All you need to do is pick the strongest one, and watch out for "too much of a good thing"; that's bad for you!

The winds from all directions could be blowing in your favor to the point that you feel the need to live larger than life. You don't need to buy a four-wheel-drive Hummer because you don't drive on sandy roads. You live where there's tropical weather, and you never drive to places where winter brings snowstorms. But life is good—or is it? First, you're paying way too much for what you don't use. Second, it doesn't matter how you got your money or how much you have; you should never waste it. Otherwise, you are opening the door for trouble, never mind the fact that such an attitude shows a disrespect for money. This is not leverage by any means. Instead, it may be a stupid approach to life, one that's sure to bite you hard one day.

Use the surrounding leverage to empower your life with as much leverage as possible, as long as it fits a useful purpose and isn't used for junk laying around. You don't know how much junk you have until you move to a new residence or are having a yard sale. Greed makes us never be satisfied with what we have. Define the difference between your need-leverage and your want-leverage before you begin the process of getting either one.

Need-leverage: Taking into consideration our chaotic and complicated lifestyles, we no longer thrive by normal means. We need more strength to stay ahead of the game. A wise move is to combine what your ancestors gave you with what your surroundings have available. The next move is to find areas that are crying for an urgent leverage. And the third move should be to wipe away your sad tears and replace them with tears of joy. You also need to think of the future, and get its leverage now, if you can. Let's say you believe in global warming, and you own a house in a town that's at or below the sea level. You already have experienced flood damage caused by torrential rain, and you intend to live there forever. You need leverage of some kind to protect you from floods after the rain and from sea rise later.

So to what area of life should give priority? I would tell you finances. You know that once you have taken this big elephant out of the room, the party will go on until sunrise. Money dominates our entire lives. Once we have the money, we have built all sorts of need-leverages. Remember that nothing can open the doors of financial leverage better than higher education. That's because education is that important in all areas of life.

Want-leverage: Want-leverage lives in the danger zone. You may enter at your own risk. The products there are beautifully crafted to impress you. At a shoe store, you spot a pair of winter boots that seem to call to you, "Hello, baby! Please take me home!" With a bright smile, you reply, "Oh, I'm definitely taking you home, baby! I must have you!" You have more than enough pairs of winter boots, but this one is different. Right now your life has no meaning unless you own what you describe as the most beautiful and comfortable pair of boots you've ever seen. Obviously, the designers and marketers have hit the nail on the head. Something has served its purpose well, and your credit card is about to serve you.

This scenario is familiar to us. Instinctively, we are hypnotized by the notion that more is always better. That may not be too bad, once we understand the game. The danger is that this philosophy has forced many individuals with lots of money to go bankrupt. If you are one of the youngsters—especially the boys who only wear brand-name sneakers that cost $150 and up—watch out! You must quarantine the hypnosis of want-leverage, or you'll never be an adult.

As you walk past the window of leverages, the following items are what you'll see on the display:

The numbers: Years ago, farmers aimed to have many kids and use farming equipment. They wouldn't work as hard as previous generations, yet they harvested more. Now, we rely on fast and powerful toys to make our lives easier and to propel our means of prosperity to a diversity never seen before.

Financial stability: If you have a big refrigerator, a large freezer, and a big garage, you can take advantage of foods and items on sale and save lots of money. You'll hire a maid or landscaper to free your time, which in turn allows you to make extra money and enjoy hobbies, such as golfing, hunting, skiing, or climbing. If you are wealthy, you take care of yourself through exercise and balanced nutrition, guided by professional trainers, certified dietitians, and great chefs. You live extra-large.

Specialty: Being an electrician, plumber, or carpenter saves you a lot of money on house repairs and renovations.

Parental support: Your mother is a lawyer, and your father is a businessman. Clearly, you have a better chance to have a bright future than the regular kids on the block or less frustrating than the unfortunate kids who live in the ghetto.

Bilingual/multilingual: You double-down easily.

Ranks: The president, CEO, and CFO of a large company have reserved parking, usually close to the main entrance. It serves them well in stormy weather or when they need to leave work in a rush.

Zoning: If you don't live in a ghetto neighborhood, you won't lose a good night of sleep due to loud music coming from the next block or from the apartment above yours. You won't be disgusted by the smell of urine or the sight of spit, broken beer bottles, vomit, and rotten leftovers in sandwich bags on your streets. And you will not be terrified of being a bystander who becomes the victim of a shooting.

Transportation: A four-wheel-drive SUV will allow you to travel on roads covered with many inches of snow. In an accident, the force of the impact is absorbed by the car, saving you and your passengers from injury or death. Also, driving your car while others walk in bad weather gives you a sense of empowerment, as arrogant as that may sound.

Your driver's license: If you maintain a clean driving record, you are ready to take a job as the driver of a taxi, school bus, truck, Uber, or any other driving jobs.

Clean record: If your criminal shows a couple of domestic disputes that went bad, you have only a small bump on the road. If your criminal record is a mile long, you can be sure that you're traveling along an uneven road with bumps and potholes. Then you'll continue through ditches and over cliffs and horrifying precipices and will need to be on the lookout for quicksand before you get to your destination. A clean record is the best leverage you'll ever give yourself, especially now that the wagon of opportunity is running low on available seats. We are more than seven billion people, remember?

Power: Nations race to get nuclear bombs to become untouchable (leverage rocks, even in stupidity). And then there's this:

For the many years I've lived in Brockton, Massachusetts, many businesses have fought to survive in a spooky part of town. A small gas station was the first to go, leaving an even spookier spot for a business. A couple of hundred yards away was a small house that served as a printing shop. It didn't survive for more than a year after the gas station closed its doors. After a couple of years of no activity, someone tried to turn the former printing shop into a small restaurant. The majority of clients seemed to be the ghosts of the former printing shop. As a result, it didn't take long for the owner to close the doors and go home too.

The area became a dump of empty beer bottles, cans of sodas, and used condoms. A fire station located on the other side of the road didn't make any difference. The zone was just not business-friendly. Yet someone else had the guts to give it another shot.

First, the area was fenced, giving the indication that some activity was about to take place. Then the small house and gas station were demolished, so everyone thought something big must be coming to replace them. The construction began couple of days later. After three days of work, it became obvious that another gas station was being built. The project moved fast, and the public knew who was driving it, as a sign attached to the fence read, "Cumberland Farms coming soon."

I told my son Carlos that no business would thrive there, to which he replied, "But this is Cumberland Farms."

The construction continued moving at lightning speed, and things took a good turn. In less than three months, the construction was finished. The whole area looked three times bigger. When you drive by, you simply cannot resist the view, which is bewitching at night. The lights shine brightly and give a vivid panorama of the wide-open space with a one-story building, the tip of its roof standing neck to neck with a three-story residential complex a few yards away. Clearly designed to capture attention and imagination, standing taller than itself is this beautiful place houses a large eight-pump station with a display panel and a seven-inch screen at each pump to display advertisement videos, short clips of comedy, and news. The surrounding area is filled with plenty of parking spots, including spots for the disabled, as well as walkways and a well-cared-for lawn. It feels like you're in a paradise in the middle of a desert. Inside the store are features designed meticulously to capture the imagination and to entice shoppers. You'd feel guilty going in to only pay for your gas.

Once it was a spooky spot in town that was visited by one or two customers per hour; now it's a store where you'd like to hang out all day to chat with the attractive, friendly staff and enjoy the steady flow of a variety of customers. The design team deserves a pat on the back. My son was right—it's Cumberland! And their gas prices were among the cheapest in town.

And there's more: About three weeks before the grand opening on the east side, a small used-car business next to a small Cumberland Farms on the south side of the town went out of business. This small Cumberland was a new station, almost a duplicate of the one on the east side. Two towns over, there was a relocation of a Cumberland, close to the small original one. The new one had the same features as the two new ones in Brockton.

Apparently, two leverages played a role here. The first is money. The second is reputation. And combined with the people behind the scenes, this is an exhibition of the power of leverage in pushing businesses ahead of the game. These two new gas stations were designed to kill many birds with one stone. You can, for example, stop in to buy gas and for the shopping you would have done at a convenience store, except at this gas station / convenience store you'll find a greater variety of products available and the customer service of the big grocery stores.

This example serves as a reminder in looking for opportunities where we can use our leverage to make our lives better and cash in on the benefits that come with it. We don't usually appreciate our leverage until it's gone, or we don't see the need until we find ourselves stranded for the lack of it. Leverage can be your best friend forever. Get as much leverage as you can, and put it to work to help you stay ahead of the game. I hope that you are listening, Generation Loser.

10

The Shadows of Death

THE SHADOWS OF DEATH ARE eventualities with the power to throw us out of our comfort zones and hinder our ability to succeed. Parasite shadows (the ones given to us by destiny) and induced shadows (the ones we give to ourselves) follow us everywhere we go. Parasite shadows include brain damage, poor intellectual inheritance, bad temperament, and physical defects. We could also be born poor, born in a country that faces endless war, or born and raised in a violent ghetto neighborhood. In these cases, we have to accept and find ways to minimize the harm that parasite shadows bring to us. Usually, we adjust ourselves to the reality of our illnesses and disabilities, as well as to the entrapment of our environment, and we move along to achieving outstanding goals.

Induced shadows, on the other hand, mostly originate from our choices and behavior. Let's say we are smart students who dropped out of school to join a street gang, or we are talented singers who let the stardom slip away by becoming teenage parents. Or we embrace the kings of the induced shadows—science and technology.

Technology gives us comfort and happiness (truly, a false sense of comfort and happiness) while it robs us blind. We can spend a day at home watching hundreds of television programs. We can also play video games, watch YouTube videos, and check Twitter and Facebook—not only at home but also on our smartphones that we take everywhere.

If you don't want to be screwed in the worst way, you must act ever so smart. But you might say, "What's the big deal? This is the generation of open communication and engagement worldwide. This is the millennial generation!" You would be absolutely right. The big deal is that these activities can be addictive and can ruin your life. Many of us check Facebook and YouTube for funny videos or for posting something at work. If we get caught by a supervisor or a snitch makes a move, we could be called into the office or even be escorted out the door.

Here's a clearer picture: Say you leave work at midnight and get home at 12:43 a.m. You shower, have a light meal, and check Facebook or YouTube. You watch a movie on your laptop or watch an interesting TV program. You may want some badly, but you don't want to disturb your partner, who's sleeping like an angel. You turn to online porn for assistance ... and surprisingly, three o'clock has arrived. You rush yourself to bed. At six thirty in the morning, the alarm buzzes you awake. You take your daughter to the bus stop. Since you're too tired to go to the gym, you take care of some of the items on your to-do list. Time flies by. You have to leave for work now.

You perform poorly but give an excuse to your supervisor. Because the online activity is so addictive, you run the risk of doing just about the same thing as the night before. You check a video of cats pulling stunts. You scroll down to take a quick peek at a couple of videos and then one more. The last video is so funny that you have to forward it to a couple of friends. It seems that you can't get to bed before three in the morning every day. Your errands suffer so that you can catch up on sleep. Lack of enough sleep, which is brought to you by induced shadows of death, will put you on a blacklist at work due to your poor performance. Many of your projects will never take off, and the ones currently in development could come to a complete halt. Be honest: under these circumstances—will you ever start that needed online course or finish a program at the community college? I don't think so.

The Trio-Plus-One

The shadows of death can be divided into two categories: harmful and deadly. The harmful shadows bring discomfort, stress, and a headache for some time. Of course they rob you of your drive, but they leave you only wounded. Once you do some work, you will heal in no time and continue your journey. On the other hand, the deadly shadows bring all kinds of depression, frustration, and disinterest in life, with a lifetime effect. They hunt you in the sunshine and haunt you in the darkness. They torment you when you're awake and give you nightmares when you sleep. Yet the tragedy is that either type of the shadows of death poses a serious obstacle in your path. Both combined can hurt you so badly that you might never recover. You will keep going deeper and deeper into the abyss and never be seen again. This usually happens when harmful shadows have piled up, or the deadly shadows are greater than all your powers.

The trio-plus-one is a bunch of harmful and deadly shadows ganged up to cover you, head to toe, with the blankets of hardship. They are known to you, but they are not your friends in any way. They protect each other, support each other, and cooperate in many ways to take you down or stop you from advancing. Once one member tackles you, you're in danger of being stomped on and ping-ponged by all four in a single match. Who are they? Drugs, alcohol, cigarettes, and prostitution.

Drugs: Drugs are one of the shadows of death that carries the double-edged sword for slicing and dicing two of the most important ingredients for survival: money and personality. To earn any legitimate money, you must have employment. Doing drugs messes up your skills and education, which leaves you unable to qualify for a decent skilled job, never mind having a staff under your command. Landscaping, burger flipping, dishwashing, janitorial service, working in a warehouse, and other unskilled jobs are the only venues available for your employment. Since the number of applicants in this area keeps growing while the job availability lags, employers choose those who are fit, drug-free, independent, seem reliable and safe, and are team players. Negative drug-test results and no criminal record have become the master key to employment doors. You might dodge the system and pass a drug test, only to get fired due to your poor attendance, underperformance, or doing something stupid driven by your being high.

Steve, a forty-three-year-old man, had been working for a food distribution center less than five miles from his house. The company's policy stated that any new hire must pass the drug test before being hired. There was no random drug testing, but there were mandatory drug tests when any employee was involved in an accident while operating machinery. And any accident had to be reported immediately to the supervisor. Refusing to take a drug test or a positive drug test meant immediate termination.

On a particular Friday, while working on a forklift, Steve hit the racks when he was backing up. Since no one saw the accident, he didn't report it. Before the end of the shift, someone noticed the damage on the racks and informed the manager in charge, who reviewed the surveillance tape for confirmation.

At the time of the accident, Steve had been earning more than twenty-five dollars per hour. He had performed his duty well, and the company was happy to have him on board—until tragedy struck. This father of four minor children, with his marriage in decay, was now unemployed. Steve clearly remembers having better days. Drugs, one of the members of the trio-plus-one, was to blame.

When you are a drug addict, your friends and family no longer lend you money because they can't afford to lend to those who never pay back. Illegal ways to get money might now be your only option. Robberies of gas stations and convenience stores, house burglary, and elderly assault come to mind. Any of these actions can worsen your situation, send you to prison, or get you killed. If you go to jail, your criminal record makes it even more difficult to socially integrate and find employment. This causes your frustration to mount and boosts your bad temperament. If you survive the slicing and dicing, you will be severely cut off from your power to be a productive citizen, and you will become the harbinger for the shadows of death.

With an inability to get and hold a job, your drug addiction will press on your shoulders. Your relationships will be down to casual sexual encounters with the same kind of person (like attracts like). The irony of life can easily surprise you with a pregnancy and make you a victim of circumstances, on top of the devastating consequences of a drug addiction that already is eroding your foundation. In recent years, the consequences of drug addiction have led to an overdose epidemic, where thousands of youngsters have lost their lives in seconds. On one hand, there's the overdose caused by increasing the dosage to get the same results, and on the other hand, there's the overdose caused by drugs that are simply more powerful, due to the impurity of the drugs. It's sad that the ways to get addicted to drugs continue to increase, and once you're an addict, the world spins too slowly for you to move or too fast for you to catch up. You are in limbo, dazed and confused. That is not who you are, but you've lost all your potential. The drugs have sucked you dry.

Alcohol: As long as you're twenty-one years of age or older (younger in some countries) you won't go to prison for alcohol consumption. But it could give you most of the problems that drug addiction can. You can't drive or operate certain machines and equipment. From here, things go south on a fast track, damaging your health quicker and more drastically than drugs do, in general. You could be on the path of losing the love and care of your family and might become homeless.

Cigarettes: Smoking regular or electronic cigarettes, cigars, blunts takes your money and gives you health and social problems. Depending on the severity of your addiction, you could find yourself spending more than $450 a month on cigarettes alone (equal to a monthly payment on a brand-new car). Health complications are in the number-one place with the shadows of death. They kill us silently and slowly, with lung cancer as the leader.

Prostitution: Some things are ugly, detrimental, shameful, and socially unacceptable. Prostitution can be all of that and more. That makes prostitution one of the shadows of death with long-lasting, bad repercussions. Even when life circumstances force you into prostitution as a temporary measure, and you have strong determination to clean yourself up and get on a dignified road for your journey, you'll face strong challenges when you quit. First, you'll lose your integrity and dignity. Second, you might never recover. Third, you might never be able to clear your name. In some cases, even after you clean your name, your dignity is still affected by your despicable past; your cloth is washed, but the stain is still there. And then, for better or for worse, prostitution is in most of the world.

Sadly, the other members of the trio-plus-one (drugs, alcohol, and cigarettes) are only getting more powerful and delivering more devastating, deadly blows, especially to youngsters. My impression is that millennials decrease their potentials by all kinds of malign tumors, with drugs, alcohol, and cigarettes pushing hard on the gas pedal.

Any shadows of death come with the destructive power to eliminate you from the game, but drugs, alcohol, and cigarettes are the invincible soldiers of the shadows of death, and they are ferociously in action. And they are slick. They attack the innocent and indefensible—the young millennials. They come with a sugar-daddy face, but as soon as they get hugs and kisses, they unleash the evils on you—the addictive agents—unmercifully. Once they have you, they have you. The time, money, and sacrifice you need to free yourself become a torture that many people cannot endure. Should you be messing around with these three powerful agents of the shadows of death? I don't think you should. Believe that smoking herbs, taking drugs, and drinking liquor all are addictive and very bad for you. Take prescribed drugs only—although it's better if you take care of yourself so you don't need to take any drugs at all—and follow the recommended dosage. Yet watch your dependency like a hawk. Also, keep your skepticism about the legalization of some drugs, such as marijuana, alive and well. Educate yourself on illegal drugs before you swallow, sniff, or smoke any of them.

Usually we get hit with a false sense of time empowerment. We are young, beautiful, and invincible, with a lifetime of luxury ahead of us. We think there's no trouble we can't get out of, safe and sound. I wish life was like that. The reality is that freeing yourself from any addiction takes self-determination for detox and rehabilitation. After all is said and done, you have to start a new life from scratch, far behind the game, with serious work to do before you catch up. Statistics are not encouraging either. Don't rely on the power of time to lay back and let the shadows of drugs, alcohol, cigarettes, or prostitution take you where you shouldn't go. And if you find yourself there, fight to get out, and enjoy the fresh air before you become shackled and trapped. Fresh air is good for your body, mind, and spirit, while the trio-plus-one is simply toxic.

Please develop the ability to recognize them from far away, and then run for your life.

Obesity

Obesity is an active, number-one member of the unmerciful shadows-of-death squad. Alone, it brings health complications and physical restrictions that take away more than half of our potential.

And it can fatally stab us with its most poisonous knife—diabetes. Diabetes whips us head to toe, front to back, from beginning to end. It drains away almost all our powers as it wraps us in a blanket of thorns and poison ivy and gets us soaking wet before throwing us in a torture chamber. Obesity's soldiers use a variety of bullets and continue to improve their whipping skills and strategies; they do not discriminate. Even when we have a break, our lives will still be full of restrictions, our motor skills will be always under attack, and our desires will be severely quarantined. A healthy person, fit and proactive, goes through rough times in his or her lifestyle. An obese person with diabetes goes through hell. I cannot think of any shadows of death capable of reducing us to zero more than obesity. Please educate yourself as much as you can about diabetes, and then take cover and more cover.

Illiteracy

When you are illiterate, your life is a struggle. Illiteracy nowadays is pretty much a low-level of education that doesn't allow an individual to keep up with technology. A high school diploma takes you nowhere. In fact, someone with only a high school diploma can almost fit in with the illiterate people—and that's just in the employment area. From there, everything becomes even more dreadful, frustrating, and discouraging. It is true that technology has made our lives easier, and we believe it will continue to do so, but to take full advantage of technology, we must have an education greater than merely the ability to read and write. Holding diplomas and certificates from low-level education doesn't cut it anymore. If you are illiterate in this current era, there aren't many trains welcoming you on board. And the train you need the most, such as good employment, left the station a long time ago.

If you earn a paycheck from an unskilled job, the shadows of illiteracy have nailed you to the cross of poverty. The sun rarely shines in poverty, and illiteracy takes away the moonlight. Don't listen to negative voices that shout about the hardship and/or impossibility of getting a higher education. And if you can't, make the best of what you have. If you are in for the fight, whatever level of education you have can turn you into a successful individual. Fight to escape this shadow of death, and earn a degree—not in the next generation but now.

Breakups, Splits, and Divorce

Breakups, splits, and divorces can fit in one basket as items of the same kind. Individually and collectively, they all bring consequences that fit in the world of the shadows of death.

Breakups: Even when a breakup comes after a short-lived romance, it can dump a heavy load of emotional stress that can turn into frustration or depression. Females are easier prey for this shadow because they're wired with a higher degree of love, care, and nurturing.

Splits: Considering the fact that a split is a stepping away from the kitchen that has become too hot, it can bring surprising consequences. Either partner could use a trick to gain a full commitment due to a pregnancy. Suddenly, you have to go through the hell of having an abortion, which, in this case, is almost impossible without a ferocious argument that could kill all possibilities of a reunion. Having to raise a child in a split relationship is no fun. And if child support is enforced by the law, the train of chaos has started its engine, and you are in for a bumpy ride for at least eighteen years.

Divorce: The consequences of a divorce are more devastating than those of a breakup or split because divorces come with more strings attached. Usually, we have invested time, love, and dedication to building something great. Before its completion, a storm has brought it to ruin. Rebuilding it from the scratch again can be a challenge impossible to endure. And if happens after many years of marriage and there are children involved, the shadows of death are doubled or tripled.

Keep mind that I've only touched on a few shadows of death. It's your responsibility to picture realities that can be translated to shadows of death if they attack you. Keep in mind also that any shadows of death can slow your progress and paralyze your potential, thus hurting your chances of living a happy, productive life. To avoid that—whoever you are, wherever you are—fight to get the best from life. We inevitably face many aspects of life that, at some point, will become shadows of death. Everybody does stupid things that can turn into monstrous shadows of death. So the game here is not to aim for a life with zero shadow attacks; that's impossible (although it doesn't hurt to try). The game is for you to find ways to dodge as many shadows as you can and minimize the consequences of the ones that have tackled you. Taking care of small malfunctions means blocking the arrival of big problems. This is one of the many principles in a strong philosophy used to deal with the shadows of death. And here we are again, facing another aspect of life where the young and beautiful are vulnerable because of age and immaturity, and they are severely disempowered by living circumstances and the surrounding influences.

Whatever factors are used to classify any group as the loser generation, the millennials are a generation where such factors are in greater number and span, and the consequences are much more daunting and last much longer. Nowadays when you're taken down by one member of the shadows of death, it takes longer to recover, and harder work is needed. Such a reality is true not only for millennials but for all of us in Generation Loser.

The sacrifice is definitely horrifying, but letting the shadows of death cover us from head to toe is not an option. In the end, the choice is yours. I recommend that you pick your fights wisely and take nothing but victory. Shadows of death are very strong, but you are stronger. Don't forget that.

11

Sports, Entertainment, and Frustration Bond

WE BEGAN BY FOOLING AROUND to kill time and boredom in a very simplistic way. Without realizing we were doing so, we also developed physical, mental, and emotional strengths. And it felt great because we were fulfilling the demands ingrained in our human framework. Playing was our greatest entertainment, so we played with Mom and Dad, brothers and sisters, and friends next door. And later, we invited more friends. We created small teams and challenged each other. We invited the people who couldn't play (or didn't want to play) to watch us. They became fans, encouraging us to play more and take the games more seriously. To make things more exciting and expand the goodness of the games, we spread the news to friends, districts, towns, states, and nations. We grew, diversified, and created federations. And we continued to grow and diversify. And then we decided to create an arena where only the best of the best could compete for the world championship—the Olympics. Great things were getting better!

But then came big money, and with big money came greed. Greed brings cheating, corruption, and the key that opens the gates of hell. The simplistic games we played for excitement became sophisticated, major money generators—sports. Gambling found its way in small, simple games and then to big teams, players, and owners. This reality forced parents to push their kids to practice sports at a very young age, hoping they'd make it to the high school teams and eventually to a national league.

After years of practice, there will be the time to try out, which is another daunting matter, thanks to recruiters. (History tells us that whenever there's a competition, there will be a struggle and unfair games.) If you're qualified and able to pull some strings, luck might strike. After that, the compromise to please the fans—they expect a good game all the time—the struggle to stay competitive, the pressure of socioeconomic demands, among other sport-related stressors, almost dictates that players take serious action to measure up. One way is to learn to be unbreakable. They hide the pain of minor injuries and push the envelope so they can play in every game. Sitting on the bench would hurt their value. Football players, for example, take physical punishment quietly, including blows to the head. Taking it like a man or going the extra mile to please the fans is one thing, but going through hell with injuries caused by a vicious opponent is another thing. The effects of such an act will show up after retirement in the form of changes in personality and/or physical and mental degradation.

Then there are the greedy big shots in charge of the crazy, filthy, and despicable games behind the scenes, with match fixing, selection of opponents to be taken out, and doctors choosing the best players to experiment on with a new drug. We never know which card will be pulled next, but we know it won't be a good one. And it gets worse! Once a scam comes to light, people get arrested, names are removed from Halls of Fame, trophies are taken away, and titles are stripped, hurting sports' dignity and leaving fans disappointed.

Fortunately, we don't let cheaters take away our sports devotion, and we stay loyal to our teams. The worst is that these dangerous tactics are becoming normal in our culture. If you wonder why sports got so bad, the answer is money.

Sports have become an industry to which everybody wants to belong. It's a money generator everybody wants to have. Everyone wants to get in as a player on the field or as a behind-the-scenes agent for the money and fame. The big dogs driving the games from behind the scenes aim their focus on TV ratings instead of prioritizing the excellence of the sport and the well-being of the players. Big corporations use the elite players to advertise their products and spend crazy amounts of money on the best commercial spot for special televised games, such as the Super Bowl. Another ton of money is invested in bringing us what we want at the stadium or on TV. Money from the big dogs pours everywhere, as "money makes money." Well, where there's money, the devil is dancing with his evils, waiting to strike hard.

But sports have found new playgrounds in different venues and have expanded their meaning too. The Olympics now does not just represent the best athletes; it's also about representing nations' economic power for international recognition. When Team USA plays Team Russia, the game is a battle of which nation is better in the eyes of the world, rather than glorifying the sport.

The sports we practiced became the games we played, or the games we practiced became the sports we played. Whether you are a player or a fan, you must act smart and not be a loser.

Entertainment

Since entertainment is vital to us, its wings have extended to different areas. Years ago there wasn't much entertainment other than sports, bars, dancing, and social events, like weddings. Then came movies, followed by television. The 1936 Olympics in Berlin,

Germany, became the first sporting event to be shown on television. Slowly, the entertainment in homes grew as the diversity of programs kicked the ball all the way up to where we can watch movies, sports, and comedy on our laptops and smartphones. Yet sports stands tall because they give the opportunity for friends to gather together at a buddy's house with booze and food to entertain themselves by watching a game. It's also cheaper, safer, and more convenient than going to the stadium. And some peaceful gambling may take place—I think it takes place all the time. Somebody might go home not only boozed up, with a full stomach, entertained and happy, but also with extra cash in his pocket, thanks to sports.

Frustration

We humans are exposed to many things for keeping the body, mind, and spirit balanced. Sunny days, our favorite coffee blend, fast-moving traffic, courteous drivers on the road, a smiling face behind the counter, a pretty secretary—each one alone boosts our happiness. Conversely, a rainy day, a bitter cup of coffee, a traffic jam, jerks on the roads, an angry face behind the counter, or a rude secretary elevates our depression level and could ruin our day. It is hard to get around these depressing factors (we should try our best, though) because we evolved like this. Sports happen to be a two-faced friend.

When we watch the game at the stadium or at home, and our team is winning, happiness runs freely in our blood. We love the world. Life is great. We go home, probably drunk, to a nice party under the sheets and then to a good night's sleep. We get up early for work. We can't wait to get there and start commenting on the game and brag to our nonfan friends. The week goes by fast. But when our team plays badly and loses, rage and anger gush from every pore in our bodies. We hate the world. Life sucks. No one better mess with us at home! We go straight to the fridge for a cold beer or straight to the booze cabinet. Night comes, and we use the wife for stress and frustration relief, and we're guaranteed to have a nightmare. We don't feel like going to work. When we get there, we don't want to talk to anyone. The day is the longest ever, throughout which we curse a player or two and hate the whole team. There's double the stress and frustration if we lost a bet.

Day by day we are more engaged in sports, and so is our money. The happiness brought to us is more celebratory, and the frustration and madness are more intense, more devastating. But we cannot turn our backs on something born within us and beneficial in so many ways. We are born addicted to playing as the main entertainment and fuel for our happiness. From a very young age up to the time we become a child again, we never say no to games that entertain. We can play for hours and hours. When we don't, we feel like we are missing something great. Well, we are! Nothing gives us more happiness than playing. We admire and cherish the energy children have, playing forever. That happens because playing brings happiness, and happiness is life's greatness without prejudice. We need to play like a child every day and at the same time be smart sportsmen, especially now that sports have become such an evil monster that we are trying to tame.

The current era demands that you keep a foot on solid ground if you want to be successful and ahead of the game. Practice the sports you have the skills for. Be a fan of your favorite sports. Watch games on TV. Go to stadium as often as you can, as long as you don't hurt your means of success and survival. And remember that the more you engage in sports, the less time there will be for you to invest in the fundamental aspects of your life. The more you spend on sports, the less you will have to help you build leverage that propels you in life. Think of yourself first. If you are a player, play for the cause, clean and smart. Your effort and skill will shine brighter and farther and will be better appreciated.

As player or fan, understand the bond between sports, entertainment, and frustration to get the best out of it, rather than frustration, the enemy, and the empty pocket. Then you won't be a loser, even if your generation is.

12

Education

EARLY EDUCATION IS THE BEST foundation of a prosperous life. And I'm not talking about teaching our kids to count from one to ten and to distinguish colors. I'm referring to the whole range of activities that empowers children's learning ability, starting with fun games up to smart toys and creative tools. Exposing children to a supervised world of danger and interaction with nature and its creatures is another area where the children have been hindered— made losers already by the parents' ignorance, lack of understanding, and financial means. The millennial children, unfortunately, suffer the most. And once a child is hurt in his early education, the chances of achieving excellence in later education are severely reduced. Those of Generation Loser seem unable to repair the damages and lack the grit to change this reality.

Despite the wide range of possibilities and a serious effort from the government to educate every child, education hasn't bloomed in the entire garden. It continues to follow the traditional, normal pattern. On rough terrain, only a handful of flowers bloom. Since there isn't enough water or sun, only the strong flowers survive. On flatlands, despite some challenges, the blooming score is from decent to pretty good for the entire population. And on fertile lands, there are more than enough roses dancing around and blocking the view of the little guys, making it seem like we aren't all parts of the great meadow.

The kids of poor families are the least able to advance; the kids of middle class achieve many goals; and the kids of the rich class grow up to become successful individuals who run the lives of the rest of us. During the three stages of education (home education, school education, and higher education), this trend still dominates.

Home Education

All parents work hard so their children can have a good education. Parents who have had a good home education want to pass it on to their children. This challenge is increasingly difficult in all social classes and obviously is much harder for the poor and middle classes. Children of parents who are poorly educated don't create a home environment that inspires good morals, let alone the taste for education. They live a lifestyle dominated by low standards, under the whips of poverty. We haven't yet provided the solution for this problem, while the birth rate in this social class is the highest. On top of that, home education has been tackled by so many predators, such as finance, the laws of the country, outside influences, and the dominance of media and video games.

Finances: Parents don't have the financial means to cover the basic human needs, which sours their home environment. The challenges of their lives don't allow for financial support for building a solid home education. The focus and efforts are on getting the means for survival. This task is increasingly more difficult, despite economic improvements.

The laws of the country: The government should step in and enact laws to protect children from domestic abuse. Many parents have bad tempers and go through hard times filled with stress and frustration. When they are angry, they could go too far and abuse children unintentionally. That is why a great number of parents have been convicted of domestic abuse more than once, usually resulting in children growing up missing a mom or dad at home.

The parents who are capable of giving a good home education often choose time-out as the only punishment for children's misbehavior and disobedience to avoid getting in trouble with the law. The line between punishment and abuse is very thin. Most parents cross it unknowingly. And when it's up to the legal system to judge whether or not the line has been crossed, trouble knocks on the door, and the parents are the ones to answer. On top of that, when children understand their protection by the law, they take over the kingdom. The parents become completely powerless and must move smartly to avoid trouble. Keeping their mouths shut and hands to themselves is a far better choice than cutting a deal with a prosecutor.

In common child-abuse scenarios, the parents go to counseling and follow court orders. In extreme cases, the parents face jail, and the kids are taken away and placed in foster care. Despite credit that should go to foster parents, foster care is, at best, a secondhand family. And the priority is not home education; rather, it's ensuring that another child has a roof over his or her head and food on the table.

Aware of family law, foster parents do their best to care for children accordingly so they don't fall through the cracks. And so, they only give so much love to avoid facing legal issues in court. At the first sign of trouble, they turn over the children to social services, possibly at the first opportunity, to then send them to another foster home. It is basically up to the children to behave and obey, or leave and face the consequences. Usually, they leave.

They grow fast; in no time they turn eighteen years old. Now on their own on the streets, they possibly are on the way to becoming criminals. They have experienced trauma, deception, and lack of love from their biological parents. They know nothing about home education. And the law of the land is to blame. Even though this reality is predominant in large countries, cities, and towns, Generation Loser is blessed (or cursed) by the supersonic speed at which news travels, and their world is basically one big nation/city/town. Will a kid who, by law, can't be physically punished for misconduct and is bounced from one foster home to another have a strong home education and become a respectful, successful adult? Impossible!

The outside influence: Two major players seriously influence kids, both at home and outside home: marketing and advertising.

Marketing spends tons of money on research and development of ways to satisfy the need they create. They choose culture and traditions for our kids to follow, as the complementary values to home education. Supposedly, this enables children to integrate easily with other cultures. And that seems like a great idea, except it not only comes at a cost, but it also has consequences, where the new values imposed by marketing strategies will clash with the traditional values of the parents. Let's say surveys have concluded that the miniskirt is what teens prefer for summer clothing, but parents disapprove it because they think miniskirts are too revealing. Or maybe going to a mall and outside activities with a bunch of friends is socially empowering, but the parents believe that trouble always comes when teens gather together.

In reality both, the marketing and the parents are right. And the toddlers and youngsters, due to immaturity, will choose whatever marketing promotes because that's where the fun is! In addition to that, marketing has a powerful source: advertising.

Another ton of money is used in advertising to bombard your house with advertisements through television, newspapers, radio, and so on. The content of programs designed to educate kids is poor and boring. Children choose to watch adult programs, which is not a problem under a parent's supervision, but parents are never home to filter what children can and cannot watch. Besides, so many programs approved for children are just stunning. And the technology comes in to make everything better and more interesting through the internet and smart devices. How do we stop our children from watching pornographic content online when all they need to do is click, tap, and watch, twenty-four/seven?

The dominance of video games: This is another big elephant in the room. Games designed to educate and empower the mind don't cut it. Kids play them when there's nothing else to shake the boredom off. They only play for a while because after forty minutes, such games become boring. *Call of Duty* and other violent video games are on center stage. They are interesting and are played with friends and people online.

We try to squeeze quality time with our children into our busy schedules, but for many reasons, the quality time is reduced to trips to the mall to shop for school clothes and school supplies or playing video games with them at home. Unfortunately, playing video games falls short of the expectation because we cannot match the children's level. Playing with us is boring, so they play with their friends and other players. On top of that, while we keep waiting for the conclusive results on whether violent video games modify children's behavior, the game goes on, and parents watch their kids' aggressive behavior increase in direct proportion to the time they spend playing violent video games, especially when they lose over and over again.

The children who grow up with a very poor home education will have a low moral standard, learn the culture of the streets, and have media as their guardian angels. These are the flaws of the past we still allow to dominate today. And we are worsening the consequences as if we've forgotten that the best homes create the best minds.

School Education

The second major step on the road to prosperity has a twelve- to thirteen-year journey. Your child will be educated, with academics and skills development taking center stage. They also will learn social norms and social integration. Teachers, the assistant parents, have enormous responsibilities and challenges with children of different ethnicities and backgrounds, on top of local, state, and federal laws and school's policy, rules, and regulations. These extraordinary individuals work at their best, sharing love and care for the children, while ensuring that they have a strong base for every purpose of life. And it seems that no one appreciates that.

If we make a detailed analysis, the result will be stunning, with staff pushing austerity to the extreme, and teachers using the little money they earn to buy school materials so the students don't feel left out. I think this is an ugly shame on government. An even uglier shame is that big, rich nations like the USA lag behind developing countries. Rumor has it that the educational system in rich nations has been in crisis. Lack of creativity is one of the missing ingredients.

From an outside quick analysis, we find that we don't pay teachers enough, let alone a lot of money. People with a passion and a calling for teaching feel obligated to look for another career because the money they earn as teachers is not worth it the stress and other related job demands. And there are layoffs in teaching more often than in other areas of employment. We lay off teachers, make school budget cuts, and use gimmicks that leave teachers with no choice but to go on strike. We even shut schools down. We've forgotten that we desperately need to boost education, bringing young and innovative minds into the game. We've been making moves that worsen the already losing conditions for young people to earn a rich, basic school education.

Higher Education

The rapid advancement of science and technology along with the new business philosophy dictated that higher education is a mandatory tool for individuals seeking to excel. College degrees are the first set of ladders to climb, followed by university or specialization. The higher you climb, the greater and more beautiful the view is. But higher education is very challenging, if not the most challenging. The challenges begin at enrollment. Unless you win a scholarship, you must rely on your parents, who are struggling with their own financial hardship, to cosign for your student loan. This reality is even more daunting when you aren't the only child, and your brothers and/or sisters are already in college or university.

When you must count on your parents' support for your higher education, you could have to hold your breath for a little bit longer before you take the first steps in making that dream a reality. What is bad about this is that your brain will become lazy and thus hinder your motivation to resolve the tuition problem. Forget working two jobs to save for higher education as a way out for millennials. They are not cut out for that endeavor, and drugs and smoking are after the cash they have earned, stolen, or borrowed. What a tragedy!

The next scenario is the one that demands you to be a soldier, fighting a war on two fronts. On one front you fight for your employment. You must be productive, keep good attendance, and embrace all the sacrifices to stay employed. Note that this battle is increasingly harder. On the other front, you fight for your higher education. Because you can't enroll full time, and you study under stressful conditions, it will take longer to graduate. Even for simple online and correspondences courses—say you just want to upgrade yourself—there's a burden to carry that can be really heavy if you are married with children, and your partner is a jackass. Triple the load and stress if you are a single parent. Quadruple it if, on top of this, you have to care for your elderly parents because your brothers and sister are ungrateful.

And think about this fact: A twenty-seven-year-old in the United States, with $67,000 of school debt will pay off the loan when he or she is seventy-three years old. Graduates from universities will make far less than what they've hoped for, and in most cases, they will work two jobs in order to survive. Even when the conditions are favorable, the uncertainty of the future makes people think twice about enrolling in higher education because the future is becoming very scary, and its predictability is no longer so unpredictable (the prediction is showing an ugly face wearing a nightmare mask). Well-educated people are going through financial hell, committing despicable acts, and exhibiting shameful behavior. Who wants to bother with higher education? That's a shame because higher education is supposed to give a boost to our social-economic lives and take our personal integrity to a whole new level, instead of causing stress and frustration from the inability to find a job to pay back school loans.

But let's dig deeper for a better understanding. Philosophically speaking, to leave higher education alone sits well. Practically speaking, it does not. Well-educated individuals committing despicable acts have turned off the power of their education. They became the shameful torches of literacy. Imagine how tragic their lives would be without education.

The second greatest benefit of higher education is found in employment. It gives you some advantages over other applicants, and it eases frustration. And education is way more than what it seems to be; education transformed the human species, and the human species transformed education. The transformation is not going to stop or take a break any time soon, if ever. And so, you must pass high school, and move on to the real learning. Education is anything but easy or free of stress, frustration, and anxiety. It's the complete opposite. But once you make it to the door, you might as well go in, endure the pain and sacrifice, and then collect your trophies. It is true that you could come out with tons of school debt, worries, and uncertainty that make you lose sleep or have nightmares. But you must stay true to reality, with a positive attitude to fulfill the prophecy. You are born with the ability to read and write for a reason. You cannot sit back and watch your genius evolve. That's not how things work. The genius in you is waiting to be set free.

Remember: "With great power comes great responsibility." And with greater power comes greater responsibility. You may not like your responsibility, but you must embrace your destiny. The beauty of life is in thanking those like you, who got up, took a deep breath, got in the higher-education room, endured the sacrifice, and brought out the best in themselves. Education strengthens body, mind, and spirit and increases your wingspan and sight. Don't let any kind of obstacle stand in your way. And keep in mind that staying current and focused on innovation are the supplemental tools that help ensure your greater success in the near and distant future. Raise your appetite for continuous learning. It not only makes you smarter but also keeps your brain active, which can serve you well as you age. Don't wait until the war gets here to learn how to fight. Instead, learn to fight and upgrade your fighting skills in a time of peace for the times of war, or you aren't ahead of the game.

Allow me to remind you that the education high-rise has no penthouse. And the higher you climb, the greater is the view. There's not a single corner of life where education cannot shine brightly and steal the show. Whatever is making you a loser is dodging the rays of education. You must not allow that to happen. As the world seems to slip away from under our feet, education is our great savior. You have to have it if you wish to cherish the best life has to offer.

13

Employment

THE MEDICINE WE NEED THE most can't be found anywhere. Even when we meet all the requirements, we are left empty-handed because there's just not enough to go around. The companies are doing their best to stay alive, running their businesses with smaller staff and bigger support from science and technology. This reality has become the new business norm, but it means a shortage of the medicine—jobs—which has become critical worldwide. But the new business norm is not the only culprit of the job shortage. Many factors also play a huge role here—globalization, bad economic conditions, and late retirement, as well as the millions of people entering the labor market every year, including recent high school graduates and everybody else who's reached employment age. The future of employment doesn't look promising.

First, population growth is estimated to reach ten billion in 2050.

Second, we have been unable to stabilize the employment assembly line and plan improvements because we have been too busy fixing broken parts in many sections. Months after we fixed the housing bubble of 2008, China/USA relations went sour over the South Asia territory. Once that was calm, North Korea tested intercontinental missiles and vowed to turn New York City into a sea of flames. Then Russia raised its voice in Syria, out of fear of Western global domination and to tell the world that the Soviet Union was no more, but Russia still stood strong to "Western bullies," especially the USA.

China, Brazil, and India were the new players that boomed faster, while the rest of the world watched, only to face decline triggered by corruption and political schemes, which suddenly and surprisingly brought a very sour taste to the Brazilian population after the World Cup in 2014. The oil boom brought the prices down to an unimaginable level, forcing a large number of oil-related businesses to close their doors, leaving thousands behind. And Venezuela got the knockout punch from the oil prices.

Each of these phenomena attacks the employment wagon direct and indirectly. The companies fear a loss of profit, and the uncertainty of the future forces them to watch their pennies like a hawk. If you see the employment world getting where it needs to be and doing what it is supposed to do, you must be high, on drugs, or hallucinating.

In the 2008 presidential race, Barack Obama was riding on the "Hope and Change" slogan. People were tired of stressful lives under bad economic conditions. President George W Bush and "his" wars (Iraq and Afghanistan) were to blame. Even though unemployment dropped from 8.5 to 4.5 during Obama's two terms as president, we couldn't wait for him to go home. The reason why we were unhappy with the economy, despite the low unemployment, is a complicated puzzle to piece together. Quite honestly, the majority of us aren't equipped to understand this puzzle, let alone put it together.

In the 2016 presidential race, people feared Obama's strategy, pushed forward by Hillary Clinton, which, in part, gave the victory to Donald Trump, who, for better or worse, spoke the language of the people and made the promises they wanted to hear, especially in manufacturing. Yet the employment mess cannot be cleaned up as easily as we think. Unfortunately, the gloom and doom will stick around for some time.

Is there a way out of this? Let's make an assessment to find out.

Double work, same pay: Here's an example of a miniature assembly line with a disturbing chain reaction: Harsh economic conditions worldwide lead to wars, natural disasters, bubbles, and corruption, which leads to forcing businesses to cut corners so they can stay competitively profitable. Cutting corners increases pollution, and people will complain. Government steps in to tighten rules and regulations and increase business taxes. The increase in taxes forces businesses to reduce the task force and freeze raises and hiring. Employees find a better job (supposedly) and quit. The extra work is spread out to the reduced task force. The work is now harder but the pay stays the same. And there you have it: employment chaos!

The rat syndrome: When rats have nothing to eat, and you're sleeping, dinner is about to be served. Only after you wake up will you notice that your exposed toes have been assaulted. Why? Because rats aren't as dumb as we think! They bite softly and blow on the wound immediately. This means your brain doesn't notice any pain or reason to wake you up. Similarly, many jobs we take are simply soft roads to failure. Having multiple part-time jobs is an example. When you have three part-time jobs that consume your entire day, you lose big, even if you are making good money. You are going through bits of employment, far from a career. Before you know it, ten years have gone by, and you don't have a real job. You're broke or barely surviving in disempowerment. Uber and Lyft are very convenient ways of making a buck or two—or even a lot of cash. The problem is that in the long run, those easy bucks will keep you broke. Sooner than you think, you will get used to them, and not care about empowering yourself for full-time employment that supports your financial responsibilities to retirement. You will be replaced by driverless cars. (Sure, this stretches the truth a bit because it'll take time before artificial intelligence becomes our trusted driver. Then again, we could be surprised by science and technology's speed of delivery.) Unless you are 100 percent sure that the rat syndrome is a temporary measure, don't mess with it. You could lose a toe or two.

The minimum wage war: No one is earning enough money. That includes the government. Little money and unemployment is a twofold problem for the government. First there's a decrease in tax revenues collected directly from our paychecks and indirectly from our purchases. Then there's the increase in social services' responsibilities as more people need government assistance to make the ends meet.

Businesses and the middle class are forced to face increases in health insurance, property taxes, and so on, and even losing income tax credits.

Forbes magazine publishes wealth pyramid every year. People who made the top ten last year don't want to lose that position this year or the next. In fact, everyone on the list below the number-one spot want to move up to claim the number-one spot. In order for that to happen, more profit is needed. Cost control takes center stage. Payroll reduction becomes the first sector that's hit, so unless the profit margin is really great, good raises won't happen.

Employees at the bottom, especially those earning minimum wage, have no way to survive without a considerable amount of help from the government. They cry for a pay increase, but employers don't want to hear that. They shout for an increase in the minimum wage, but the government doesn't want to hear that either. Employers fight the minimum-wage increase under the pretext of having low or no profit, driven by bad economic conditions, competitions, and bogus but convincing excuses. An increase in wages would mean a reduction of the task force and definitely a freeze on full-time hiring. A full-time employee is entitled to the company's benefits, but that leads to an increase in the company's expenses.

When the government understands the cries of the employees, a dilemma is laid on its lap. The government wants the love of the people, and it would like people to make lots of money, which would increase the consumption of goods and services, which would benefit the people and the government. But it doesn't want to mess with pay increases because if businesses lay off employees or relocate to another state or country due to labor costs, the government has to deal with the loss of tax revenue, on top of the headaches of the unemployment increase. As much as it's unfair that employers pay a wage that doesn't cover the cost of living and give raises that don't offset inflation, this war is not going to see peace any time soon. I guess the best way to get out of this abyss is to keep looking for better-paying jobs and reduce your expenses until the government does the right thing.

Employed, feeling unemployed: The same plague that's attacking the minimum-wage war is spreading its virus to the low, middle, and upper-middle classes, precisely because monthly earnings don't cover monthly expenses. Even with good pay and people sticking to their budgets, there's a struggle. For example, just when you finally get on the positive side of your budget sheet—most of your must-have expenses are covered, and your want-needs are on standby—you find yourself forced to buy supplemental goods and services that have become a must-have. You need to get a new computer, a tablet, a phone, and so on because what you have is obsolete. Or the fees for the registration, title, and inspection sticker for your car have gone up. So many businesses haven't increased the starting pay for more than twenty years. How can we not feel unemployed if what we earn is far from enough?

Finding a job: Finding a job is a daunting task. Sure, unemployment is generally low, and the economy has improved globally. The outcome would mean more jobs are available, except things are never quite like that. Once you jump in the water, you realize that it's not as warm or as pleasant as you thought it would be.

Staying employed: In these modern times, keeping your job is a heavy responsibility. You must attend to the demands of the company and show your worth through excellence in performance. Your diploma and interviews got you in; now it's time to prove that you can deliver. Keep in mind that you are on the radar. Everything you do and say is carefully measured in your favor or against you. Rookies are entitled to some initial mistakes, but don't be laid-back; be proactive. Any extra effort is sure to bring a nice surprise.

If your employment package comes with the opportunity to move up, and you have what it takes, go for it. Start the journey from day one. While doing your best to excel and prove your worthiness, learn as much as you can about the company. Familiarize yourself with as much as you possibly can, but be careful not to push the wagon too soon or too fast. Ask as many questions as you possibly can, observe the dynamic of the company, and don't feel shy about offering your suggestions, as long as you don't step on anybody's foot. Take your job very seriously, and whatever self-improvement comes to you, just embrace it. That could mean searching for a different view of the company as to its longevity and prosperity and then looking for areas of improvement in your department. Build a respectful, friendly relationship with higher-ups and elder employees. It's better if you come with a different perspective and ways of doing things while still within the company's rules and policies. Offer to train in different tasks or to be transferred to other departments for cross-training. It makes you a more valuable employee, and it gives you extra points when there's a vacant position in any department. Obey the company's rules and policies from day one, beginning with attendance and breaks. Aim for a perfect attendance and never take extra minutes on your breaks.

Prioritize your safety and that of others. A work injury is problematic for you and your company; you get a red mark on your safety page, and you could be transferred to a position or department you don't like to prevent the possibility of reinjury. You could lose your job if you are found at fault. Companies and workplaces must report all accidents to the Occupation Safety and Health Administration (OSHA). Companies can be fined if there's a bad accident. Therefore, showing your diligence to safety and the safety of others is a big plus for you.

If you are serious about staying employed and moving up the company's ladder, do your homework. Be aware that you need to deliver what is expected of you, as well as rooting yourself strongly in the company. In doing so, you will be armed against three enemy soldiers: the employees below your level, at your level, and above your level.

Employees below your level: These employees carry a double-edged sword. One edge gives you the greatest information about the company and tells you who the reasonable bosses, stupid supervisors, and unqualified managers are. It points out great helpers, as well as the employees around whom you must watch your back. The other edge of the split sword can chop off your wings and slice and dice you. This happens to new hires with an attitude. If you don't want to be a victim, give employees below your level better respect than they give you.

Employees at your level: Employees at your level are the tigers with fangs, ready to strike you dead. They have a close eye on you because you all are after the same prey. Your strategic move is to love your enemies while you maintain your attack weapons and defensive mechanisms and keep them within easy reach. You strike at night and silently. Be a good team player, humble, with a cooperative attitude during the daytime. At the same time, protect your castle from all hostility. Make it clear—preferably by handling your job flawlessly—that you are well qualified for your job and you can execute your tasks without anybody looking over your shoulder. Don't welcome support with open arms. It'd be better if you could wear a sign on your forehead that reads, "Unless I ask, don't help," along with a smile on your face. Don't reveal your plans to move up, or your transparency will close the windows of opportunity for your advancement. You are facing strong, smart players. You must find stronger cards than theirs and think carefully about your every move, after predicting theirs.

The employees above you. The employees above your level are more dangerous than the employees at your level. They are where you want to be. You must secretly worship these team members without losing your integrity. You can truly use their help. At the same time, be careful because once they read your intentions, they will set traps. You are their replacement. They know that you want their jobs. They are not going to let you send them to the unemployment line. The encouragement in the interview about making a career in the company was a chocolate bar given to you as an enticement to devote your life to the company because they saw your potential. That sweet talk is now turned around. You're watched not for your performance—you've proven your worthiness—but for your moves and intentions, which are considered smartly dangerous.

If you are an employee with zero possibility of advancing—say you're poorly educated and without skills—you still can play smart games for keeping your job, especially when so many employees with management skills today are working in low-tech jobs. They have a great advantage over you, which translates to greater respect for the company, management, and coworkers. You need to go the extra mile to be more productive than such coworkers. Be an outstanding team member and, above all, have a respectful attitude toward your team members and the company's rules and policies.

If you are strongly secure in your job, you're lucky and are doing your work right. Yet there still are measures you can take so you don't visit the unemployment line.

Entrepreneurship: Entrepreneurship is the best way to maximize your potential, and it's the best employment you can ever have. The reason is that you are your own boss! You work the hours you want and for as long as you want. You steer your own ship to the port you want at the speed and comfort you like—you create your own way to make money instead of working for companies that pay you what they think is fair. But entrepreneurship is not as rosy as it looks. If you don't know how to play the cards right, don't even approach the table, or you'll go home broke and with enormous debt on your shoulders. If you have what it takes and are sure of taking nothing but success, drop everything, and start your entrepreneurship journey.

Generations ago, employment was a rich mean of survival. It held the middle class strong, with possibilities to advance easily. Even poor communities that had family members employed lived well above the average. And many factors contributed to the prosperity of employment. Agriculture was one of them. People who chose to get a higher education weren't faced with exorbitant student loans, nor did they have a hard time finding jobs after graduation. And employment allowed them to easily repay the loans they did have.

Then things began to shift dramatically. Agriculture became unreliable, population growth exploded, and the exodus of rural and suburban people to large cities exploded, making crop products even more expensive. Employment became the number-one tool for our survival and prosperity. Higher education became the only way to achieve a decent employment. With everybody looking for ways to enroll in colleges and universities, tuition costs skyrocketed. The wheels of life kept spinning out of control … and here we are in the employment plague worldwide. Not a pretty picture at all. Worse is that this employment plague is keeping college graduates in their parents' houses, while the stress and frustration of school loan repayment deplete their motivation. High school graduates are sadly boxed in, almost certain to live in their parents' basements forever. And of course it's just a matter of time before drugs, prostitution, and other crimes grab them and don't let go. This assessment is not encouraging at all.

Yet it doesn't have to be so barbaric. And yes, there's a way out.

Forget the problems that we created yesterday and the consequences we are paying today, with higher prices for tomorrow. Forget that yesterday the employment world was friendly, and jobs were abundant. Forget that no one can find good employment anywhere. Forget that you're part of Generation Loser, doomed to failure. Forget that the government is responsible for this entire mess. Remind yourself that you are in charge of your destiny. You may not like your current employment. You may not find employment that fits your needs. You may find yourself angry, frustrated, and discouraged, but you won't give up on your quest of getting the employment you want. Thinking and acting outside the box is a good approach that's guaranteed to serve you well.

Make employment work for you, instead of your working for employment, whether you are employed or looking for a job. Say you have to travel forty miles to your workplace and face traffic jams. Move closer to your job or find one closer to your home. Also, stretch the cash of your employment as far as it can go by taking good care of your finances and by watching your spending like a hawk. There might be simple measures you can take to stay afloat and ahead of the game in any corner of your life, especially the corners crying for attention.

Don't forget to empower yourself for good employment, in good and bad economic times, and have an invincible attitude at all times. These empowerment tools will bring success and happiness to your life. Find them, and never let go.

14

Finances

CENTURIES AGO PEOPLE HAD FEWER needs and wants, and wants were not taken as needs. Help was easier to find, as people were in better positions to be Good Samaritans. They knew how to care for their finances. That's the opposite of what we've been experiencing in recent decades, and it makes us look like we know and understand nothing about finances. Indeed, we know how to take care of our finances. When our finances such, we know how much they suck, especially now that everyone must be self-sufficient, which comes, sadly, at a very high cost.

We are hit by many destructive economic forces that leave us financially handicapped. A bad economy is one of the destructive forces attacking our financial power and making life suck. Droughts, excessive rain, natural disasters, and the schemes of Wall Street are some of the destructive economic forces responsible for bad regional economies. Wars and international political games are responsible for a bad global economy, leaving the population in mediocre land. These undesired phenomena continue to expand, attacking everybody in all generations, but the millennials are whipped more unmercifully. Too many economic snipers have our finances in their scopes, and they pull the trigger without bias or prejudice. We know and understand our situation. We're trying to win. But the game is getting harder, and we've run out of tricks.

We can't tackle all financial predators. Most of them are too big for us to pick a fight with them. Let's focus on what brings a penny or two into our pockets and helps put food on the table, starting with money generators.

Money Generators

Employment: Employment is the first main source of income that fuels our finances. Unfortunately, it continues to disappoint us. No matter how disappointing employment is, however, we must get a job; otherwise, we'll live stressed, frustrated, and desperate.

Supplemental income: The extra cash you earn from a part-time and side jobs, such as doing car repairs in your driveway, mowing and landscaping your neighbors' lawn, yard work, snowplowing, minor house repair, and so one, should belong to your supplemental income.

Sadly, nowadays everybody—except the wealthy—must have a supplemental income to balance their budgets. Luckily, supplemental income comes in more ways than we think. We simply need to pay more attention. One way is with something I call invisible cash.

Invisible cash is money that comes from our routine financial activities. We never see it. We only see its benefits. Clearly, we need to pay more attention and appreciate it. It comes in many ways, shapes, and forms, such as the following:

Credit cards. Luckily, we are always improving life from all angles, as creativity keeps innovation and competition on their toes. Credit card companies have followed every step of the way. As a result, the annual fee is history, the late-payment fee is almost history, and a cash-back reward is their "appreciation for your business." So we save a buck or two every time we use the plastic. Clearly, credit cards don't just take our money; they help us make money too. And as we become experts in paying on time, our financial management improves. This is great, especially as we're moving fast into the cashless world. It's like we hit two birds with one stone.

Credit score. A credit score shows our financial management skills and the ability to pay back loans. It flashes its power when we have to finance a large item that costs a lot of money. Here, the benefits of good credit include our being approved for a loan right away, as well as saving on interest charges, where differentiating between a bad credit score and an excellent one can mean saving thousands of dollars. The higher your credit score, the lower the annual percentage rate. This is a clear-cut benefit. There are other areas where a credit score's shine is becoming wider and brighter. Your employer-to-be will check your credit score as a qualifying item in your hiring, or a landlord can deny you a lease, based on a bad credit score. So learn the ways to have a credit, and then build it as tall as it can be. You'll save some money during the process and lots of money when it reaches the ceiling.

Relationships. Relationship benefits extend way beyond love, care, sex, and companionship. A relationship is an ace of hearts in finances. Say you're able to provide for the family alone, but your partner makes as much as you do or more. You're doubling down and more. This would make it a nice money generator.

Health, nutrition, and fitness. When you think of this trio, you may easily ask, "Where's the money?" Health, nutrition, and fitness take money from you rather than giving it to you. Therefore, there's no money—except there is. When you strive to stay healthy, including having a regimen that includes balanced nutrition and good exercise, you save money by not needing to pay for doctor visits, emergency room charges, and other hospitalization-related charges and medicine. You also save money on foods your crazy taste buds wanted but you refused to buy. You don't need it; junk food is loaded with sugars, saturated fat, cholesterol, and sodium. In fact, there's a substantial amount of invisible cash in health, nutrition, and fitness. Try to stay away from your doctor for a year. Then make an estimate of what it would've cost you if you had gone for whatever reason— say, a $70 copayment on two visits, $20 on prescriptions, and $15 on gas and wear and tear of your car. Pull that $105 out of your purse or bank account, and put it in an envelope named "Crazy savings." And there you have it! Some invisible cash, out of the clouds!

Philosophical principles. Social activities, entertainment, drinking, unnecessary spending, and flamboyance are some of the activities for which you should stay within the budget. Respecting what you have empowers you to grow. Say you usually go out with your buddies twice a month for drinking and entertainment. Skip a month here and there.

Budget. Running your life on a budget means that you live within your means. This will stop you from spending on the intruders of want while it allows you to eliminate items that seemed important but that you can do without. And the greatest benefit of a budget is not even the invisible cash. It's the control it gives to one of the most important sectors of life: finances.

Education. Prioritizing education is equal to 90 percent of financial stability.

Staying ahead of the game. Watching your money like a hawk ensures that you will not run into nasty financial surprises.

Bargains. Anytime you find a bargain, you save a lot of invisible cash, no questions asked.

We are conditioned to appreciate what we can see, touch, and feel and to despise invisible things and things we don't understand. So here's a small hint to help the magic come out of the clouds and stand tall for you to see, touch, and feel. Let's take the cash from a bargain on tires, for example. A set of four tires for your car costs $600, but you got them in a Black Friday sale for $490. You saved $110. Place the $110 in your piggy bank or in an envelope you've marked "bargains" or "invisible cash." Adopting this principle with all bargains could result in substantial savings at the end of the year. The result is clean, visible cash that you can touch and feel. If you play this game and keep your tokens and chips, at the end of ten years you could have a good twelve grand of visible cash, which can be a down payment for a house.

We are surrounded by invisible cash. Be alert and look harder. Grab as much of it as you can to empower your money generators and to make your financial world shine.

Since we are vulnerable to a financial crisis, when we get hit while unprepared, we will ride on the train of desperation. Give your money generators the attention they deserve. Also keep in mind that you should upgrade the generators so they never let you down; it's better yet if you can replace them with better and bigger ones. It's also a great idea to have as many money generators as you possibly can, but please don't consider your parents as one of the money generators. Are you listening, millennials?

Finally, whether you have one or many money generators, you must respect the power you receive, or you could run the risk of spending nights in darkness. You should not waste money left and right on things you want simply because you make lots of money from different sources. Build an empire before you invite the rich and powerful. It doesn't matter how much money you have; if you don't seriously guard and multiply it, you will go broke. Take your finances seriously. Protect them from contaminating agents, evil shadows, and everything that's trying to get your money.

Who's after Your Money?

In general, everybody's after our money. In particular, it depends on who we are and what we have. Advertisers focus on children and are the real creeps that chase our money. How do they do that when kids don't have any money? Advertisers aren't stupid. They go after the hands that feed the kids. Once they hypnotize kids with a flood of ads, kids beg and cry until they get what they want from their parents.

The next creeps are our brothers and sisters who assault our piggy banks—creeps without shame, respect, or consideration.

As we reach working age, the number of people and things after our money increases considerably. Government, advertisers, our friends and siblings, our parents, our needs, want-intruders, health care, sports, entertainment, and booze are all after our money through tax on our incomes, shopping, borrowing, board settlements, the basic needs, items that aren't important but feel good to have, and our choice of lifestyle. For men, there's spending money on the women with whom they're desperately trying to party with all night.

You'd better believe that the marketers and advertisers stay really busy by chasing our footsteps when we get our first jobs as teenagers; they know that teens are stupid, careless, listen to wrong voices, and pretty much buy everything they sell. It sounds like they whisper in teens' ears that a pair of shoes that cost less than $150 are for uncool people. Of course, teens believe them. The advertisers hypnotize them, and maturity fails them.

From a simplistic perspective, the ads seem very effective, or we fall too easily into the advertisers' laps. From a deeper perspective, we are not having a fair fight. Advertising is not a simple game. It is a science whose philosophical principles and objectives are aimed at making us believe that we must shop, shop, and shop some more. Enormous amounts of money are spent on research about human behavior and spending patterns, categorized by race, gender, group, and ethnicity at different stages of life. Thus, advertisers know that parents go that extra mile to make their children happy, predominantly in their first ten years. Married women are targeted with kitchen appliances and furniture ads, married men with tools and equipment, and the elderly with safety and convenience items. Let's call this a psychological enticement.

Other money is spent on biological enticement. This one leads studies to the conclusion that malls and other shopping centers must be designed to respect certain characteristics of human behavior environmentally. The zoning must be carefully chosen; the architecture must be flawless, including the beauty, arrangement, and connection of buildings; and the decoration must attend to all minor details. The outside decoration is aimed at the sparkling attraction. The inside decoration, even more carefully thinking of every single detail, is to ensure that we are not only happy there but also ready to buy--and when we go home, we can't wait to go back. The music played in malls and shopping centers is scientifically selected and played in a certain order so our natural response is to buy. The walls and floors are designed for good acoustics, so all sounds are pleasant. Even the barking of a crazy dog would sound like music to our ears inside the mall.

The advertisers and researchers have concluded that once we have a great experience at a mall or shopping center, even if we don't buy all the time, they have us in their pockets; we will return and buy. They aren't worried that we know about this trap; they know that we can't fool biology. How smart! And so the depth and seriousness of this game make us the losers. Children, teenagers, young adults, and females are the soft targets, but everybody gets hit.

And it gets crazier: Now we get messages from our banks reminding us that our checks have come in. Translation: Start spending!

In this crazy, stressful world of finance, the merciless cash suckers can suck us dry and ask for more. Basically, everything seems to be after our money, from the day we were born until the day we die. A ninety-seven-year-old was reading a local newspaper. I greeted him with, "How are you doing today?" His answer was, "One more day to see more debt. Waiting to die!" He didn't even look miserable! So the best defense is to shield your money to increase the power of enjoying life.

How Do You Shield Your Money?

This one is hard because the agents after our money continue to upgrade their games, especially the advertisers (directly) and the government (indirectly). People accuse governments of being behind the scenes in the advertisement industry. That's not so surprising because whatever advertisers sell us, the government gets a share of it. But as the advertisers step up their game, we run out of places to run and hide. The struggle to survive is all we have left. To ease the struggle, we must fight. Some of the measures we can take to stay alive and protect our money include the following:

- making a budget
- discipline in following the budget strictly
- perseverance in avoiding adjustments to the budget, unless it no longer works
- protection by putting a restraining order on the want-intruders and fighting advertisements.
- avoiding falling for appealing products we don't need and ignoring enticing prices
- having self-empathy by remembering how many hours of work, stress, and frustration it took to earn sixty dollars, probably at a job we can't stand
- learning as much as possible about finances, especially money management
- choosing the money management style that works and sticking with it
- having the philosophy of worshipping savings (It's so worthwhile—a drop here and a drop there can become a flood.)

Take these hints into consideration and add your own philosophy to create your way of protecting your money with devotion. Otherwise, regardless of how much you have, the chances are you will soon be broke and die in misery. Instead, grow your money tree as tall as it can be.

How Do You Grow Your Money Tree?

The older we get, the greater the need to save, and, fortunately, the stronger our attitude toward savings. The tragedy is that the older we get, the harder it is to save because our responsibilities increase in number and size. And it seems too late to start saving. Well, the game here is to save whatever you can, whenever you can.

Let's tackle the youngsters, as their power, time, and possibilities are endless.

You should walk baby steps with adult strength and balance. Start with a piggy bank that you will never touch. Whatever you have, share it with that piggy. When you grow it for a cause—say, buying your first car—your parents will help to keep piggy fed on a regular basis, as they would feel ashamed not to contribute to something so great that they wish they had done it when they were your age. You could also challenge yourself in growing the piggy as big as it can be in a thirty-year period. This gives you saving without hassle—you save what you have and don't feel any financial pain—and time: the older your savings, the greater the amount! A piggy bank you start growing when you're twenty years old for forty-five years will result in a nice cash stack, which will serve you really well in your retirement, especially if you find yourself battling health issues. The following steps should help you grow your money:

Take the steps of "How Do You Shield Your Money?" seriously.
Take the steps of "How Do You Shield Your Money?" seriously.
Take the steps of "How Do You Shield Your Money?" seriously.

Bargain hunting: Look for bargains when you buy all items of basic needs or desires. Do not underestimate the saving power of coupons. If only we didn't feel embarrassed to use coupons!

The uncounted for: A raise of fifty cents per hour totals $1,040 a year (minus the government's cut), assuming you work forty hours a week, fifty-two weeks a year. A raise of a dollar per hour, under the same circumstances, totals $2,000 and pretty good extra change. So, when you get a raise, whatever it is, save half or at least some of it. It's even better if you save all of it. You can save your overtime earnings too.

The lucky cash: If you can carpool, save the amount you would've spent on gas and parking, or save the money you get from people you carpool.

The rat syndrome: Take an additional deduction. Claim zero on your tax form, and authorize an additional deduction to your paychecks. You'll have a nice income tax refund or less chance of paying additional tax. If you do get a refund, don't rush to spend it on drugs, booze, strip clubs, casinos, furniture, or kitchen appliances. Take care of some important financial issues, such as credit card debt and loans of high interest, or get a better car, and then give the rest to the piggy. Your piggy swallows your sacrifice now and spits out money later. Don't be afraid to sacrifice.

The trick of the numbers: If you get paid weekly, chances are your budget is based on four checks per month. At the end of the year, you have an extra four checks (four checks per month equals forty-eight checks a year, but a year has fifty-two weeks). Say your weekly check is $500. You then will have $2,000 extra. You can use half of that to cover some basic needs and save the other half—$1,000 at the end of the year! That's $7,000 in seven years! Better yet, $35,000 in thirty-five years! And the beauty of it is that, usually, you make more each year, resulting in more savings.

Consistency: The secret of this game is consistency. No matter how insignificant your saving is, as long as you stick with it, the final result will put a smile on your face.

Training: Train yourself to ignore enticing gimmicks. You know that capitalism is the dominant global economic strategy. Capitalism is a fantastic economic system, but it can keep you broke. Its market economy philosophy is tricky. While it gives you possibilities to take charge of your life, it never gets tired of sucking up your money with the misleading slogan that you must live large. To live large, you must own assets and have cash, but that's a misleading description of living large. Living large doesn't mean you have tons of items collecting dust on your shelves or cheap junk sitting in your basement. That's wasting large, the complete opposite of what you must do to grow your money. Train yourself to resist shopping just because more is better; it's a trap, lie, and hypnosis.

Investment: Investigating is a good way to make your money make money for you. For example, after you have saved a few thousand dollars, buy a used car in need of repairs, fix it, and then sell it for a profit. Or have professional investors make your money make money for you in the stock market. (I am not much of a fan of stocks. I don't like to see the amount of my money diminishing. I try to stay away from plans in which total control lies in the hands of things, events, and people. Therefore, I only have a small stock investment. But that's me.)

Companion: Don't walk alone. Belong to a club of those playing the games you need to play. They will inspire you and raise your competitive spirit. Ask about and follow the best savings and investment practices. You can even work with a friend or two to start saving, with the purpose of joining forces on a business venture ten years from now.

The grit: If you understand the concept of saving, there will be support for your success. Of all great theories, methods, and philosophical principles, however, nothing beats your commitment and consistency. To do that, you must understand and respect the power of the numbers.

The power of the numbers: Everything is run by numbers. One hundred pennies, twenty nickels, ten dimes, or four quarters all are to equal one dollar. An item that costs one dollar cannot be bought with ninety pennies, or nineteen nickels, or three quarters and two dimes. The numbers don't add up to a dollar. Do not throw your coins away.

Evaporated money: I used to be a member of a gym where the monthly fee had to be paid by cash, check, or money order. Any member who didn't have enough money would then pay for a day of training at seven dollars per day. The owner wasn't about to let anyone work out today, with a vow of paying for the whole month tomorrow; he was not about to increase the odds of his evaporated money. Payments had to be made in bills, not in change. He was respecting the money and numbers.

In general, people avoid breaking a hundred-dollar bill for a twelve-dollar purchase. Some people say that money belongs to the devil, and once you break that hundred-dollar bill, it will evaporate in a couple of days. (The devil sucks it up, little by little.) I practice this philosophy not because the devil will take my broken bills but because they will evaporate; it's as simple as that. But how can money evaporate? Very simple! We are careless with change and small bills. Most of us leave pennies at the store counter as invalid currency, although a cashier will not cut us any slack if we are a penny short. Also, we couldn't care less about a handful of nickels and dimes. Quarters don't get much better luck either. Neither does a one-dollar bill. And items costing less than ten dollars are, in general, the biggest suckers of evaporated money. The problem is that we have to buy such insignificant items, from basic necessities to junk food and sugary drinks (foods and drinks of mass destruction). And since it seems impossible to have zero evaporated money, it's our obligation to try our best to reduce it. To be careless about change and small bills defeats the purpose of growing your money tree.

Money Management

It doesn't matter how much money you have. If you don't manage it, you can be sure that it's just a matter of time before you are broke and in debt. The tracks we've covered so far in this chapter are part of the money management assembly line. Budget is one of the main sections of the assembly line. Getting money management in good stance means a life under total control, which is something we need desperately. Your daily homework is to ensure that you are on top of your money management. This is homework a million miles away from the fun. It is, indeed, frustrating and stressful, yet not as daunting as living in the abyss of a financial mess.

There's no such a thing as a magic formula for financial success. There's the willingness for trial and error. Eventually, a formula will emerge that will work for you.

For the longest time, money has become oxygen. Wealth has become the power to buy supplemental oxygen, and riches have become the power to manage the oxygen to ensure sustainability. This means we, the less fortunate, must stretch our little cash so we can breathe. It's become mandatory that we understand some tricks and shortcuts associated to keep our finances in good standing. The secret lies in our determination to educate ourselves.

Since we have no idea when we'll start learning the philosophy and science of finances, starting in kindergarten, the fight to dominate finances—this very important aspect of life—lies in our laps. Fortunately, we have a variety of tools—our parents, professional financial advisers, online courses, and so on. And once again, our determination and commitment are the fundamentals we need to respect in order for us to have a strong financial stance.

Unless you want to get your paychecks on Friday and be broke by Monday for the rest of your life, understanding the financial game and finding the strongest cards to push you ahead of the game are a must.

One of the main purposes of life, driven by money, is happiness. And your happiness is something only you can define. After you have defined what makes you happy, including the materialization of your dreams, work toward your goals. We're living in a chaotic world. Many things can easily disturb our dreams. Therefore, while you should always dream big, make sure that your happy world is not too far away from your financial land. Be realistic about your economic potential, and focus on empowering it. A broken man is a weak man. A weak man has surrendered his soul. You are not about a lame, shameful game. You are all about making your financial world shine on every branch of your happy tree.

Although you can be a millionaire without millions of dollars because of happiness, wealth continues to be the rainbow of all rainbows. Start the journey to becoming a millionaire, and your finances will follow through. Nothing is like financial independence. Just remember that financial independence requires economic sacrifices before the glory. And because I know you are on a journey to make it big (me too), here's a nice reminder: the first million is the hardest battle. From there, money finds its way. And when you aim for the stars, if you miss, you're guaranteed to hit the moon.

15

Love, Romance, and Sex

Love

WE ARE MADE WITH LOVE. We are the products of love. We are nurtured with love. We grow up needing love and giving love. We are love. Females have and give more love than males. Whether or not we understand it, love is an affection we have for people we worship and/or want to stay close to. We love our parents like no one else, then our brothers and sisters, friends, teachers, coworkers, and idols. When puberty comes, we love those we feel sexually attracted to. Later on, we love our soul mates dearly, followed by our children and stepchildren, who get just about all our love. (I wish there was some left over to be spread to humanity for peace, harmony, and brotherhood!)

Regardless of our feelings and interpretations of love, we are outcasts when our souls don't carry much love. We are lost when we're not loved. We're on pedestals when we're loved. Love is fundamental to our emotional balance, happiness, strength, and endurance. Another sure thing is that, to our shame, we haven't been giving love the seat it deserves. We have been letting it struggle with pain and suffering, only to see our emotional world spin in hatred and disarray all the way down to lovers. It is understandable that the current times didn't come to love's rescue.

To escape death or destruction, we've taken smart measures that have kept us flourishing. We make a plan for the day and go to sleep thinking about the best way to make it work. We're focused on making a difference every day, whatever it takes, and that's wonderful. Love doesn't deserve anything less. Love is one thing that doesn't cause any harm when too much of it is given or received. Love sits very close to the oxygen we need for our survival. Add as much love as you can to your love pit. You'll live happier, and you'll allow those who come your way to benefit from it.

If your heart is empty of love, there could be an emotional unbalance you must fix. Otherwise, the consequences can hit you at any time. It could be that they already did. Even beautiful girls, who should worry less about lack of love—somehow their hearts are filled with love from birth, and it never runs out—need to stay vigilant to many suckers, such as the decline of romance, pushing a straw deep into their hearts to suck dry the juices of love.

Romance

Before my parents' generation, all sorts of intimacy was to be granted after marriage. The world was small, lifestyles were humble, and agriculture was the main occupation. A union between a man and a woman was primarily for raising a family. Raising lots of kids was good for the image of the couple and for the crop fields. As the population growth exploded, social values changed, and nature began pushing us to find a better means for survival. We slowed marriage down and began looking for our own soul mates, instead of accepting the choices of our parents and destiny. Weddings no longer happened a few months after parents introduced the bride and groom. Rather, they happened after years of deeply knowing our self-chosen lovers. There was time for talking after church, trips to the market and villages, and attending weddings, christenings, and other social events. There was plenty of time for planning the future, courtship, and sex before marriage. (Contrary to the taboo against sex before marriage, people were partying discreetly.)

I'm not sure how and when romance was born, but I know its celebration gained dimension in my generation, as we are surrounded by fancy restaurants, movie theaters, exotic places, parks, vacations and getaways, automobiles, trains, and airplanes, as well as women's liberation. The telephone made it possible for long hours of sweet conversation. Then life slipped into a higher gear, and the possibility for romance to shine increased dramatically. And so did its killers.

Each new generation brings new deadly pills and more destructive knockout punches, leaving romance in the struggle of staying alive on the battlefield of love. The world is simply spinning too fast for romance. Right now, romance seems to be struggling with its final breath. That means you have some responsibility on your hands for holding romance dear to your heart.

Sex

God realized that he needed to come up with a different strategic game for the replication of creatures. By creating creature after creature, it would take forever to fill the world and maintain species diversity. On top of that, he had to keep an eye on the devil, who was working day and night to plant the seed of evilness in every single creature. After a few different tries, God chose self-replication as a solution—asexual reproduction. But along the way, he noticed problems with asexual reproduction. He chose another way with a crazy upgrade. This brought us sexual reproduction, millions of years ago. And it evolved to become the dominant means of reproduction to this day. God's finest work is a creature in his image. We humans got the best of everything, with sex as the ultimate reward. From the big bang to contemporary humans, sex has been a reproduction winner and an unmatched pleasure.

On our arrival, we knew nothing about it. Then we began knowing. Then came puberty that forced us to learn a lot about it and to experiment. The best of it happens in our thirties, but until we die, the master of all pleasures is sex. We may like it or not; be good at it or not; have it on a regular basis or be addicted to it. It all is fine, to some extent—having it while in crisis is wrong. From all perspectives, letting sex live in crisis land is disrespectful to God or a neglect of an evolutionary phenomenon that started about fourteen billion years ago (the big bang).

Numerous factors make us forget the importance of sex, and various side effects bring us to misery instead of joy and satisfaction. We should make it imperative that we keep its crisis factors under control, but sex is the very essence of life, no matter the angle we look at it. This ultimate life reward shouldn't be messed with. You may forget all the mystery and focus on the importance of sex, and then, without bias or prejudice, give it the valor it deserves. Fortunately, even in its most simplistic way, sex is very joyful, and we are surrounded by enough supplements to have great sex for life.

The Supplements

The list of the supplements of sex could extend from here to China. Some of them are common and most are personal, even secretive, and are driven by many factors, including sex drive, personality, and economic power. From food, drinks, aphrodisiacs, and favorite positions, all the way to strange, dangerous, and absurd actions, we cannot run out of sex supplements. But we're going to talk about the common ones, such as masturbation and pornography.

Masturbation: Masturbation is a half version of something we do in privacy for pleasure and reproduction—sex. It is healthy and natural. In fact, if we are not sexually active, and we have no health conditions that inhibit our sexual desires, we can only resist masturbation for so long. A wet dream, one of the unconscious ways to release sexual tension, is an indication of the urgent need to have sex or, if we can't have sex, to masturbate. So our bodies confirm to us that masturbation is healthy, and doctors recommend it.

A friend of mine, happily married for seventeen years, once said, "A good masturbation is better than any sex." I am not so sure about that, but I get the point. But the taboo still impedes us from taking masturbation as the natural, good thing that it is. We do it and pretend we don't. We even lie about it, thanks to the taboo. Back in my day, we had a trick—to join a group of boys and girls, get comfortable, and say that people who masturbated had hair growing out of their hands. Instinctively, everybody would check their palms. Busted! It worked all the time. With teenagers, there's no mercy, so it wouldn't matter how hard anyone tried to prove their innocence; everybody was guilty as charged. The girls would make fun of the boys for weeks!

But taboo or not, masturbation, like sex, should stay private, or there could be embarrassment and consequences.

A father caught his son masturbating and was upset about it. "You're lucky it wasn't your mother who caught you," he told the boy. I found that remark absurd but not surprising. I know of a married man who slept on the couch for days because his wife caught him masturbating. She took it as an act of cheating. She asked her twenty-year-old sister, who was in college, to move out. She assumed that the younger sister had been the reason for what happened.

The bottom line is that masturbation is biological, healthy, pleasurable, and recommended. (Did you know that in the jungle, monkeys teach boys how to masturbate? Yes, they do!) Teenage boys seem to need it more than girls and adults. But we have to monitor our sexual activities. A decline in performance could be a sign of a masturbation side effect. And there are, for sure, more masturbation side effects on which you should educate yourself.

By the way, it's not a good idea to get out of bed, stand up, and masturbate in front of your partner who's not in a mood to party, and say, "See! I can do this without you."

Pornography: The sexual revolution began its journey in the 1960s. The entertainment media brought the mystery out of the bedroom and into everybody's living room and outdoors, mainly through magazines and other print works. And then pornography took the lead and dominance. For decades, music videos have been aimed at arousing teenagers through sexual expressions that most people call exotic, some call erotic, and others call pornographic exhibition. (And it continues to be more revealing because there's a competition among female pop stars as to who's pushing Madonna's legacy to the extreme, it seems.) The internet and smart devices came to add salt to the wounds, as they enable pornography to be carried out in everybody's pockets or pocketbooks. It's a business that beats all other online businesses. The numbers aren't lying; we love pornography. And we should. But behind its goodies lies harmful potential that deserves our attention.

Teen girls complain that their boyfriends ask them to shave their pubic hair and act more like porn stars. They also complain that boys are trying to act like porn stars, being very aggressive in the process. I am quite sure that, to a lesser extent, adult females are going through the same pornography problems with their partners. It's almost impossible not to feel the temptation to match the porn stars. The problem is that when we fall short of the expectations all the time, we become frustrated. We feel like we or our partners aren't measuring up. We try harder next time and come out with even more frustration. Yet the knockout punch comes when we get addicted to pornography. If pornography is taking you to uncharted territories, the following is for you:

Have you forgotten that pornography is a movie, a fake reality? The location is carefully selected. There are the actors and a director and assistant director to call the shots for the following:

Sexual positions that give the cameramen the best angle

The frequency of moaning, groaning, screams, and going wild

The time to switch position

Instructions for "Action ... hold it for ten more seconds ... look over there ... move your hands this way ... go deeper and harder," as well as selecting the final position for the ejaculation and fake orgasms.

Have you also forgotten about the editing, where a cut-and-paste montage makes a three-second shot last an eternity? Don't forget performance enhancement drugs!

What you watch and hear is far from real because sex in pornography is for money. In your house, sex is for love and has no cast, only and your partner(s). Everything flows naturally and is driven by love, passion, and desire. You choose positions that make the penetration easier and the action more pleasurable for both of you. And you don't need to fake anything, unless you want to. There is no applause for a good job, and there's no concern over having to do it again because some shots didn't look good enough. Therefore, you will not allow yourself to match what you've watched or fall into pornography addiction. Otherwise, you have defeated the purpose and have become the victim of too much of a good thing—and that's bad for you.

To emphasize the claims that pornography is a good thing, let's remember that we didn't invent it; we inherited it and will pass it on. We discovered it in curiosity and spying. The conversations about sex among groups of girls and groups of boys are not the reality of Generation Loser. It has always been there. Freedom of speech and expression weren't abundant generations ago, but people were always digging the sexual adventures of friends and other people. And we cannot resist stealth walking on someone having sex and finding a good spot to watch. We can't resist peeking on a girl or guy getting undressed. If we walk by a house with lights on late at night or early morning, we peek for sexual activity. If the party is on, we are definitely watching and recording to show to our friends. Some idiots will even post it online. Any one of these instances could trigger our desire to masturbate. And watching pornography is for sex, masturbation, or both.

Unlike girls, guys embrace pornography with passion and will probably pay any price for it (to give us a bad reputation), but masturbation and pornography are sex supplements that serve all, and serve well. And so, males and females, let's not underestimate the benefits or ignore the consequences. Let's use our heads to eat the fruits and throw the seeds away. Sex is of capital importance to us. We should welcome any supplement that makes it even greater.

The Time to Start

The time to start having sex depends on many factors, such as personality, cultural tradition, and opportunity, among other things, including food and drink. Even though we begin to be biologically ready at puberty, a significant percentage of teenagers from all walks of life experimented with sexual activities before puberty. The number is definitely boosted by the internet and other means to access sexual material. So the time to start having sex cannot be written in the stone. Common sense says that if you're not sure, and you don't know enough about it, it's not the time for you to start.

To start having sex too young is a clear sign of poor knowledge about sex, and that has many consequences that can bring lifetime regrets. There should be no need to rush and run the risk of getting the whipping from bad sexual experiences. Some researchers found that two-thirds of sexually active girls wish they had waited longer before having sex and that of seniors in high school more than 70 percent of girls regret sexual experiences they have had.

The early arrival of puberty can produce sex drives at a time when teens aren't fully capable of understanding the social and biological consequences of sexual activities. In fact, the younger the adolescents who have any type of sexual relations, including oral sex, the higher the chances for them to catch a sexually transmitted infection or disease. Therefore, if you happened to have a high sex drive, and you started sexual activities young, you must focus your attention on knowing as much as you can about sex so you can minimize the chances of nasty surprises and lifetime regrets. There are many ways to educate yourself about sex, such as talking to your parents, friends, or school counselor; online articles; and adult videos (not necessarily pornography), just to mention a few. And the main reason for us to be knowledgeable and enjoy sex is that sex is phenomenal and extremely important in our lives. It relieves stress, frustration, and depression. It stimulates the mind and improves the immune system. It is the only pleasurable way to populate the world and stay true to the continuity of the family tree. In other words, it evens out the emotional and biological balance, among other goodness it brings. And yet it carries many side effects, some of which are deadly. Even though these effects don't discriminate by age, the younger you are, the greater the odds of being a prime target. Immaturity sells you out to the bad guys.

The Shadows of Death

Sexually transmitted infection or disease (STI/D) and unwanted pregnancy are the bad guys lurking under the bed to strike us hard after we've enjoyed a moment of pleasure. For the most part, they sneak up on us with minor infections, which we get rid of in no time, almost hassle-free. But they can also grab us by the neck and slam us down with the discomfort that turns into a serious infection or a deadly disease. Studies have concluded the following:

Each year, up to ten million American teenagers contract a sexually transmitted infection or disease, with HPV (human papillomavirus) as the most common sexually transmitted infection (STI), followed by trichomoniasis and chlamydia as the most common STI diagnoses among fifteen- to nineteen-year-olds. Combined, they account for one-third of diagnoses each year.

Genital herpes and gonorrhea combined account for about 12 percent.

HIV, syphilis, and hepatitis B account for less than 1 percent, but young people ages thirteen to nineteen accounted for about 20 percent of all new HIV diagnoses in the United States in 2011.

Teenagers do not understand the risks associated with sexual activity. They think there are fewer risks associated with oral sex, as compared to intercourse, while in reality, oral sex can transmit chlamydia, genital herpes, gonorrhea, and syphilis. This poor knowledge drives teenage girls to give oral sex to many boys as if it was nothing. They soon wake up with bitterness in their mouths, way before their first vaginal intercourse. (Once you become involved in sexual activities with more than one partner, your risk of getting an infection or disease increases, directly proportional to the number of partners.)

You may not care because none of your friends who are playing this dangerous game has ever had any sexual infection, and you feel pretty literate on this subject. Well, you could be fooling yourself and seriously shoot yourself in the foot. The numbers don't lie.

Since sexual shadows of death swim in the oceans and have strong currents to pass infections and diseases rapidly to other people—and some infections give no sign of their invasion of your privacy—it's almost impossible for us *not* to be hit. The only sure thing we can do is to stay aware of our vulnerability and do our best to dodge the bullets.

The Umbrellas

Considering the frequency and danger of this game, we need umbrellas to protect us from the sun, rain, and snow. *Protection* is our umbrella and bodyguard who is lightning fast and is powerful like the Hulk. Any time we have sex without protection, only luck saves us from the beatings of STI/D and unwanted pregnancy.

Some sex educators and Christian organizations advocate abstinence as the most important chapter of sex education, and they recommend teenagers be sexually abstinent until marriage. All say that abstinence rocks! The problem is that anyone who would have sex but abstains is missing the greatest ingredient of life. "She needs to get laid" is a comment we hear all the time about a woman known to be single and crazy. A physician asks patients about their sexual lives and recommends sexual intercourse on a regular basis for health reasons.

In the late 1960s to early '70s, our church demanded that women wear skirts no shorter than a couple of inches above the knees and that wives wear nothing that showed any skin above the knees. Those who refused would be temporarily banned from church, could not take communion, and were not allowed to have their children baptized. The worst offenders would be banned from church activities forever. The purpose was to curb sexual desires, which then would reduce the chances of having sex before marriage. So many single women chose the punishment rather than lengthen their skirts. Abstinence, despite being an ace in this game, didn't go far at the start of the sexual revolution, and it doesn't now. But there are many other powerful cards to serve as an umbrella for STI/D. Pick the ones that are easily workable for you and that goes with your morality and philosophy, whether you're a mature teen, single, married, straight, gay, religious, atheist, or agnostic.

It seems that suddenly the world's become too much of a macho man and is spinning way too fast for love and romance. And romance is not only gravely wounded but also left with the short end of the stick in the struggle to stay alive on the battlefield of love. I hope I am wrong because sex is the ultimate thrill of life. Romance is the silky road of passionate sex.

Either way, the more we understand and respect romance and sex, the greater the chances for our enjoyment of both. For that, focus your efforts on learning and evolving in love and romance, instead of priming yourself to be a sex master. It doesn't matter how hard you try; you won't master the game of sex because of its complexity and dependence on hundreds of factors. And romance (or lack of it) pretty much dictates the wealth or poverty of sex. Romance is something you can exercise without boundaries. It flows freely through all people and cultures, and it's loved like chocolate. It actually beats chocolate in its goodness to the heart, mind, and spirit.

In the end, love, romance, and sex are games like any other games. We cannot just take an empty seat at the table and play hard. We need to know the game inside and out, and then practice, practice, and practice some more. And then continue to practice. Educate yourself to the maximum extent, and be aware that in this game, you will have a bad hand, a horrible hand, and a losing hand more often than you think—that's regardless of how much you know and understand. You'll have to stay focused on the better hands coming next.

Life is a journey filled with a variety of thrills from the very beginning to the end. The party is more exciting when love and romance are in the room. They make the room so hot that you have to take off your clothes. Don't let any chill make you wear another layer of clothing to protect your skin—that's to remind you that if you're a victim of sexual abuse, gather your strength, sink your traumas and regrets to the bottom of the ocean, and replace them with loving memories. And then indulge in love, romance, and sex. Don't be afraid of taking the big step.

16

Relationships

Once upon a time (even though it seems like yesterday), the 1960s woke up, inspired by dreams full of wonder. This decade put on its best makeup, best outfit, and best high heels for a lifetime journey. Confident that from now on, life would spring instead of slowly walking, the '60s were as ready as it could be. The revolution in all corners of life is what the '60s had up its sleeve. And then it was showtime!

Nations began to ferociously fight for independence. Science and technology took Yuri Gagarin, the Soviet cosmonaut, to space and Neil Armstrong, the American astronaut, to the moon. Manufacturing and industry stepped on the gas. More important, the computer revolution started its Ferrari engine. And if the revolution was to reach to every corner of life, then relationships also got the touch. I think relationships, indeed, got a significant piece of the pie. Their wagon came to spike infidelity, skyrocket the divorce rate, and redefine marriage, household responsibilities, and freedom of sex and expression. Older generations claimed that the devil had spilled his evil throughout the entire world and that relationships were a plague. I don't think things were that bad, but drastic changes were in the air. It seems, though, that only now we're recognizing the arrival of the 1960s revolution, as the current chaotic world and living conditions are incomprehensible. And this reality makes the matter of relationships a living nightmare, especially when we find ourselves in search of a soul mate.

Your Partner for Life

When we're young, we don't fully understand the meaning of a relationship. As we grow older and learn the dynamics and meaning of life, we realize that at some point we'll have a relationship and a family of our own. Then puberty arrives to close our case; we start falling in love, looking for love, and dreaming of relationships. In societies where we have total control of whom we will marry, we plan, seek, and select.

Your partner for life comes with strong strings attached, followed by the strings of his or her family. Strumming or playing those chords can bring horrendous pain to the fingers and arm, and the sounds could be unpleasant to the ear. To avoid that, you need to pick and choose your partner for life without rushing. Even when your partner for life meets all your requirements, you'll face rough waters with deadly waves, particularly if you let the idiocy of your heart pick one for you. And once you start searching, you'll need to ensure that all stones have been turned, including personality, heredity, communication skills, and conflict resolution, among other things, before you make your final decision.

Despite the fact that there are enough fish in the water, all beautiful and delicious, none is going to jump out and land in your lap. If you want beautiful and delicious, you might try to be beautiful and delicious yourself. Part of being beautiful and delicious includes education, employment, and finances, the strongest weapons you can have for your success in general and your relationship in particular. Once you have a higher education, good employment is headed your way. With that, you're on the road to dominate the tricks of finances and to be in control of your destiny. For that reason, consider education, employment, and finances as the three most important keys to the castle of your relationship. When you get this trio under control, it's a certainty that the most beautiful and delicious will come to nest with you and, with a little bit of luck, kiss you from head to toe. Doing it right could be a lengthy and frustrating process, but it's a very wise move that will save you lots of headaches and sleepless nights.

Remember that to build a castle strong, from the foundation, is to avoid rebuilding it. The material and builders define a long-lasting castle or a castle in decline from day one. If the materials are cheap and the builders unqualified, there will be nasty surprises. A mistake in selecting your partner for life can ruin the branches of your family tree and bring termites to the trunk. It is your obligation to make each new branch stronger, more desirable, and more beautiful. And so bring the best and be with the best, not the rest.

Dance around to learn the ropes until you are thirty years old or until you're sure that you're fit for a relationship, and then think seriously about blending two bodies into one soul for life. The number-one reason you should take your time is that rushing can cause you to take whoever comes your way. Big mistake!

The Families and You

Your cousins, nephews and nieces, uncles and aunts, brothers and sisters, and mom and dad will be happy to watch you cherish your pie, hoping that you will share. On the other side, your in-laws have high expectations from you, even if you don't clearly see it. Of course, their main expectation is that you will treat their daughter or son (your lover/spouse) to the best of your ability in peace, love, harmony, prosperity, and happiness, but they also expect that you will add their well-being to your wagon too. You must accept that responsibility and try to please both families while you focus on your own family needs. Take them aboard, but don't get a flat tire. Also, while you ride along with them, you need to make sure that you are in the driver's seat at all times; otherwise, your wagon could end up in a bad crash. Some in-laws can be a better driver than you. To those, you should offer your seat, watch how they maneuver, and learn their skill so you can improve and take over. You also will need to find ways to deal with suckers in both families. Regardless of how much you do, your sister might never stop complaining that you don't help enough. And a brother or sister-in-law could suck you dry and ask for more.

You can adopt many strategies and take measures while you endure the burden of both families. Part of the strategies and measures include the respect for family values, not neglecting your responsibilities, taking advice from those who know better, and remembering that only you can find the magic bullets.

A Family of Your Own

A family of your own is your best treasure. It deserves the best care and protection. If you don't have one, you should find one. Think of this: Your kids are the only ones who can ensure the continuity of your branch of the family tree. You must give them the necessary tools to do the job. You could be short of your parents' (and everyone's) expectations but not your own family's. This implies a clear understanding of the total control of your destiny. If your own family is blended with your family, and you are constantly running to your parents and siblings for advice and financial rescue, you'd better prepare for the eternal burning of your ears—a sign that people are gossiping about you. And since it is almost impossible not to have your family meddling in your affairs, reduce the effect of this bad behavior by keeping your independence, and stand strong and far from threats. Of course you should keep in close contact and a strong connection with your family while you build your own, but you are now a branch that must grow on its own, with the obligation of making the tree stronger and better. If the branches are healthy with vivid green leaves, the trunk and roots also are healthy.

You are now split in three: one part to your family, another part to your in-laws, and the third part to the family of your own. You must attend to all three but with a priority to the family of your own.

Raising a family has become a challenge that requires physical, spiritual, and intellectual strength. The social environment—the poison of the internet and social media—make it almost impossible for you to raise your family by your absolute terms. Emotional distress constantly comes from every direction to rock a family's boat. Single parenting, poverty, unemployment, and underemployment have caused stress and frustration to strike families without mercy.

The head of the household is very tempted to rely heavily on alcohol (a slow death) as a medicine for stress and frustration relief. Chances are the children will be malnourished and have poor home education. Both boys and girls will hit the streets (a suicidal move) to relieve their own frustration, and being a runaway is within arm's reach.

As the train of chaos keeps rolling faster and faster, it will reach the split-up station. And there the hell can get even hotter. A single mom or dad is left puzzled over the parenting and employment balance. If grandparents can offer some assistance, there will be some relief, but in general, dropping children at a daycare and returning after work to pick them up has proven to be the norm and an impossible task to balance. One child poses a daunting struggle. Double the number of kids triples the amount of struggle. What about the money for childcare?

Single parents (as well as the majority of the population) earn barely enough to cover the basic needs with sacrifices already. The absent parent (generally the father) must chip in for child support and education. When the courts have to step in to enforce the child support, more often than not the relationship with the ex-spouse is sour and on old, rusty tracks. It is stress, frustration, and desperation, twenty-four/seven, to the detrimental development of the children. A broken family is a nest for a broken man. A broken man is a man whose power of integrity and strength of character have been lost or stripped away. A broken man might never find his way back.

Generation Loser is forced to embrace a relationship that is severely attacked by the struggles of raising a family, while it also faces a high probability of going through the single parenting phenomenon, leading to broken men and women. And the children are likely to follow in the parents' footsteps.

The main goal of any family is about the same as everybody else's: happiness, prosperity, and empowerment for children. In order for that to happen, children need the tools. The greatest tool happens to be education. Regardless of how well or poorly educated you are, don't mess with the education of your kids. Without it, their chances of success are slimmer, and the odds of their becoming isolated broken adults are greater.

Part of this game includes your connection to your children's school and teachers. Never miss a teacher-parent conference; ask questions and seek advice. Talk to your kids about the importance of education, and make it clear that you are there to help. Be engaged. If it becomes necessary and you have the means, find tutors. In fact, once you've determined that the education of your kids is the priority of all your priorities, help will come from all corners. Also, don't allow life and the relationship revolution to laugh at the family you're raising. Don't wait forever to think about it, and don't wait an eternity before you start taking action.

At eighteen, you're in the swinging zone. At twenty-five, you are definitely in the zone of seriousness. Prepare to seriously go to action. At thirty, you are most definitely on the battlefield. In case you are backing down, remember that from a family you came, to a family you belong, and from a family of your own you will leave, or you didn't make the cut. Don't linger in your parents' basement for an eternity—that's a hideout for losers. The longer you stay there, the more comfortable you'll be, and the harder it will become for you to face the outside.

Roll up your sleeves and go to work, aware of the tricks of your heart, and be prepared to take the necessary measures. A relationship is serious business. Raising a family of your own could be jeopardized by the tricks of your heart. Don't be a fool. Don't be a loser. Make it count.

Sending Your Sweetheart to Hell

History has shown that many things don't get better with time or maturity. The relationship is one of them. The world, our friends, and our parents constantly remind us of relationships hardships. We are not alone, and relationships hardships are not a phenomenon of the current era. It is part of who we are and the dumb things we do. And it is so because the affairs of the heart are rooted in soft ground. We adults—losers and heroes—have much to say about them. Chances are that you, the youngsters, have experienced love deception and hardship more than once or twice. We all have fallen into the wrong arms, gone to bed with bad partners, received hugs and kisses of death, or have woken up with a nightmare in our laps. And before we recovered, there we were, falling in love again.

The heart, which holds the very key to our emotions and survival, never misses an opportunity to do something astonishingly stupid, such as falling madly in love with the dumbest girl at the mall or the most punk guy on the streets. No matter how smart we are, we're going to be tricked by the heart's idiocy and then stumble, fall, get up, dust ourselves off, and move on, with a lesson learned. But this is not too smart. We could stumble and fall so hard that we pass out or die. We must find a better way, especially when we realize that nothing has more power to put our dreams' lights out or to turn us from a hero into a zero than our own hearts.

Kelsey was a distinguished student from kindergarten through high school. Her good grades earned her a full scholarship to college, and after graduating she enrolled in law school, mastering in criminal justice. All went very well during the first semester. After that, trouble started to sneak in. She needed a better part-time job to cover the expenses of her car payment, insurance premium, school materials, food and clothing, and smartphone, as well as helping out with her mom's rent. To make matters worse, her junior-high sweetheart, who'd been in and out of jail, needed serious cash for bail. There was no way she could find that kind of money, but she wasn't about to let her sweetheart suffer in prison. She found another part-time job.

Struggling with two jobs, school, and prison visits proved to be too much hassle, stress, and frustration to handle. Some of her responsibilities had to go. She quit school to work as hard as she could to support the boyfriend in prison. She soon realized that she'd bitten off more than she could chew. She was going to die from exhaustion, stress, frustration, and lack of sleep unless she dropped more responsibilities, which she did. She quit the part-time job she had held since junior high. With that came the loss of an income. Consequently, she couldn't support her sweetheart in prison as she had been doing. Going back to school was out of the question.

About a year later, she moved in with the boyfriend. Within a year, she delivered his daughter, her first baby, at the age of twenty. And a year later, she became a single mother.

She had had many calls to send her sweetheart to hell, but she ignored them. Destiny answered for her, although not without regrets that included her education, which has stayed stagnant to this day.

When we're young, we make all kinds of mistakes and do dumb things with complete disregard to the consequences, and it's all good because we learn from our mistakes and have enough time to compensate, except the world has become an increasingly crazier place. Any setback that touches our lives pushes us far behind the game. When you are victimized and badly scarred by your sweetheart, your chances of success in life are severely minimized. Actually, depending on the nature and intensity of the attack and disillusionment, you could be on the brink of taking your life or facing criminal charges, triggered by your sweetheart. To avoid the drama, you must send your sweetheart to hell and take charge of your emotions before the storm. This approach is a mandate after you've been tricked seriously more than once or twice.

Now, hold your horses! Understand where you stand and where you want to go before you start galloping into the unknown and end up in a more horrendous abyss than the one you're trying to walk away from. And don't think that once you send your sweetheart to hell that you're protected from the whips of relationships. You can't be heartless, nor should you allow your sweetheart to destroy your life. You sent your sweetheart to hell so you can prepare to conquer the love you deserve, not the first phantom that shows up in front of you. Kelsey did the opposite. Her new sweetheart wasn't much better than the one she left in prison. As a result, darker times struck her unmercifully.

Who Do You Welcome into Your Heart?

Aiming high and sticking to your dreams helps you steer your life away from tricky, troublesome love roads. But to understand whom to welcome into your heart, you need to become a bodyguard. That doesn't mean you should carry guns and have gigantic biceps; rather, you should learn the scanning skills to stay vigilant to the tricks of the heart and aware of people's hidden intentions. You must train yourself to see, smell, and feel them before anybody else. And you must be prepared because you'll be hit. When it happens, you'll be screwed, thrown off the wagon, and left for dead, except you aren't. You endure the consequences of a bad experience before you get up and continue your journey, with one more lesson in your backpack. To be aware of this reality is to empower yourself by deciding who you should welcome into your heart and by preparing for not being blown away by nasty surprises.

No girl dreams of a lazy bum as her adored one. All girls dream of being princesses. No lazy bum is going to give even an inch of that. Boys, on the other hand, want beautiful, sexy girls with nice, firm butts and big boobs, or a choice of one of my sons: "Girls who won't make me mad when I look at them or annoy me when I hear them talk." (I found that odd, but whatever. I like beautiful, smart women).

But you want to go beyond generalization and common fantasies and stick to your beautiful dreams, while you stay true to your reality. In your beautiful dreams lies the person to help your dreams comes true—to work on your projects; give you a hand when you fall; comfort you in your sorrow and sadness; be there when you least expect it; and love you forever for who you are. And you will respond in kind. If he or she doesn't come, you must go get him or her.

Conquer the Love You Deserve

Conquering the love you deserve is a challenge that requires serious commitment and hard work—nothing that you don't have to dominate, but it would be a wise move to prepare well for the challenge. The question is this: Where do you go to conquer the love you deserve?

Venues: The sky is the limit, but you must be true to the span of your wings and power of your engines. Respect the capabilities of your aircraft, and be aware of all restricted and prohibited airspace. If you're living in poverty, rich boys and girls are out of your league. If you're poorly educated, high-class individuals are off limits. If you don't believe in God, churches and other venues of worship are not your circles. If you are a drug addict or stuck on welfare with three children, your wings are broken, and your engines are sputtering. You have some serious work to do. Basically, you cannot go to a cranberry field to find banana trees.

Although your package sets up your venues and boundaries, you shouldn't feel bad if your package is almost empty. No one has a full package, and many of the people with the best packages have fallen short. Be in the open. Prioritize social activities, such as nightclubs, movies, cruises, and community events that involve a diversity of ethnicity.

I would not suggest going to bars. Usually, we're there to forget someone fast or liberate ourselves from deadly stress and frustration. With that said, however, I know someone who picked a husband at a bar and lived happily ever after. I guess it is true that we can find love in a hopeless place. I just wouldn't bet on it, nor do I recommend it.

Just consider that the greater your package, the greater your chances of conquering what you deserve on high ground. Regardless of what you have up your sleeve, you should do all you can to conquer the love you deserve. Empowering yourself is a strong card in your hands.

Empowerment: Empowering yourself demands that you have at least two of the most valuable players—education and independence—and many other good players on your team. Fortunately, once you have education on your side, you've placed your right foot in for your independence. Getting your independence means that you have the intellectual and financial abilities to live on your own. Being independent ensures that you will not give in to the one who seems able to give you a roof over your head and food on the table but is not your dream one. Of course, the hardship of living independently nowadays is a daily pounding headache, and Generation Loser seems to be cursed by that. Still, falling into the wrong arms or falling for the wrong reasons can be cancerous. No tragedy compares to living single, as your jackass of a lover left for someone prettier, or she found someone else who parties better under the sheets and has more cash than you. Education and independence come handy to support you during such hard times.

Your players on the bench are whatever you want them to be. I would recommend that health and fitness top the list. (By the way, single or married to your dream or a punk, health and fitness should be your best buddies forever.) They will support your legs while you're on your quest. And since you must live while you're searching, you cannot be so consumed by work, family, friends, and other responsibilities that online dating becomes the only venue you use to conquer the love you deserve.

Fortunately, there are plenty of fish in the ocean for you to take home for a spin and then go your separate ways. Yes, you can have your sexual needs satisfied without any compromise while you're searching for your significant one. How can you do that, though, if you are sick all the time, mentally disturbed, and physically frail? To be healthy and fit is to carry an attractive package. When who you deserve arrives and takes a look at you, he or she won't turn around and go home. And since no college graduate will go to a ghetto to look for someone he or she deserves, and no beautiful person wants to ride broken wheels, you need to empower yourself with the strongest cards—education, health and fitness, and money—before you take a seat at the negotiation table.

The negotiation table: Our lover is a special person who possesses specific characteristics in line with our desire and preference and with whom we wish to share intimacy, love, and care until death do us part. Therefore, our lover is not a commodity we buy in stores or order online. We ought to set ourselves on the journey of finding him or her. Unfortunately, the odds of finding the perfect match to the picture in our minds is about zero. To avoid dying single because you couldn't find the perfect lover, you might have to let go of some ingredients. For example, your perfect lover doesn't have to be tall and have brown eyes and black hair. The person's color, ethnicity, or religion shouldn't matter much anymore.

You must go to the negotiation table to make a deal. At the negotiation table, you'll meet lovers with many powerful cards (an illusion), who are ready to make you a loser. Also the daredevils of your heart—passion, love at first sight, and strong emotions—team up with the illusion to make you a loser. On top of that, you have to be on the lookout for the trickiest trick of the heart: temptation.

We men like to keep count and make a list. If something is available, you're damn right we're smacking it. We tone down this macho attitude as we age and become smarter—or more careful—but so many of us have been tricked or lied to, or we pulled out too late. As a result, we woke up on the train of chaos, speeding to hell.

Say the girl walking your way has a breathtaking beauty with a dazzling smile. Your heart tells you, "Oh damn! That's what I call love at first sight! I am hurt. I am badly wounded. I am gonna die if I don't have her! I've got to get that divine angel! My savior!" Your friends tell you to stand down and think it over, but you insist that you must close the deal before you lose this opportunity. Clearly, the illusion and the daredevil of your heart have hypnotized you, have you in a choke hold, and are dragging you to the gas chamber. Or the phantom walking your way doesn't have any features to match the picture in your mind but somehow seems to be a character you can party with under the sheets and add one more to the list. Later on, you tell yourself that you don't really understand what happened, as your adventure ended in a nightmare of responsibilities you can't afford. Undoubtedly, you forgot all about prevention.

The prevention is to wear a few layers of protection before you fall flat or drop your pants standing up. A condom is one example. Dropping the attitude of the macho man in pursuit of the number would also be a great help for winning the battle against temptation. You are not a better man than any other man simply because you've slept with more women than any other man. The same applies to other genders. You could also empower yourself to be strong enough to resist the temptation. No matter how delicious he or she looks, stick with the plan.

The purpose of this ordeal is for you to understand that you are not going to find anyone with a full package. Then anyone who has more than 50 percent of what you have dreamed of is a deal. Your heart will be happy, and you will be satisfied. The remaining 49 percent (the less the better, though) is to be worked at after the deal is sealed. That's how relationships stand strong and endure. Prioritize personality, education, and philosophical principles as the defining ingredients of the true nature of an individual. These human traits will bring other qualities that you want your significant other to have. You played your cards right at the negotiation table, and now you're a big winner.

You could be one of the lucky ones who's empowered from day one. You don't even need to think about your cards; they are all aces. Your parents are wealthy, and you graduated from the best schools in town. Born with a silver spoon in your mouth, you sip gold and spit silver. You are on top of your game. From here, all is greater glory ... until you wake up from a nightmare to face a real tragedy.

I didn't have any trouble recognizing that the new hire who came to join the night crew was a Cape Verdean. I wasn't sure about our acquaintance, but I had no doubts that I had seen him before. I don't like to be intrusive, so hours after the supervisor introduced him to us, I greeted him in person as we ran into each other and then went our separate ways. A quick first impression told me that I wouldn't have a beer with him, but we could be friends. Besides, I needed to know if he really was the person I thought he was.

A few months later, our friendship was good, and as it turned out, I was right about my assumption: We not only lived in the same town but also had been schoolmates.

In our dialogues at work, we talked a lot about crazy teachers and crazy adventures in our high-school days. One slow night, we covered a few interesting stories. One of the stories started with the skinny, seven-foot-tall, very eccentric yet excellent English teacher. Some senior girls often dragged him into a sexual conversation or did whatever they could to get a noticeable erection and then tease him about it.

Then we turned our dialogue to the hot girls of that time. Maria John was on top of the list. Somehow I held off on talking about the crush and misadventure I had had with Maria John, but our conversation ignited the fire under the burning ashes. Despite all the years that had passed, my passion never went away; only my chances did. And my heart was about to drop in disbelief. Contrary to what we had imagined, Maria John didn't continue her higher education abroad. She's still shines but not as a big star, as we predicted.

We talked about other hot girls who were not the star that Maria John was but who had bright futures. Unfortunately, they became nobodies after marriage.

The awkward spins of life can turn us from hero to zero and star to shame in the blink of an eye. No matter what cards we have, if we don't pay attention to the game, we'll lose. And our quest of conquering the love we deserve will turn out as an ugly failure, with a jerk to ruin our lives or a bitch to drive us nuts until we drop dead.

Girls, you are beautiful and irresistible to men. Don't stand there saying, "Come and get me for free!" And don't allow any rooster to take over your henhouse and throw you into the abyss. Once you conquer the love you deserve, you have conquered the world. You are ahead of the game, empowered to win almost every hand. And the chances are that you will never have a scar on your heart. Yet keep in mind that the only thing guaranteed in life is death and you can turn whoever you have as a soul mate into the love you deserve.

Insanity

We nurture, worship, and indulge in the goodies of life and hang on to relationships' roller coaster like no other creatures. When good is good, it's so rewarding. When good is bad, it's very painful. When it's painful, insanity is in charge. And the insanity of relationships comes in many ways, shapes, and forms, carrying destructive power. And that's not a good thing. Trapped and abusive relationships are some of the insanity that stops us from getting the best of relationships.

Trapped relationships: It is so sad to be in a relationship that has taken away our freedom and happiness. Sadly, more people than we think are in this situation. Here are some of their possible short explanations:

"He had everything in his name."

"I didn't want to lose what I had."

"I didn't want to be shameful."

"The next thing was going to a shelter. It sucks there."

"He convinced me that it was my fault."

"He told me that no one could love me like he does."

"He said that he would do all he can to make the world see that I am nothing but trash."

"I stayed so my kids can have a father."

"I am getting old, and I have kids."

"It is my destiny."

"I love him."

It is unfortunate that we go through bitterness in a relationship, but we must admit that a large share of the blame goes to us. The bitterness almost never comes unannounced and with sucker punches. We make mistakes and don't bother correcting them. This is a bad attitude. Worst of all is that we ignore the signs pointing toward a trapping relationship. We see the storm clouds, shrug our shoulders, and then bitch about getting wet and blown away.

But no matter how you got trapped, creating a strategy to freedom is the best remedy for the situation, unless you can live happily when trapped. I doubt that people would believe you.

Abusive relationships: We have come a long way in respecting our soul mates, but we are still stunned about the horrendous cases of abusive relationships, which include emotional and physical punishments and often end in homicide or suicide. Even when the reality is not so savage, in an abusive relationship, you're used and abused, getting pounded in every possible way, without any respect at all.

"The longer you hang on, the worse it'll get." This is common advice from the people putting their two cents in to your rescue. Absolutely true! Some excuses for enduring the insanity of relationships do make sense; others don't. Relationships and marriages of convenience, such as the ones for economic or citizenship reasons, are crazy and dangerous but make sense. To be in an abusive relationship as a victim of circumstances makes sense too, but you would have to leave when there's a possibility. Any other reason makes no sense. And obviously, if you don't get out when the door is open, you might not get out at all.

We know of cases when authorities stepped in to solve domestic abuse incidents. The victim rescued her soul mate, and days later, he stabbed her to death. You have the obligation to fight for the survival of your relationship, but when it seems hopeless, leave while you can. Or you're insane.

Those who left could've said:

"The day I left I had a gun to my head."

"I left so my kids can have a mother."

"If he gets away with it, he will never stop."

"I just couldn't take it anymore."

I support those who take destiny in their hands with a vow to protect their freedom, liberty, and dignity.

Victim of circumstances: People might think your excuses for staying in an abusive relationship are a cover-up for something shameful or compromising that you have done, such as the discovery of cheating or dark secrets. They could also assume that you left your relationship because you are a bad partner who left before getting caught cheating. To that, I say never allow people's ignorance and prejudice to influence your behavior. More often than not, people jump over your purity and accuse you of something they are guilty of. You could have taken all the necessary measures to avoid impregnating your soul mate and receive sour news.

My coworker didn't like kids. We asked him why he got married. His answer: "For sex." His wife was fine with it, which made us believe that she too didn't like kids. We couldn't understand people who do not like children, but they both worked hard and seemed like a happy couple. Many years into their marriage, out of the blue, he told us that he was a father. Just about a year later, he became the father of two … and then three … and then four! We were surprised; he didn't like kids! So we asked him about that.

He answered, "She lied and tricked me."

Leaving the wife now was practically impossible. The child support alone would keep him broke and sailing in stress, frustration, and disappointment. For better or for worse, he's victimized and trapped. Yes, it's insane!

In many cases both men and women go the extra mile to make a pregnancy happen for a variety of selfish reasons, resulting in someone's becoming a victim of human despicable evilness. The arranged, forced marriages, for example, are some of the sad, inhumane realities—the victims of circumstances in the insanity of a relationship.

The insanity of a relationship is shameful, but if it happens to be the only way to have honor and glory, so be it. Regardless of how you became a mother or father, "I stayed so my son can have a father," or "I left so my kids can have a mother" ought to be obeyed. Whether you like your life or not, once you bring a soul into this world, you own it. There are no other priorities other than those that will ensure the dignity and happiness of that soul. There shouldn't be any dreams of yours before his or hers. There should be no paradise before his or hers. There should be no one before him or her, not even you.

And you have no time to think about madness, revenge, or bad luck. You only have time to make sure you won't be a cowardly scumbag who neglects on his responsibilities or a despicable mother who shames motherhood. You stay in the relationship, or you leave it, as long as the only purpose is the full well-being of your child. It's hard for a father to leave with the child, but all of the above applies to you, whether you remain lonely and single or are in another relationship. Your child must not endure your victimization. Your child must cherish your love, care, and nurturing, period.

And by the way, when friends tell you to leave and just pay child support, leave your friends instead. You do not want the regrets of a jackass father biting your sorry ass on your deathbed.

Trapped in abusive relationships: This one is the worst of the worst. You are not only unhappy and without freedom but also being beaten like a dumb dog. It could be that the reasons for being trapped in an abusive relationship are giving you hell. I sympathize with those who are trapped; it's a tragedy no one should have to endure. My hat's off to those who fought hard to stay but had to leave. I give glory to those fighting to stay and prayers to those who must leave but are staying.

If you are an abuser, you aren't worth more than a rotten rodent on the road, no matter who you are or claim to be. And this is not just my opinion; this is your verdict in the courts of humanity. It could be that being abusive is the only way you can show that you are the man in the house, or it is how you show superiority. This behavior is triggered and driven by an inferiority complex, bigotry, narcissism, or some serious mental disorder. Seek help before tragedy strikes! Quarantine your evil and unleash love, compassion, and respect to guide your thoughts and actions at home, or stay single for your sake and the sake of others. Otherwise, it's only a matter of time before you return home to find an empty house with divorce papers on the kitchen table, or criminal charges knocking on your door.

Divorce/Separation/Split—Winners and Losers

On the divorce/separation/split battlefield, there aren't winners, only losers and losers with the short end of the stick. No one wants to be there because dissolving a relationship is a betrayal to the children, a shame to the relationship, and an emblem of an ugly failure. If you dodge being blown up, the flames can barbecue you for life. While it has become so easy to divorce, separate, or split, the consequences continue to be more devastating. Cleaning up the mess of divorce is a lifetime responsibility of the ex-husband, and it can be very costly. Generation Loser gets no mercy.

You can be sure that anyone who doesn't fear divorce needs to wake up and smell the roses. A separation that involves children can be just as devastating as a divorce. Splitting from a relationship might not be as devastating, but it certainly leaves a long-lasting sour taste.

Life can reveal its ugly face to you and might leave you in a situation where taking a knockout punch and then repairing the wounds and broken ribs is better than leaning on the ropes and taking the punches, in the hope that the opponent will run out of juice before you fall.

After every stone has been turned, and the conditions haven't seen even an inch of change, a second chance is no longer deserved. It's time to begin packing. Do whatever you must do so you don't worsen the situation, but leave when you're ready.

Be true to the reality. The road will be rough and the ride bumpy for a while. As long as you stay focused on the paved roads ahead, you'll not feel the discomfort of the ride. Besides, you have tried your best but it's continued to get the worse, with no end in sight. Life has demanded that you embark on a new journey, whatever it takes. You should obey.

We haven't found ways to benefit fully from a relationship. Each new generation seems to be more cursed on that aspect. Generation Loser has fewer tools to reverse the curse, despite the increase in possibilities. In fact, the increase in possibilities defeats the purpose by propelling relationships' hardships. You have to hang on, and be strong and prepared for everything.

Stand up for your relationship to the last drop of your blood, mourning no relationship.

17

Parenting, Teenage Crisis, and Management

Parenting

SOME THINGS IN LIFE ARE so important and look very easy, while in reality they are complicated and worsened by the entanglement they face. To be a parent is, among so many other responsibilities, to endure the teenage crises and not drop everything and run for cover, as hellish missiles are unleashed by teenagers' outrageous behavior.

Triage dictates that we skip the scrapes and work on the lacerations, stabs, or gunshot wounds. By this standard, we will tackle parenting in its crucial phase: teenagers at home. Better yet, we will lay out our response to teenagers who complain all the time that we parents make their lives a living hell because we don't understand what they go through.

That's simply not true. We parents understand the burden on our shoulders as our teens walk through life. We've been there and done that. Hundreds of factors make our jobs stressful and complicated—and more so with each generation. Generation Loser seems to be the worst to tame and maintain.

The followings are some examples of the hellish gates we have to go through for you, our teenagers:

Providence: It is our responsibility to provide a roof over your heads, food on the table, and clothing for you. The necessary work for providing these basic needs has become complex and overwhelming. We take jobs we don't like. We stay in relationships not meant to be, taking physical and emotional abuse. We lose friends. We go through hell at home, at work, and everywhere. We try our best not to show you our anguish, pain, suffering, and all other emotions that would hinder your happiness. Our dreams, plans, and projects stall or get crossed off because we have a greater responsibility to attend to—you.

Your education: The hardship of life nowadays makes it almost impossible to give you an education that propels you to greatness. The struggle of providing you with the basic needs leave us physical and financially exhausted. We don't engage in your home studies, can't follow your progress, and can't enroll you in the best schools in town. We are forced to send you to public schools and hope that you'll make it to college.

Your entertainment: We are unable to engage in your entertainment world (video games and media interaction) because it is expensive and time-consuming, and it does not improve your odds of success. Even if we make the necessary sacrifice to take you to outdoor activities, such as the park or zoo, sailing, beaches, and so forth, you are not interested, as you find these activities, as one teen said, "boring, antiquated, and gay."

The invisible monsters: While you see yourself as a normal teenager, your temperament makes our work twice as hard. We must be on top of everything and constantly think about ways to deal with you so you don't get hurt, and you don't hurt people around you. Jokingly, we say there must have been a mistake at the hospital.

The hereditary bond: When you were a baby, we were all you ever wanted. You refused to go to people you didn't recognize, and you ran from strangers. If you were lost in the store, garden, or at the park or mall, as soon as you were found, you were brought to us, the parents. If a tragedy strikes, we are the first ones notified. When you misbehave or get in trouble, we are the first ones called. When our parenting methods are such that your well-being is in jeopardy, the authorities take you away to foster homes, but only when there is no possibility of keeping you with us. And if you commit crimes and atrocities, we, the parents, will be labeled bad parents. These are the parents/children bonds translated as *responsibility* in the eyes of the law and society to reinforce our obligations to care and answer for you until you're adults. In fact, even after you're the captain of your ship, we parents are your copilots. Even if you reject us, we still stay ready to answer your calls. The hereditary bond made us this way.

The betrayal: Humankind is wired to give love, care, and respect to everybody and expect the same in return, particularly from lovers, family, and children. We cannot go on giving forever without receiving something in return; eventually, we'll stop giving. The problem is that this genetic demand is something you refuse to attend, and you couldn't care less about how we feel about it. For your information, that attitude not only leaves us with a spear in our hearts while we swim in a pool of betrayal but also dumps cold buckets of ice over our determination to endure parenting.

Stubbornness: Nothing leaves us angrier than your stubbornness. We take time explaining the reasons why you shouldn't do something or behave in certain ways. You turn around and do the opposite. We ask you why; you say that you don't know, which leaves us infuriated.

The look ahead: First, you are what we hate that we were, so we guide you away from the troubles and stupidity we faced in our teen years. Second, you will take care of us when we can no longer take care of ourselves. As you refuse our guidance and walk your walk on troublesome roads, we fear your failure, which is translated as doomed days in our finals years and a hellish future for you. This leaves us frustrated and worried as well. Don't you dare think that we are nothing more than an impossible elephant in the room, ruining your party, or that we don't understand.

Teenage Crisis

The teenage crisis is, unfortunately, not a distasteful phase of life that a destitute fifteen-year-old of a third-world country has to go through. The teenage crisis is a critical phase of life that all human beings face. It is earlier or later and less harsh or harsher on some teens. But what defines the teenage crisis generally embraces all teenagers in all walks of life, no matter where. Like everything else in life, the more we understand what goes on, the better the chances of success.

The early bird: Under normal circumstances, the teenage phase starts at around age thirteen. Many factors, such as genetics, food, environment, and culture, trigger an early puberty phase, and it's earlier for girls than for boys. Having to go through the changes of biological puberty can bring additional stress, frustration, and traits. It also can bring many other consequences. Say you are a fourteen-year-old physically developed like a seventeen-year-old. You could be a victim of your appearance. The older kids would want to hang around with you. This could be troublesome for girls; your friends could push you to do things too advanced for your age, resulting in boys taking sexual advantage of you, or you could be a victim of rape or teen pregnancy. On the other hand, you could have social integration difficulties, as kids of your age consider you too mature, and kids older than you might not want to hang with you because you act dumb.

Both boys and girls could see their level of stress and frustration rising due to early puberty. Find ways to fit in your age group, keeping in mind that you could go through some tough times, and be sure to let your friends know that you're not as old as you look.

The late arrival: The late arrival of puberty brings the opposite consequences of those brought by early puberty. You are likely to be left behind because your maturity is lagging. Life puts you behind the game. But late arrival of puberty is not a death sentence. You won't suffer much more than some teasing and rejection from your age-group friends. Or you could find yourself very inexperienced and virgin at age nineteen. It's nothing to worry about, as long as your overall development is normal.

Teenage Extension

In different countries and different cultures, there may be different ages at which a person is recognized as an adult by the society and laws of the land. In general, that age is eighteen. Many children see their teen world extend well into adulthood; they act silly and make lots of stupid mistakes. This is fine, except that the teen extension will hold back your progress, and society will label you with ugly names—slow or retarded comes to mind. And there could be more related damaging consequences.

There you are at twenty-five, racing cars, stealing cars, and shooting randomly in the park and committing other criminal acts. At sixteen years of age, you could get away with it with small disapproval from society and a slap on the wrist by the law. Now, all of society condemns your teenager behavior, and your punishments by the law is that of the fully grown adult that you are. With that said, benign silly things that we did as teenagers, which brought laughter and happiness, should never die, no matter how old we are.

The Toxic Gas

Despite what we know and think we know, we are still so far away from having a total understanding of teenagers. Teenagers once were considered as rebellious creatures, doing stupid things all the time. A simple definition is that the teen years are a transition from childhood to adulthood. But both definitions are far from the real thing. Let's have a fair assessment as to what makes teenagers who they are and act the way they do. Biology, sociology, psychology, education, heredity, environment, and anthropology are some of the tools we rely on for this assessment. Although technically, anthropology includes all of the above, breaking this definition into bits and parts will help us understand more clearly the complexity that surrounds a teenager's world.

Heredity shapes a personality right from insemination. From this very beginning, whatever ingredients we receive from our ancestors will cook for about twenty-five years, and then there we are—short, tall, sexy, handsome, thin, fat, muscular, skeletal, weak, powerful, smart, genius, musician, or sports star and down to despicable rapists and serial killers. The phenomenon that was defined as an individual's choice, such as homosexuality, has been proven to be hereditary, reaffirming that no matter how stunning something is, we inherited it—although heredity traits can change for better or for worse, according to the goodness or evilness of our daily surroundings. If our family is poor, there's a high probability that we will be raised in a ghetto. Without much there to look up to, teenagers have no chance for a smooth transition, even if they have good personalities. The negative forces of their environment, along with a hostile home environment, add to a teenager's innocent evilness. Regardless of color, gender, or ethnicity, teenagers from ghetto and poor families go through more trouble in school and with the law.

On the other hand, if their environment is rich, any tendencies toward bad behavior will be mitigated by good influences. In a good home environment, supported by peace, love, and understanding, there's money for after-school programs, psychiatric diagnosis, and therapy, and inspiration joins forces to stop the teenagers from self-combusting. Most important, the parents help teenagers in trouble instead of making matters worse. This is a huge help because during our battle of transition to adulthood, we don't understand what is going on. Even though we think we're in charge, we are actually acting crazy and impulsive. And unfortunately, millennial teens get more fuel to the fire than buckets of water.

We parents should confess that in so many instances, we demand the impossible from our teens. They could have done their best, but we get angry with them. We simply forget that their brains don't allow them to do better, and we fail to realize that they are immature and going through a crisis. Our negative reactions are toxic to them.

The Taste for Danger and Disobedience

There's almost nothing too dangerous for any teenager. Many risky behaviors bring the consequences right away, sometimes severe punishments, yet as soon as the next risky behavior knocks, they rush to open the door and engage fast. My son William had problems with house keys. He lost them once. I explained the consequences, and we came up with a strategy to avoid losing them again: "Keep them in your backpack at all times. You come home, unlock the door, come inside, and put them back in the backpack."

Three days later he lost them again. He got a reprimand. A few weeks later, he lost them for the third time. He got a mild whipping. Then his problems moved to inviting friends over. I had no problem with that as long as I was home. He understood that. He still brought friends over when I wasn't home. I found out and whipped him again.

Three days later I received an email from AOL about a threatening message, full of foul language, that my son sent to someone. I was angry, but when I confronted him, he said it was his friend. I paced from room to room, boiling inside, too angry to whip him because it would definitely end up in him being hurt. Yet I had to let the anger out. I punched the bathroom wall, which made a big hole.

Then William moved to dangerously risky behavior. A neighbor told me that he was jumping from a second-floor window to impress friends. I realized that he was having a tough time doing the right things. I was sure that he didn't like what was happening and that he wanted to please. I simply asked him to stop dangerous behaviors like that.

When we adults talk about when the boys were younger, he and his brothers, Carlos, and Claudio, laugh about the crazy things they did. They don't understand how they did what they did, including things I didn't even know they did!

Teens running away is another example of the taste for danger and disobedience. Say you are a sixteen-year-old girl, living with your parents. You have a roof over your head, food, and running water. You have your own bedroom, TV, clothes and shoes provided by your parents. You run away because your curfew is ten o'clock every night, unless you're granted permission otherwise. You pack your bags to go live with your friends. You sleep on the floor and share a closet, and you can't touch the fridge. After two weeks, you bounce to other friends because things became hectic. Hunger and frustration are consuming you. And you continue to bounce around until you're nineteen years old, a complete junkie now. You beg your parents to take you back, yet you have to obey the old rules.

Here's another example: your friends at the park tell you to steal a car and take the gang uptown. You don't think twice. You proceed with your risky behavior, get caught, and call your friends to bail you out. Or, the worst of all, you join a street gang to prove your toughness, or you'll fire guns in the park.

Many adults are in jail for gruesome crimes they committed in their teen years, including killing of their parents, brothers, or sisters. The blame falls on the demons in charge of their devilish actions. It's so tragic that almost all our diabolic actions happen during the high school years.

High School

High school is the bittersweet holy grail of teenagers, as the stormy times are about to calm down or become good times and great experiences. Best friends forever, high school sweethearts, driving, the first job, and sneaking out of the house through the bedroom window to the movies and house parties form a large pot of good and bad experiences. Then there's approach of freedom—the eighteenth birthday. High school is also the start of the construction of the road to paradise. But on the other side of this green land lies some seriously vicious predators.

Teenagers in high school are under a lot of pressure that comes continuously from many directions. Responding to such pressure is a heavy burden on their shoulders. On top of that, the urge to fit in or be different pushes them to despise adults' advice and disrespect the laws of the land because they think the adults' advice is archaic and filled with taboos and that the laws of the land are nonsense that stands in their way. In fact, they believe that crime is a normal teen behavior, misunderstood by society.

They also feel obligated to show how powerful they are. Guns, knives, swift fists, and the gang become the main means of showing toughness. They select the friends that have the same approach as theirs and abandon the ones who are focused on getting good grades. Another crazy teenage behavior in high school is fast driving and car racing to impress the girls. So many lives are lost as a result of this foolish behavior.

Girls, you aren't immune to high school shadows of death either. In a lesser degree, you are sliced and diced by the same sword when sneaking out of the house and giving fake excuses to go to the mall or see a friend. In reality, you are going to hang with the boys. You go the extra mile to look prettier than your friends and cool and attractive to boys. More often than not, this behavior brings ugly consequences.

But this is the way of teen life. How can that make this generation a loser or in crisis? The millennial generation faces a life struggle all around them. The behavior and conditions may seem the same as the previous generations, but the consequences are far worse. In some states, three driving citations will send you to special driving classes, contrary to decades ago, when you were required only to pay a fine to keep your license. Having no license is a handicap. Taking actions to the extreme for the fun of it costs more nowadays. Also, the odds of a teenager's having a long criminal record is greater than in previous generations. A criminal record can give nightmares and block the shine of your power for a long time. In fact, from all corners of life, millennial teens are surrounded by obstacles that are just about impossible to overcome. On top of that, the distractions, control, and domination of their world are taken ever so seriously by the big boys behind the scenes. It is crisis inside and out for millennial teens.

Communication

All living organisms and creatures communicate with each other. We humans set ourselves apart from the rest and live interesting lives because we have speech as the greatest component of communication. Teenagers don't know that—or they don't care. I think that's a tragedy!

After thousands of years of language development and evolution, we still don't understand that communication is a silky road to a peaceful interaction between people and nations—a warm, cozy blanket for all relationships. Yet whatever we have been making of communication, it is hard to sell it to teenagers. Sadly, that's quite understandable, as teenagers feel the urge to be dominant, to be the leader in the shining spotlight. They also believe that instead of listening, others should listen to them. A short dialogue between a teen brother and sister, for example, could be an exchange of sympathetic words such as the following:

"Clean up your room, pig!"

"Make me."

"Are you doing your homework?"

"No, I'm going to the moon. Obviously, I'm doing my homework."

"Did you see my phone?"

"Are you blind? Is right there, idiot!"

"Where are you going?"

"Somewhere."

"Is that yours?"

"No. It's yours. Obviously, it's mine!"

"What are you eating?

"Food."

"Who you talking to?"

"Somebody."

"Can you pass me that?"

"Can't you see I'm busy?"

"You're playing the stupid video game. Pause it!"

"I can't pause this game, stupid! How about you not asking me to do things for you ever!"

"Your attitude will cost you someday."

"Who cares?"

Pretty straightforward, isn't it?

Their interaction with parents and other adults isn't far from that either. Say you want to start a chat while in the car with your sixteen-year-old son:

"How was your day?" you ask.

"What you think? It's school."

You swallow that and change the direction of the dialogue. "My left shoulder's bothering me."

"That's not my problem."

You see that he's upset. You ask, "What's the matter?"

He chooses to stay silent. You ask again, only to get the response, "I don't wanna talk about it."

Explaining to teenagers that communication demands that the receiver listen and decode the message from the sender would be a waste of time. Teenagers use the war of words for communication.

Nowhere to Run, No Place to Hide

The teenage years—adolescence, human devilish phase, age of puberty, coming of age, time to be stupid, or whatever we want to call it—is the most turbulent period of development. It lasts about seven years. The first five years are the most intriguing, crucial, and mind-blowing. And here's why:

At age thirteen we enter the childhood-to-adulthood transition battlefield. This battlefield is dominated by physical and physiological changes that unleash their strongest soldiers for a simultaneous attack on our little bodies, minds, and spirits. On top of that, our grandma, grandpa, mom, dad, siblings, cousins, doctors, teachers, priests, nuns, and the governments join forces to tame us. And then there's the reinforcement on standby, so that all exits are covered while the melee keeps pounding us. We can scream, cry, wet our pants, and beg for a bathroom break or just waste our time because everywhere we look, there are familiar soldiers who suddenly don't know us, don't speak our language, and are ready to strike us hard. Their mission is to stop us from becoming psychopathic serial killers, despicable citizens, or socially unfit creatures. They know that once we reach adulthood, there's no going back. There is only one chance to do this right, and they cannot blow it.

The less terrifying phenomenon, such as the first menstrual period; development of pubic hair; the growth of the breasts, buttocks, and height in girls; and the first ejaculation, voice deepening, appearance of facial hair, and the growth of the penis, height, and muscle in boys are common teenage portraits easily recognized. The daunting monsters are the invisible developments such as the enlargement of lungs, heart, and (the king) brain activity. The less terrifying phenomena and the daunting ones combine forces to go to work on teens. Oh, yes, they're in hell, being whipped left and right from head to toe. Their outrageous behavior is the language of their pain, stress, and frustration in the eyes of their parents, as the drastic change occurs from adorable angels to despicable devils. For this much change and chaos, there must be a King Kong in the room. Yes, there is—the brain.

At about ten years of age, our brain size is 90 percent of its normal size, not reaching its full size until age twenty-five. Despite the fact that the brain weighs only about three pounds (2 percent of the total body weight), it uses 25 percent of our calories. And so it is not the size of our brains that cause the chaos in our teen ages; it's the complexity of its activities. As the commander in chief, brain responsibilities include the assurance of the normal development of our five senses, which ensures our fitness for the challenges of adulthood. For that to happen, the brain orders our eyes, ears, noses, feelings, and taste buds to work nonstop. The activities of these senses keep the brain going crazy, analyzing and responding to the information it receives. And so, this process of breaking to rebuild stronger is not a pleasant or peaceful experience. Since this is a one-size-fits-all, there's no escape; you are your worst enemy. As if this is not poisonous enough, the toxic gas will finish you off.

Crisis Management

Facing crisis is a bitter experience that can suck our resolve right out of our souls and leave us sailing in turbulent waters. We curse life and destiny, and we blame God, the world, friends, enemies, and families for our crisis. Managing parenting during the teenage crisis is an almost impossible job that must be done well. The same bugs that bite in home education for our children return to bite again, and they spread their venom on the parent-teenager battlefield. Teenagers of Generation Loser are once again hit unmercifully by two different whips—the one swung by humankind and the other by genetic order. Parents are sucked in and whipped, sometimes more unmercifully than the teenagers.

All the glory and paradise of the first five years of a child's development, which brings the greatest happiness to parents, is gone and replaced with the flames of hell. Fortunately, the crisis is, to some extent, a good thing. Each time we face it, we learn valuable lessons and accumulate experiences that help us navigate the next time around without as much frustration and despair. In the meantime, we ought to alleviate the pain. We must do two things: (1) understand that life comes with crisis and (2) believe that we are empowered to manage any crisis, at any time, regardless of circumstances.

Management is the ability to perform tasks in ways that lead to intended goals. Any business in good standing is rooted in good management. Likewise, any individual or family whose life is moving smoothly has good management, and it deserves good credit. Parents need all the help they can get to manage life when the teen years of their sons and daughters arrive. Let's touch on a couple of crisis zones that demand a remedy, and inject the medicine before they become disaster areas.

Emotional distress: From every perspective, the angels you cared for since day one have changed drastically. They are now refusing to listen to you, and in disrespectful tones, they demand that you don't touch their stuff, order you to stay away from their business, and tell you to leave them alone. These teenage reactions, among others, surely sting your heart and bring you to tears. Resist the pain, hold your anger, and keep your emotions strong.

The battlefield: Teenagers engage in wars of words at any time, and they are good at it; actually, they are experts at it. Responding in kind means a loss on your part. To stay alive and win, digest the words that have sense and spit out the stupid and offensive ones. Find a strong branch to hold on tight. This tornado is a fast-moving storm. It will soon give way to a rainbow again. Besides, you put out a flame with an extinguisher or water, not hay and fuel. Also, watch the edges, where the fire is more intense. If your teen gets heated when you give lectures, ride your police horses in good weather only, or use extreme caution. If all proves worthless or makes the situation worse, don't ride your police horse at all. And remember that your sermons are better appreciated when delivered at the right time to the right crowd.

Tough love: Somehow we fool ourselves into thinking that we must ensure the well-being and education of our kids until they take charge of their destinies at eighteen or, for most parents, at twenty-one. At that point we free ourselves from parenting duties and obligations, except parenting is for life. Our responsibilities simply diminish, not vanish. Love, care, and guilt sneak in to make parenting an eternal endeavor. Unfortunately, some teenagers just do not help home parenting see its sweet sixteen. They push their luck and trigger tough love, a relief resource no parent likes to use because nobody wins.

Parents, when you have to use tough love, consider the circumstances, which are different for girls than boys, and seriously picture the outcome before you act. The first question to ask yourself is, "Will they succeed or fail miserably?" Here's one prognosis: Daughters are likely to become junkies on the streets who will do anything for a buck or two for drugs, cigarettes, alcohol, or a place to crash tonight. Sons have a high probability of joining gangs and drug dealing. When you hear about their troubles, particularly the daughters, your heart will tremble. If you continue to ignore the situation, tragedy could strike; your help could've come a little too late. You could lie to yourself, but deep down you're suffering from emotional distress. And this could be the best scenario yet. Some teenagers need a reality slap to wake up, but tough love might not do the trick.

If there isn't any other option, don't forget that tough love is a monster living in sensitivity land, where emotional whips swing from all directions. Prepare yourself to be bruised, but minimize your pain and suffering—and that of your teen—by explaining the reasons for your tough love. Don't use the heat of the moment to unleash your authority with a finishing move. Also, keep communication channels open. Parenting is for life, and tough love is a temporary measure for crossing temporarily troubled water. Your rebellious teens will soon realize their mistakes and seek your forgiveness. Although life in general runs through valleys of shadows of death, nothing can compare to teenage crisis management. Once again, the double-edged sword is slicing and dicing; your demons beat you up severely, and your inexperience with the challenges of life management will come to finish you off.

Teenagers, management of your life consists of fighting the demons causing your trouble. I hate to sound negative, but I'm not sure that you have what it takes to fight them off. You don't know what you don't know, and you refuse to admit that you are in crisis. You don't understand what's coming your way with its consequences, yet you think you are in charge. This attitude, driven by your demons, can turn you into a bad crisis manager. When we tell you what it takes to make it—wit, wisdom, grit, blood, sweat, and tears—you stare at us for a second, as if we are from a circus, and then burst out in laughter. Well, the clown in the room is, actually, you. But wait just a minute! Teenagers join the military and become great soldiers who carry out highly sophisticated missions and endure demanding daily duties that only can be successful through sharpened skills, determination, perseverance, and good judgment. And so, yes, you can fight the demons. Besides, "If there's a will, there's a way."

Fighting the Demons

Fighting the demons consists of strategies to defeat stupidity and stop tragedy from striking. The brave, daring, invincible attitude we carry within, as well as the refusal to accept orders and guidance from people, especially family, are part of teenagers' normal behavior, though translated as stupidity in the eyes of the adults. The tragedy is that teens can't see such things as stupidity because their demons don't.

Teenagers, the demons cause internal turmoil, manipulate your acts and behavior, shackle your legs, and chop off your wings. Unless you fight the troublemakers, you'll be paralyzed, without anything strong to hold on to, when adulthood arrives. Understand that you cannot take this fight all by yourself. Until you accept guidance from others, you won't be wearing protective gear for the fights ahead. You are simply limping toward the greatness of life. And you know that a castle on the sand can't withstand a storm.

Exceptional teenagers might have been born with skills and virtues that spring them ahead of the game, but they improve themselves. Their attitude is the one you need to copy: obedience to parents, family member, and society; big dreams and perseverance; always raising the bar and adding new adventures. They march strongly and focus on greatness. That's why they are exceptional and exceptionally ahead of the game. You must follow their paths within your means and become an inspiration as well. You might not become exceptional, but you'll boost your inherited power to fight evil and turn yourself into what you want to be. This fight is yours, but it's not an easy one. You should use the army available to you— your parents, family, and society—and make sure that your parents are your SEAL team, commanders in chief, and allies. Here's why:

While you need all the help you can get, society gives you friends, best friends, and peers to support your pursuit of happiness. It also gives you great books and technological tools to help you understand your surroundings. But your family (grandmother and grandfather, parents, siblings, uncles and aunties, and cousins) share a strong blood tie with you. They are willing to chip in so you can become the best you can be. Yet the full responsibility for your victory lies on your parents, who are, indeed, your greatest lifesavers; you are their best creation. They stand before you to fight for making you a star. They empower you to fight the demons. Besides, you are in hell and won't get out until years later. You need buckets of ice to cool you off. Your parents have all the ice you need. So try your best to quarantine your rebellious side and embrace understanding and compromise in the free flow of mutual respect, and there won't be a single demon standing in your way. Show appreciation through your willingness to learn the ropes now and cash great rewards later.

Learning the Ropes

"Why do I need to learn the ropes?" you might ask. And the answers, long and inconclusive, would be that contrary to what you think, you don't know everything; you only know a little bit more than nothing. The devil in you is leading you to the edge of the cliff. Out of the three distinct phases of life—childhood, teenage, and adulthood—the teenage phase is the most challenging. And last but not least, learning, as well as teaching, is vital for the continuation of humanity.

From the readings of cave paintings to all other forms of recorded history, each generation learns from previous generations and teaches the generations in front of it, which in turn will teach the future generations. As soon as we are able to talk, the urge to learn (curiosity) drives us to ask endless questions. Learning the ropes is not a human creation. It's written in every creature's DNA. Teenagers who neglect to learn the ropes are the biggest adult losers. Hell came down and found them handicapped and unprepared. They got burned badly. And it wasn't cool. Since you don't want that experience, let's see what it takes to learn the ropes of becoming a great mind instead of a disgusting loser. Let's start with the learning circles.

The learning circle: Your learning circle is the team you create. It should include your parents and families, your friends, teachers, and Google. Your family is the captain and quarterback. There could be a situation where your team sucks or your parents are, in your opinion, stupid or unable to teach the ropes right. In this case, you must split off and build a better learning circle. Be careful in doing so to avoid walking into a trap or ambush. For example, teens leaving home vow to be a better parent than their parents, but they later find themselves worse off as victims of a bad split and deadly sins.

Bad split. When you split off from your family, teen rage can easily make you careless. As a result, you could get involved in countless fights, get expelled from school, and have endless jail time, which builds up an extensive criminal record. If an extensive criminal record substitutes for your high school diploma, you can be sure that your game will always be increasingly complicated, frustrating, and even suicidal. You've turned yourself into a loser. So when you have to split off from your family to learn the ropes, make sure you're not trading a great horse for a donkey with bad teeth.

Deadly sins. Teen's risky behavior is an easy path to try smoking, do drugs, drink, steal cars, and exhibit reckless driving. It may take a long time to bring death, but you can be sure that from the day you start smoking, doing drugs, or drinking, your slow death starts its engine. Smoking, especially cigarettes, sucks the oxygen from your lungs; drugs and alcohol could leave you jobless and homeless before rotting your liver; car theft has landed a stunning number of teenagers in jail; reckless driving has proved to be the deadliest immediate consequences of risky behavior, with a significant number of teens killed in car crashes every year. Some statistics say that six teens, ages sixteen to nineteen, die every day in car accidents in the USA.

And here's the big one: once you lay your hands on a gun or knife for "protection," you should smell the odor of corpses and picture your funeral or a long stay behind the bars. Are you stupid or something? There's no need for this type of protection when you stay away from troublesome roads. If your temperament is such that you cannot stay away from troublesome roads, fight yourself harder. Develop the skills to spot trouble, and then run away as fast as you can so that any deadly sin will only dream of catching you. This is a philosophical principle you should practice in your teenage years and throughout your life.

Taking the hit vs. dodging the bullets: As you move along on your long, stressful process of becoming an adult, life throws hard balls at you. Learning the skill to make the best choice between facing a problem head-on or avoiding a problem becomes very important. Taking the hit doesn't mean you volunteer your head for sacrifice, nor does it mean letting stressors knock your body, mind, and spirit off balance or let stress, frustration, and depression fog your path to success. Taking the hit means you're aware of your situation and you deal with it in a way that you'll come out of it as a winner. Stress, depression, frustration, and rage are some of the hard balls life throws at teenagers.

On the other side of the river lie the strategies for avoiding the hard balls. Sports, music, after-school programs, or any activity that keeps the body, mind, and spirit active are a big help. YMCA is the best because of the benefits of learning social interaction and discipline, among other things. Unfortunately, we do a bad job there. I'm surprised about the number of teenagers in my neighborhood who admit to smoking weed and cigarettes because they are stressed out all the time. Some of them add alcohol to the train of tragedy. A cigarette relaxes you for two minutes and then gives you a crazy desire to have another one twenty minutes later. Until you get it, your stress level keeps going up. Soon you won't live a day without puffing a pack or two. And drugs give you a high, a great feeling that allows you to navigate through heights of the mind and leave all your problems down below until you crash and burn. With regard to alcohol, remember that it doesn't help until you are drunk and have forgotten what's causing you stress and other troubles. This is a drunk move.

Those of you who rely on cigarettes, drugs, bullying, gangs, intimidation, rage, and vandalism to kick out stress are simply making fools of yourselves. You're trying to solve a problem with a bigger problem. This is a no-brainer! Find ways to dodge the bullets without the possibility of ricochet.

When it comes to choosing between taking the hit or dodging the bullets while learning the ropes, you face a delicate situation. Don't let your impulses overtake your reasoning. You're sailing in very turbulent waters. Find the humility in you, and reach out to those who have been there and done that or can build bridges. What you learn or don't learn now will serve or haunt you for life.

Victim of Circumstances

Being a victim of circumstances means that your crisis is chaotic and its management is under attack. You, who were raised by a single parent, foster parents, or stepparents, will face harder times during the teenage years. Fortunately, the system comes in to ensure that your father gives financial support, but the most important thing, emotional support, is not mandatory. Although financial support is important, any child would prefer a visit or call from his or her father. Some parents don't understand the importance of emotional nurturing. They not only become estranged but also seek revenge, using the children as a bargaining chip. Moms allow only the recommendation of the courts, and the fathers simply abstain from visiting the children. What astounding stupidity, with the greatest loss for the children!

The bond between children and their foster or stepparents is far from the bond by blood. Stepparents need to find ways to deal with your personality that is far from their family tree. Your stepbrothers and/or stepsisters could throw the "You're not my real brother/sister" card in your face. And there's worse. Some women may go through menopause in their late thirties or early forties. This biological change clashes with raging teenage hormones and their going through hell at school, at games, and on trips with friends, bringing frustration and humiliation, among other things, only to return home to face hotter flames. It's not a pretty scenario.

Unfortunately, once life throws you in the victim-of-circumstances ring, you can't escape the turbulence. No teenager can. What you can do is to avoid coming out of it as a loser. Keep your cool and the situation under control. Any time you feel the heat, get out of the kitchen. Keep your head up, and function straight. Develop ways to see smoke from far (wherever there's smoke, there's a fire), and take a different route. Don't burn yourself by trying to prove you are invincible. You are a winner but not invincible yet. You'll be a loser if you do.

This may seem like an impossible task, but you must try your best. You're a victim of circumstances, through absolutely no fault of your own, but it doesn't mean that you're a sacrifice to the gods. You can win this game if you believe in yourself and embrace the challenges—and let your parents tag along.

Teen Parents

To all teens, boys and girls, when risky behavior lays a pregnancy in your laps, you can be sure that you've screwed up badly. The main reason is not even the frightening aspect of becoming a parent when you know nothing about parenting. The main reason is that you can destroy your life and mess up the lives of your loved ones, especially children. Your parents are the first victims because, in most cases, they are the first ones to rescue you, probably by raising your kids. This tragedy affects girls more than boys, as they have to drop their dreams to become a single mother, raising a child without support from the baby's father, in general. Also, teen moms have a disadvantage in the market for love. Yet boys who are teen fathers also have shot themselves in the foot. This is a crisis that imposes a strong demand for a good management.

Life continues to increasingly depend on finances. To have finances that don't suck, you need good employment. Good employment requires a higher education. A higher education requires your commitment. Once you have a child as a teen, you've given yourself responsibilities you're not ready for. As a result, the path to your financial paradise is washed away or has obstacles that could be impossible to overcome. Right here, right now, you're being sliced and diced and simultaneously passing the pain to your kids and their future.

According to statistics, the number of teen pregnancies has gone down. But casual sex—mostly driven by weed and drugs—is still the reason for a stunning number of teen mothers.

Girls, the world of romance, love, and sex is complicated and is capable of dumping a tragedy in your lap in the blink of an eye. You have to use your head to avoid traps filled with lifetime scars and regrets. You are a very special winner from the day one. Don't let your special gifts vanish in front of your eyes. You deserve the best. Anything less should be forbidden. Once you have the best at the right time, your odds of winning are greater. You must see that your generation is not friendly to teen pregnancy, despite its decline. Vow to avoid becoming a teen mom at all costs. It takes just one little accident to chop off your wings and turn you from a heroine to a "zeroine."

Boys, your fate could be as doomed as that of the girls. If you are a teen father, you too have shot yourself in the foot and chopped off your wings. Don't think this is funny; the joke will be on you.

Over-the-Counter Medicine

Communication and understanding are the over-the-counter medicines that are available on every street corner for a low price. They are the best medicines to fix any type of teenager/parent issue.

Parents, put yourselves in your teenagers' shoes. If there was poor communication and lack of understanding from your parents during your teen years, now is your opportunity to make sure your teenagers don't go through those same gates of hell. Conversely, you can give your teenagers the helping hand you got in your teen years.

All teenagers would have exciting lives if they didn't have to go through a crazy crisis. Sadly, this is tough luck. But there's a remedy tree right next to you. The greatest medicine for crisis management is a small package that contains pills, including humility and determination to make a difference. It's not light, but it's not heavier than you can carry. And the beauty of this is that once you swallow the humility and determination, the taste in your mouth will be pleasant. The voices of great minds will whisper the following reminder in your ears: "When you have to cross rough waters, listen to expert swimmers and to those who build bridges."

Take the bull by the horns. Choose small ones first, and gradually pick bigger sizes. This fight builds strength, endurance, and confidence to deal with the crisis in adulthood. Rely heavily on communication and understanding as your favorite over-the-counter medicines for all the sickness of your teen years, and don't let your bad temper stand in the way. It alone can destroy your life as it robs you of the opportunity to succeed and forces you to waste your precious time in jail, where you will be surrounded by criminals ready to make matters worse for you. Remember that once you swallow a bad pill, you can count on a bitter taste in your mouth and an upset stomach that could last longer than you'd expected. You know better.

Personality Clash

So many factors bring a small fan instead of a powerful air conditioner to cool off the room where parents and teenagers are frying each other. Some parents are intolerant, and they need to be the king at all times. Their parenting philosophy is, "Do as I say or else." Other parents are control freaks, allowing zero room for teenagers to experiment and take charge. And a small percentage of parents are both. When the full-grown, messed-up personality of parents clashes with the developing personality of teenagers, who could be on their way to becoming their parents (intolerant control freaks), there can only be war. Parents fight for respect and dominance. Teenagers fight for freedom and superiority. Since the parents must do parenting, and teenagers must have their space to evolve, both of you must come to the peace-negotiation table for the final fight, and neither of you will go home a loser.

Once both of you understand who you are, you can take the necessary measures to change what you can, avoid situations that increase your already high level of stress, and instruct yourself to accept a larger burden of stress than other people do.

A parent's personality cannot change, but the parenting strategy can and, for some parents, must evolve. Therefore, parents, take a closer look at the way you deal with your teenagers to ensure that you are not pouring gasoline to their burning fire.

On the other hand, teenagers, you must understand that you can't have it your way all the time. It wasn't like that for anyone. Nothing has changed so drastically that millennial teens can have it their way, all the way.

Stress

It's not Monday or Friday the thirteenth. You had a good night's sleep that followed a romantic moment, sealed with passionate lovemaking. How is it that you feel stressed out? The answer lies in your internal stress. The interaction among our thirty-seven trillion cells exerts lots of stress. We don't usually notice the effect of this interaction because this stress is balanced. When some bad guys, such as virus and bacteria act up, the battle between them and our immune system, for example, generates enough stress to tilt the plates of the internal stress balance. As a result, we feel stressed out but don't know the reason. We ride on the gloom-and-doom train without making any sense, or we go through terrible turbulence while the fight goes on. Usually, our immune system wins and restores the balance in a few days. And we're happy again.

By contrast, when we get irritated easily, angry over simple things, and toss and turn all night long, we are a victim of external stress imbalance or a victim of a combination of both internal and external imbalances. Life is now a complete nightmare. People better leave us alone and stay the heck out of the way. Since this is not fun, and we cannot escape all the stressors lurking everywhere, we must manage stress in order to enjoy life. Yet let's be careful not to make matters worse.

Some common stress-management remedies are a temporary stress relief definitely not worth the try. They carry powerfully hidden harms, with devastating lifetime consequences. Unfortunately, drugs, alcohol, cigarettes, and casual sex are some of them. The combination become tools ready to slice and dice unmercifully. You want to avoid that at any age, particularly when you're young. The younger you start fooling around with drugs, alcohol, cigarettes, and casual sex for whatever reason, the longer there will be beatings. And the consequences will get more tragic as the years go by. To avoid the drama, use a smart way of managing stress.

If you are surrounded by people who are shadowed by negative energy, or you live in a ghetto, your stressors are diverse, abundant, and powerful. It almost will be impossible not to be stressed out all the time, inside and out. Realizing that should push you into getting better friends and move to a different neighborhood, town, or city. Understanding our heredity, body, and environment comes as a powerful card in stress-management games.

Stress management calls for activities and the practice of a philosophy free of outrageous side effects. Since only you can determine what those can be, it becomes your responsibility to make a list that combines the common stress-relief activities with what works for you, and then select the best choices. Here are friendly activities for reducing stress:

- walking in the park
- walking at the beach
- dedicating time to, or developing, hobbies
- dancing
- watching movies
- having sex
- listening to soothing songs (be aware that some soothing songs can be depressing)
- laughing—jokes, comedy movies, stand-up comedy
- participating in social activities and events

Internal stress cares for itself. That doesn't mean, though, that we should relax and let the river take its course. We still have the obligation to help. A great helping hand comes from good health in the form of a balanced diet and exercise. As a matter of fact, it's killing two birds with one stone: We help the internal stress to stay balanced, and simultaneously we get a boost in fighting external stress. Happiness seems to be an even greater helping hand. The higher the level of your happiness, the great your power to fight stress. When you get hit, you'll be back on your feet in no time, dancing around, happy again. Prioritizing your focus on being happy ensures that the plates of your stress balance will always be tilted to your desire.

Remind yourself that life marches toward increasingly more stressful situations. You've got to empower yourself to face whatever stressor comes your way. You are in the ring. Avoid the punches, take the punches, and throw knockout punches. Some fights will be Mike Tyson-style—intense and short. Others will go twelve rounds with a bloody nose, black eyes, cuts, and bruises, but you're the winner. When you're prepared for everything, you can't lose!

In the end, stress management in a parent/teenager ship is all about parents' obligation to be more understanding, forgiving, and supportive, and teenagers' obligation to be more respectful and cooperative. The ship will still face storms and rough waters, but both the parents and teens join forces to go through them safely, or they go around them, glad to respect the principles of common ground.

Common Ground

Let's assume that common ground is a small room where smart, intelligent, genius, and less-than-genius; breathtakingly beautiful, impressively handsome, and incredibly ugly; young, grown up, and elderly; short, average height, and tall; and black, white, green, and yellow from all walks of life gather for refuge. If everybody shouts, no one can be heard. The swiftness and power of the fist or how loud someone can shout are definitely as useless as pointing out each other's flaws.

Among many other things, understanding and cooperation would be in your main survival kit. Parents, try to understand teenagers and give them room to breathe. It doesn't matter what is bothering you—shadows of death, bad days at work, or something mysterious. You must drop that at the doorstep, shake off any excess stress before you enter, and be prepared for surprises that might not be so welcome.

Teenagers, you have to chill out and drop your complaints and accusations. Honor the parents' expertise, granted by experience, and open your minds and hearts to welcome them. You need independence and freedom to explore the world, discover your potential, and materialize your dreams. Your parents shouldn't deny you that right, but you simply cannot force your way in or out. The common ground is the main stream of your inseparable relationship, a bond by blood. You can't deny it or pretend it doesn't exist. When it goes into crisis, you and your parents *must* save it. You're all for one and one for all. All must live and help live. Parents, you shouldn't make your teenagers feel choked. Teenagers, you shouldn't push your parents off the cliff. You must get along.

Regardless of how well your parents have done for themselves, they want you to do better. For years you've entrusted your life to your parents because they knew better. Without them you were nothing. You always saw them as your heroes. Well, they still are. Don't ignore what they have to say. Don't act as if you know the game inside and out because you don't, not yet. Ask for help in drawing a chart and follow the plan instead of sailing blindly into the abyss. When you know where you are going and what to expect on the way, you will get there faster and safer.

Parents, relax, and dance in the off mode. If the captain needs your help, he or she will call for it. Understanding, mutual respect, and cooperation are the tools to help us navigate the common ground. Otherwise, we're all guilty as charged.

Guilty as charged: When everybody's right and there's no peace and harmony, everybody's wrong. Can everybody be wrong? Certainly!

Once, my father and I were watching Jimi Hendrix's music video. At the end of the video, there was a scene of his smashing the guitar. My father thought it was stupid.

"Why destroy the guitar?" my father remarked.

"It is fun, and the crowd always likes it," I said.

"So stupid! That's a waste of money."

"Dad, they have money to buy millions of guitars."

The video was cool. My judgment was that both of us were righteously wrong. To destroy a guitar for fun *is* a waste of money. Rock bands, however, do have enough money to buy tons of guitars. My dad and I could not even agree to disagree. We were guilty as charged.

Live and help live. We ferociously raise our kids within the family tradition and culture of the land, giving little or no attention to the needs of our kids. That makes us bad parents. Don't impose your philosophy and way of life on your teenager. You two live in different worlds within the world you share. You both need to find ways to get along.

Appreciate What You Have before It's Gone

We are wired to be always looking for better, easier, and safer. We can easily leave important things behind when we are eagerly in pursuit of something we have not quite conquered. Sadly, parents and loved ones are the first we leave behind. So many individuals have regretted letting the family relationship go sour or have cried over an ex-lover. You do not want to go through this pain and anguish. Your parents could be the members of the worst family on earth. Yet appreciating them is the right thing to do. This appreciative attitude helps you sail through any rough waters and get to your destination, dry, safe, and happy. Appreciating your family gives you the key to the doors of opportunity, and it removes obstacles on the path of your journey—a perfect recipe for a healthy family relationship. When you are facing grudges and hostility, it's all too easy to disrespect and abandon. Turn around as fast as you can and apologize. You want to take advantage of an easily accessible gold mine before it runs empty. Appreciate what you have before it's gone, not only because when it's gone, it's gone, but also because it enlightens the beauty of life and propels both of you to greater greatness.

Life comes with different challenges, but no part of the road is more challenging than parenting teenagers. By the same token, the teen years are complicated for teenagers. And it is not the challenge of parenting or the complexity of being a teenager that entirely makes the relationship between parent and teenagers so hectic; it is that and the generation. The lifestyle we are forced to embrace dumps mounds of frustration on each of us every day. Parents always want to be good parents; teenagers always want to be adorable to their parents. Unfortunately, the parents aren't getting the opportunity to do their job right, nor are the teenagers able to be better. It is a crisis on a daily basis, blown out from all directions. It takes the strong minds that parents have and the powerful strength that teenagers have to bring success in this daring transition. We must combine forces to fight all enemies. We must also understand our individual responsibilities in this game and play in a way that we win as a team. Parents must ensure that their jobs are done to the best of their abilities. Teenagers must accept the harsh reality that they don't know better; rather, they learn as they go. Parents may have to carry a greater share of pain, and there might be no other way. Besides, fair or not, it's "no pain, no gain."

Teenagers, please listen to the right voices, and follow the right beacons. Life has only three main phases: childhood, teenage, and adulthood. You may not repair the damages of your childhood, but you can use your teenage years to build yourself as people of steel. Regardless of how great and strong your foundation is, you still can ruin all possibilities of harvesting any reward, and you can cut yourself off from all chances of having a great adult life. The best for you won't lie ahead; you've killed it.

You, however, are going to be better than average, better than us. You are the millennials, greatly empowered.

The following tips are supplemental tools you can rely on to ease the parent/teenager relationship.

Parents, your teenagers don't walk an easy path or enjoy peaceful times. Understand what you must deliver, and watch your driving. Don't make hell hotter than it already is.

Adopt an approach consistent with your personality, evolution, and time with your teenagers.

Bend your rules to allow happiness to flow.

Lower your expectations, and worship happiness.

Allow room for experimentation and controlled risky behavior.

Give what you have, and show humility for having nothing.

Use your superior skills.

Don't forget your hidden treasures; behind your teenagers' rage lie love, respect, and admiration.

Remember that your kids count on your love and support *not* only when you are in a good mood, only when they behave well, or only when the time feels right but all the time. Don't demand love and respect. Don't pour the pain of your regrets on them. Your kids should not pay for the sins in your dark past and your misfortune. Your kids are, after all, your best creation. Please respect and appreciate them.

Teenagers, your parents could be hiding heavy, ugly sacks of resentment behind their daily struggles, especially single parents. Try to understand the world of your loved ones and the effects on your life.

You belong at home.

A journey through rough waters demands a helping hand from those who have crossed rivers and built bridges.

Right now you're building the castle to host your royalty. It takes sacrifices and a bruised back, but in the end, you will like your finished product.

Respecting your parents is respecting your future; obeying your parents is empowering yourself. You're been trained for the kingship that awaits you. Be humble!

Build loving memories, not regrets. When you can't say or do something nice, say or do nothing.

Remember that your parents are the best wells of fresh water you desperately need. They are the hands that fed you and continue to feed you. They go extra miles all the time to make your dreams come true. You are their best creation. Please respect and appreciate them.

He who refuses to see is blind of sight and mind and shall be deaf and ignorant.

18

Self-Care

MORE OFTEN THAN NOT, WE don't give enough attention to important issues because we don't think about them as such. Health care is one example. Government understands how important health care is (of course, health care can bankrupt a nation), but unfortunately, the government always avoids this issue. I understand that health care is a very complicated matter, but I don't understand avoiding it as a solution. A sensitive issue deserves special attention, not walking away from it. It should be faced head-on, once and for all. It's already become a monster too big and loose in the wild.

From every corner, we find germs, viruses, and bacteria spitting out new sickness, illness, and diseases, while they become resistant to treatments and medications. Worse is that the way we live—globalization—a pathogen can fly and spread its malice from north to south, east to west, in matters of days, leaving us trying desperately to recuperate and catch up. And before we can take a deep breath, we have to be on the move again, chasing a different killer.

Just as we got the 2014 Ebola epidemic in West Africa under control, we woke up to the Zika outbreak in 2015–16 that originated in Brazil. It spread from South America to North America, to several islands in the Pacific and Southeast Asia. Apparently, pharmaceutical companies are developing and storing the wrong vaccines. And that explains why there's so much fear, headaches, and frustration in health care.

But health care should not be an exclusive responsibility of the government, pharmaceutical companies, and doctors. In fact, we better off taking care of ourselves, in part because no one understands the relationship between our bodies and us better than we do. On the other hand, taking care of ourselves nowadays is something that's far from easy; a million things make it a daunting, almost impossible task. And leaving an illness to run its course is like knocking on the gates of hell or heaven's door.

Fortunately, taking care of one thing benefits so many others—thank God for that! Therefore, we will focus on the big guys, such as the heart, lungs, liver, and kidneys, and then reach out to big supporters: nutrition, fitness, and sleep.

Before that, let's look into our dearest friend, the car, and its similarity to us. A car is complex machinery that depends heavily on the chain reaction of its sections for a smooth and safe operation. All sections and components are important, but some are more important than others. Then there are the engine main components, without which nothing much would happen. We make engines with different sizes and power, but the basic principle is a one-size-fits-all; the fuel goes into the combustion chamber, the combustion happens, the power is expelled, the transmission allows the axle, which has a wheel attached to its extremities, to spin, causing a forward or reverse thrust. The assembly of a car is a replica of the human biological assembly line.

Here are some of the similarities:

The engine is the car's main component. It has cylinder blocks (four, six, or eight). The heart is the main organ of a human being.

It has four chambers. The engine expels the burned fuel through exhaust pipes to allow a steady flow of fresh fuel for a steady combustion. The blood returns to the heart for purification, and then it is pumped back to the entire body. If a car run out of fuel, the engine stops. If our blood count is low, we collapse or die.

The rpm at idle is the main indicator of a fine engine. If the rpm is below 500, something is wrong, and the car could go nowhere. If the engine's rpm is in the red zone, the engine will stall or explode. The heartbeat is the main indicator of vital signs. If the heartbeat is too slow, we feel funny, ready to faint. If the heartbeat is too fast, we can have a heart attack. No heartbeat means death.

If the temperature of an engine is in the red, the engine will stall or explode. Regulators regulate the car's temperature. If our body temperature is too high, we have a deadly fever, and we can die of it. We have cells to regulate our temperature.

A flat tire gives us a rough ride but not for too far. A leg injury makes us walk funny, in pain and not for too far.

Any faulty part in a car jeopardizes its performance and safety. When we are sick, our performance is affected.

The engine generates the power. The heartbeat generates the power.

The engine, battery, and radiator are some of the main car components. The heart, lungs, liver, and kidneys are some of the main human organs.

Each new model on the market more heavily relies on computers for its performance. Our brains are in charge of our performance. The more we experiment, the greater is our brain development, resulting in greater ability to handle a variety of tasks.

We continue to improve the car design for better reliability, safety, and performance through increased reliance on computers and technology. Our longevity now is improved; it's about ninety years of age.

From all branches of health care, we have come a long, long way and are getting healthier and happier.

A car requires periodic maintenance. So does the human body. The tragedy, though, is that we care for our cars better than we care for ourselves. That has to stop. Since the apparatus of a car came from the human algorithm, we should not allow our cars to be healthier than we are. The carriage cannot be ahead of the horses. So let's take care of the big guys running our health, starting with the king, the heart.

The heart: In general, hearts come in different sizes but function in the same way. A heart is a small, powerful pump, holding lots of invisible activities inside its four chambers. Day and night, rain or shine, hot or cold, calm or windy, the heart pumps blood through the entire body for about one hundred years, without breaks, or we die. The heart requires serious maintenance for great performance and longevity. A low-fat diet, especially low in saturated fat, and avoidance of excessive amounts of sugary drinks and junk food are some of the measures we should take for a healthy heart.

The lungs: These two team members of our respiratory system are our heart's neighbors. In terms of importance, they are next to our hearts too. They don't care much about nutrition but they beg us for regular exercise. Find ways to exercise four times a week at a fitness club or home gym. Walking, jogging, running, biking, swimming, dancing, and sports are some other exercises you should incorporate in your physical routine as the best remedies to your whole body, mind, and spirit for health and happiness. The greatest gift we can give our lungs is to avoid smoking tobacco products. It's better if we smoke nothing at all, for other good reasons.

The liver: As another hardworking organ in our body, the liver is always begging us not to intoxicate it with toxic stuff, including alcohol. Please listen to its cry. It allows you to have alcohol in moderation. Why do you have to reach the land of stupidity and drink way more than your tolerance and cause trouble? Your liver just wants you to respect alcohol. Not much is asked, especially considering the amount of money you'll spend on alcohol now and on hospitalization later. It is wise to respect the demands of your liver and all other organs.

The kidneys: They care about what we eat and drink. And their crying is for water in its purest form. Not through juices, sodas, and other beverages. Have you forgotten that you can survive up to seven days without food but only three days without water? Drink up as much as you can because quenching your thirst means your kidneys will thank you for the important tool they need to do their job effectively, and it ensures that you'll never experience the pain and misery of kidney stones.

Taking care of these four major organs ensures the health of others organs and, ultimately, the health of our whole body, without much hassle. Nutrition, fitness, and sleep—the three big supporters—play an important role in taking care of our health.

Nutrition: We need energy for our survival and performance of our daily activities. Science has determined that we need 2,000–2,500 calories as the recommended daily value to sustain ourselves for a day. This number can be lower or higher, depending on our metabolism and daily activities. If you have the recommended daily amount but still are hungry all the time, or if you are a hard laborer, such as a farmer, miner, landscaper, or carpenter, you definitely need more than 2,500 calories per day. (A crazy workaholic with a fast metabolism like me needs 4,000–4,500 daily calories.) If you are a couch potato or a clerk, you need fewer than 2,000 calories per day. Malnutrition or overnutrition can cause numerous problems to your health.

We have been victimized by both malnutrition and overnutrition. Because we are not turned into a skeleton or King Kong overnight, we don't respect our diets as much as we should. Worse is that even when we face the consequences of a bad diet, we slack on our obligation and commitment to bring the house in order. And the millennials are lost at sea, which is such a shame because as we are living longer, we must care for our nutritional world; so far, that's one of the best streams of happiness.

There are so many things involved in maintaining a healthy diet, and it has become increasingly harder, but this challenge is winnable and worthwhile. Our well-being is directly connected to nutrition. All our organs will suffer or benefit, according to the bad or good stuff we eat and drink. Healthy life in the future depends on what we eat and drink today. So be smart about what you feed yourself.

Fitness: Whatever you make as the backbone of your fitness world—say, the daily routine in your basement, daily walk at the park, four-day exercise routine at a fitness club, swimming, dancing, running, jogging, or martial arts—you always do better when you have nutrition as your best friend standing right next to you. The two are so intertwined that they become inseparable lovers, with fitness being the one to propose.

Here's what I mean: The more you exercise, the greater is the need for balanced nutrition because nutrition fuels your fitness. From here things only get better. Nutrition and fitness form a strong bond, with all partners putting their best efforts toward a common goal—your health. Accept nutrition as a must-have in your fitness world, and then focus on the benefits that fitness brings to your organs that are working hard to keep you alive. Commit yourself to fitness for its necessity and outcome. It's sad that Generation Loser, especially the millennials, have substituted nutrition and fitness with herbs, drugs, and video games. But I am confident they eventually will wake up and smell the coffee. Later is better than never.

Sleep: After sunlight comes night, darkness, or time to sleep. There's not much else we can do in darkness because we can't see much. That, however, is very dangerous in the jungle, where predators have an advantage over us. We had to find cover in the caves, and that was a smart move. Family members and friends stayed inside for their safety and the safety of others. This reality made it an excellent time to huddle together for fairy tales and adventures of the day, fooling around with children and family members, and then taking care of the affairs of the heart, before we crash down for a good night's sleep. The Creator timed our biological clocks so darkness coincides with sleeping time, which allows the body, mind, and spirit to have the peace and quiet they need to rejuvenate and dream. Eight to ten hours later, the sun pushes the night aside, allowing us to see clearly and far again. We're now ready to go on with our regular jungle business.

Sleep wasn't invented by man for his pleasure, nor is it the side effect of something stupid humans have done. As a miracle of greater importance than we think, sleep is part of what defines us. Simply put, sleep is very important to the health and survival of all creatures, especially human beings. First, the brain, working like a maniac to decode information it receives from our senses and dispatching answers to every little single part of our bodies at lightning speed, needs a break. As we go to sleep, it gets that break, even though it's still doing some light, important work to keep us alive and safe. The brain wakes us up to a loud noise, pain, and suffocation to fight death. Keeping us alive, whether we are awake or sleeping, is the responsibility of the brain. And unlike most of us, the brain takes its job very seriously. We should learn from it and not mess with what it needs to do its job.

Fortunately, if we try to deny sleep to our body, mind, and spirit, we'll lose. The brain, the chief in command, will refuse to allow the energy flow we need to stay active and alert. Our legs won't support our bodies anymore. We'll collapse and stay knocked out cold, snoring like an animal. Oh yes, the brain doesn't mess around. You can fool anybody but your brain. If you want to be a jackass and not giving it the sleep it needs, it will use whatever means necessary to get it. Besides, you know how miserable you are when you suffer from chronic insomnia. And so get enough sleep. Too much or too little sleep is bad for you. No sleep at all will bring serious health complication that can kill you.

The right amount of sleep varies from individual to individual, but eight hours are recommended for an adult, more for children.

Babies are always sleeping, as their brains have more work to do in trying to figure out the world and life, and elderly need less than everybody else. The rule of the thumb is that your body tells you what is enough sleep. I am sure mine does for me. I show respect and suggest that you do the same, as much as you can.

We go about our daily business, facing problems, creating problems, and solving problems, with less and less time to travel to the imagination land to mesmerize us. We seldom think philosophically about the complexity of humankind. We are crafted with wisdom, passion, and vision. All the millions of years of evolution, revolution, and mutation, among other mysteries that played a role in shaping humans, gave us one of the greatest rewards of life: happiness. There are many strings attached to happiness. Health is the main string. They must be tuned at the right pitch so, when strummed, they sound musical. The world falls fast, furiously, and painfully on us every time we are out of tune.

A small paper cut brings unimaginable and incomprehensible physical pain. A small blister on any of our toes brings torture when we wear shoes. A small headache is very annoying. A migraine leaves us in desperation. A persistent cough brings lots of misery. A fever and bad cold can keep us in bed for weeks. The flu can easily kill us. A toothache, ear pain, and cramps send us in a rush to hell. A small pimple on our buttocks causes so much hassle. Thank God these pimples usually attack only one buttock at a time!

How about using crutches because you have a broken leg or holding an arm still in a cast because it's broken? Taking a shower would be a show worth watching. A broken back or neck leaves us simply restrained in most physical activities. If many sections of the assembly are sick—say, our shoulders, low back, and joints are hit by pain and arthritis—or we're severely hit by stress, depression, and anxiety, we feel so crappy that we do not want to live. Any sickness or illness, physical or physiological, robs us of our abilities to be what we are meant to be: able and happy.

We all have fallen victim to illnesses, but no sound individual enjoys being ill. It then becomes our obligation to fight for our health and ensure that the fundamental organs (heart, lungs, liver, and kidneys) are the priorities of all priorities. These four main musketeers share a common task of keeping us alive and well. They must work in synchronization, or one takes the punch and the rest will feel the pain. If one dies, all will die. Luckily taking care of one means the benefit to four and to the entire body, but the focus must be on keeping the plates balanced. Taking care of only a few sections of an assembly of health will not guarantee a smooth operation of the whole assembly line. There is no such thing as taking excellent care of your liver and neglecting your kidneys or lungs but counting on being healthy.

Theoretically, maintaining good health is very simple: eat right, exercise, and get enough sleep. Add sexual, spiritual, and mental balance as the supplemental ingredients for your health. It could take much more than that, but we must endure in this fight. As individuals, regardless of our power and money, we are worth less than a penny in the streets without good health.

Don't let anyone fool you by saying that staying healthy is as simple as drinking a glass of water. That's a lie. Good foods are expensive, organic foods are even more expensive and hard to find, and they might not be as organic as they are advertised to be. The big boys are fighting hard to keep you hooked on bad stuff that kills you slowly and unannounced. Rumor has it that the government is the first devil, feeding us poisonous foods and releasing laboratory viruses for political gains. I am not sure about that extent of government evilness, but you can make the necessary sacrifice and commitment, and stay healthy, no matter what. Give your major organs the best they need to perform their tasks. You will save money and celebrate life with plenty of joy and happiness. Chart your health branches, and aim to get A's and B's only. You will love it in so many ways. And so, once again, eat well, exercise, sleep, and have plenty of sex. Life will reward you daily. And when you are elderly, you'll collect the jackpot.

19

The Science and Technology Evolution

TIRED OF CHASING AND SPEARING animals for food, a genius gave us a light: the trap. We still needed to chase the animals and use spears and rocks to kill them. We realized the danger was still there, as we needed to come close to the prey. The brain of the cautious guy ran in circles, and ... voilà! The sling! A decent size of rock released from a sling has a deadly speed, especially when it's released after good momentum. But the original sling was rudimentary and invented poorly, and it was very inaccurate. Clearly, there was a problem. Well, we found the problem and fixed it, and ... voilà! Science was born! And it brought a sling with a pouch.

Soon after, science married technology. In less than nine months, innovation and diversity were born to honor the science and technology family tree. That tree was about to shame the jungle. Only humans could climb it and monkey around from branch to branch. Our ancestors drooled in astonishment and then bowed to us, probably very jealous.

Now hunting can be done in the thickness of the forests or in the open wild, from a safer distance as well as a close encounter, with less danger and greater accuracy. This translated to an increase of variety, safety, and productivity. And right next door were the stones, smiling right at us. They wanted to help. We approached and found out that they had way more to give than what we ever thought possible. And for that came the Stone Age.

How dearly we embraced it, determined to never let go. We created diversified kinds of stone weapons and objects to fit our needs and pleasure for millions of years. Ultimately, the invention of firearms and shotguns gave us the incredible supremacy in the jungle. We then organized a meeting with all other animals, especially the ones that had been looking at us as a delicious meal, including the lions but with the exception of the chimpanzees. The agenda of the meeting was to set the record straight, and so we spoke.

"Right here and right now, we're beginning the journey of infinite discovery and innovation to prove our supremacy over all species, current and upcoming. All you can do is watch us leap into the abyss and bring lights that eventually will make us invincible and immortal. We humans have just begun to rule forever and ever, until … well, until robots and other things or creatures take over, as the product of our greatest creation or shameful regret."

This last note is a reminder that we find ourselves too busy enjoying the benefits of science and technology, and we don't pay attention to the crazy evolution and side effects, which have brought drastic consequences to humanity.

Sooner than we thought, the evolution of science and technology took a fast pace while we walked. And it has left us behind, unable to ever catch up before its next move. Let's not even mention military science and technology, whose evolution left the fast pacing to jogging, to running, and now flying. The reality is that every time we pay close attention to science and technology, we find ourselves wondering if they are friends or foes.

Friends or Foes?

Some things are hard to identify as friends or foes, such as science and technology. To be fair, science and technology are both friends *and* foes. And they haven't changed their character or behavior with evolution. They innovate current reality to bring better, easier, safer, and faster, while they stay on constant lookout for new areas of improvement. We developed a trusted relationship with them. We never doubted their power to make our lives easier and to empower us to venture into whatever dreams we happened to pursue. Although wealthy people see more benefits in their luxurious lifestyles and get wealthier as they embrace science and technology, in general we don't have any problems opening our doors for the science and technology evolution, which is a good thing because they would burst our doors and get in. The millennials simply adore them, as they should!

If it wasn't for creeps and scumbags marrying their evil to science and technology, we would be enjoying the thrill of life brought to us by the evolution. If you have doubts, just look around. I am sure you can find plenty of reasons to join the crowd, take your hat off to science and technology, and shout, "Hallelujah!"

In the meantime, we know that for each action, there's a reaction. To everything beautiful, there's an ugliness. To each tall, there's a short. To each side, there's an opposite side. And every good host has a bad counterpart, whether visible or not. Aside from the actions of the bad guys, science and technology spit out malice while acting on their good deeds. And there's no other way. We can only learn to live with such malice because science and technology are not going to stop their interesting journey. With each step they take, evolution follows. We must be ready to open the door when they knock and adapt to the new reality they bring.

In the early 2000s, a shoe distribution center in Brockton, Massachusetts, was prospering with the minimum help of technology. Yet even better days were on the horizon and soon reached the company. Joseph, the shipping manager, was getting dizzy and frustrated in the new world to which he was forced to adapt. He was falling behind. Fed up with the disrespect of the employees and higher management, he walked up to the president's office and demanded an explanation. He was surprised when he was told that he was lucky to have a job.

The company had installed a conveyor-belt system in the warehouse. Receiving and shipping were now computerized, faster, and more efficient, doubling and tripling the amount of the daily transactions as compared to before. It was lots of headaches and reprogramming, but it was all part of what any innovation goes through—lots of corrections until perfection or acceptable performance was achieved. Joseph wanted to go back to the old ways of doing business, which he believed would get rid of all headaches. Millions of dollars were spent on the new system, and the results were already great. Joseph was out of luck and in danger of losing his job. Eventually, he adjusted to the new ways but not without resistance. Eventually, he was no longer needed as a manager.

Whether the science and technology evolution are a friend or foe, resistance to it is a losing game. A smart move is to open your doors, let them come in, and then stay alert to the windows of opportunity they open. Or just ride along with extreme caution because everywhere we go, science and technology have taken over. It can hurt many aspects of your life, especially finances and leisure time. We know that the world is all about the internet, video games, smart devices, and apps. The smart devices, getting smarter and more useful, cost more with each new release. As soon we find ourselves happy with what we have, we hear that a new version is out and is much cooler and easier to navigate, and it has many more features than ours. And the advertisers have made us realize that we've got to get that. It costs $800, but there's surely a good deal out there, maybe even one that comes with a free phone. It's astonishing the number of millennials who work two jobs in order to pay almost $400 a month for their smart devices and a car equipped with smart devices.

Now that we've made sacrifices or done something stupid, yet to be regretted, we want to enjoy our new toy as much as possible. We go online all the time and everywhere. Every two seconds we send photos to our friends about insignificant things we find interesting. We update our profile picture every other day. If our work is hands-on at all times, and we are concerned about company's spying games, we painfully wait for break time to search for the next funny video or a sex video that YouTube or Facebook hasn't removed yet. We check for pictures or videos of chicks with impressive boobs or amazing butts. We rush to watch a hacked celebrity sex tape or pictures of a celebrities wearing see-through clothing with nothing underneath. While we enjoy all of that, our thoughts fly back and forth to what's waiting for us at home—video games or more Facebook, Twitter, Snapchat ... These have become our best buddies with special treats. We engage until it's time to go to bed and start a new day. It's fair to say that, sadly, the science and technology evolution quickly are taking over our lives.

How Do We Benefit the Most?

Many factors, such as a thirst for new, cool, different, fast, furious, and exciting, means that youngster don't feel the chill from the science and technology evolution. That could be scary. In June 2016, the British voted on the Brexit referendum, which determined whether the UK would leave the European Union (EU). The young voted no to Brexit. The elders voted yes. The young adored the freedom to travel without visas among the EU members. This was fun and exciting at all levels. It increased the cooperation and opened opportunities in so many venues. The elders, on the other hand, saw the EU as a drag to Britain, which now had an obligation to the outside world. Bailing out the country members in financial trouble was one of the obligations the elders didn't like. And the greatest problem, as they saw it, was immigration. The fear of an increase in crime and concern about job losses and social benefits triggered by the free flow of immigrants pounded the elderly, who don't give a damn about business opportunities, social development, and cooperation. They give a damn about social security, security of the country, and prosperity of the nation. All of those were, in their minds, hindered by EU membership.

This split is natural. Youngsters are careless, and elders worry too much. We're here to meet in the middle. That means working together for the greater good and to better ourselves. We are not going to get equal and same benefits. Complaining about any side effects is a drag to the advancement. Therefore, we must be on the same page in order for us to take the most benefits from the science and technology evolution.

Youngsters, don't just sit there and enjoy the glory in your hands. Use it to put yourself on the path to becoming an entrepreneur or someone able to make heads turn for what you've achieved and helped others to achieve. Move beyond users to become great participants, inventors, and creators of the new toys. A look ahead tells us that it is mandatory that you empower yourselves to take charge now and proceed with caution toward tomorrow. Pouring your faith increasingly in the hands of science and technology as the sole leader of your destiny is like the blind walking without a cane or guide dog. You need to be in charge.

Seniors, you can use the same strategy. Use the apps and other tools to monitor your heartbeat, blood pressure, sugar level, and so on. If you have time, play games to keep yourself engaged in challenges, physically and mentally. Now is the time to give it all you've got, not to slow down because you see the finish line.

And to all of us, let's watch our pockets and use science and technology to spring us ahead in whatever way possible, regardless of our ages or generation. We must evolve too so we can reach greater heights. In fact, in considering what science and technology have given humanity, it's clear there's not a mission we can't accomplish.

20

The Angels of the Land

DURING OUR CHILDHOODS, WE DIDN'T quite understand the concept
of divinity and its mystery. And it got even more puzzling when we
were told that God is the omnipotent Creator of everything, the
angels are God's family members, and that they know more than
Mom and Dad. (It was hard for us then to believe there could be
anybody better than Mom.) But in the end, we accepted what we
were told and felt safe, protected by God and his angels. As we grew
older, this mystery was no longer mysterious.

Down on earth, we have impressive forces too: families,
government, education, and employers supported by many little
angels, such as friends, society, and nature. Each one alone is the
very tool we need for our success, and as a whole, they are a jackpot.

Our families are the first guide to put us on a path to success.
The government provides infrastructure, security, and safety, as well
as a vision and inspiration throughout our route. With those in place,
our path is pretty much smooth, all the way to our destination. Then
comes education as the greatest tool to turn our dreams, wishes,

and desires into reality. Last but not least comes employment. Our families, government, and education push us far, but we need a job to advance farther and reach the destination, the materialization of our dreams. This is to say that we need the support of everybody and everything in order for us to complete our journey successfully. And fortunately, we have them.

You may ask, "If angels of the land are that great and promising, why do we live in pain and suffering and watch most of our dreams go down the drain?"

Here's the answer: Many things are the contributing factors to this mishap—misconception, too much of a good thing, and the crowded market are some of them.

Misconception: Unlike angels of divinity, angels of the land aren't here to drop miracle packages at our doorsteps or to flip a finger and there we have it—all our dreams turned into reality! By contrast, angels of the land demand our full commitment and hard work before we can indulge in the harvest. We don't seriously respond to this demand because of the following:

Too much of a good thing: Too much of good thing is bad for you. Let's get this out of the way. You, part of Generation Loser, are consumed by "easy does it." The side effects make you laid-back, which in turn locks down your wit, wisdom, creativity, and grit. God used to give us lemons, and we made lemonade to hydrate ourselves. Now God's giving us lemons, water, and sugar, yet we're dying of thirst. As a result, you fall behind.

Crowded market: Science and technology advancements bless each new generation with innovation and new tools for excellence. This widens the windows of opportunity as it allows more people to jump on the wagon of success. In a crowded market, everybody scrambles for the best bargain. If you leave your shopping in full faith of the angels of the land alone, you will go home with the cheapest product for the highest price. That's not a bargain; that's a bad deal. My grandfather's philosophy would serve you better.

Grandpa inherited a fair amount of farmland. Kids and adults were constantly trespassing and taking some of the crops. One day Grandpa saw a bunch of kids on the property about a quarter mile from our house. He uttered all kinds of blasphemy and threats to them. He was really heated.

Grandma, a living angel, said, "Paul, don't you worry. God will take care of them."

"Rose, God is very busy. He doesn't have time to take care of everything!" Grandpa shouted furiously at her.

My grandpa was one of the people who believed that God is there for us if we are there for ourselves (Put your hands on; I shall help you). Like millions of people, I too believe in that philosophy. But regardless of philosophical principles and taboos you may despise, in order for you to see and feel the empowerment of family, government, education, and employment, you must be proactive, energetic, and focused on taking care of your business.

This is the twenty-first century! You are no longer the only convenience store in town. If you don't stand up to the competition, step up your games of innovation and quality control, and sparkle in your customer service, for example, your competitors will take all your customers. You don't wait for the government to lock up all thieves and shoplifters or wait for your family to watch over your business. You hire security experts to prevent theft in your store.

We have no control over our families. Mom and Dad and brothers and sisters can do pretty much what they want. As a matter of fact, when they laughed at our complaints and demands, we had to suck it up. They could've been careless about our future, and there would have been nothing we could've done about it either. The government does one out of ten things we ask and nine out of ten things we don't ask. And there isn't much we can do other than shouting our anger, which is little more than cursing to the wind.

There are many other phenomena in life that escape our control. On the other hand, higher education is hard and costly, and employment is poor, but they are the angels of the land, and we can control them, even if partly. They illuminate our paths all the way to the end. But to be victorious, we must walk the walk. Talking the talk will not take us there.

It doesn't matter who you are or where you are. There's not a single dream you cannot turn into a reality when your commitment and determination join forces with your family, government, education, and employment. These angels of the land rule in every country. They spread their wings widest in USA and significantly in other developed countries. But even in the darkest corner of the world, you can still be a star if you are in for the sacrifice now and rewards later.

Make no mistake: If you are neglectful, the lights and caress of the angels of the land can become darkness and flames of hell. You will be crushed on things while you're burning to ashes, slowly. Take advantage of your time to excel. Ride on the wings of the angels of the land. Soar high and fast. Worry not about tomorrow. And speaking of the devil, how does tomorrow look?

21

The Future

"THE FUTURE IS A REALITY of our imagination." That's not true; future is real.

"The future is the time we don't have time for." That could be true.

"The future is an extension of today." That's not necessarily true, but it deserves some credit.

"The future is the prospect of prosperity and happiness." I like this one. So should you. Things are always quite awesome when wrapped in happiness.

The simplest and most accurate definition of the future is the time that lies ahead. Well, the time that lies ahead is never left alone because we want to know how it will be. To be full of happiness is the choice of everyone, but we have different approaches to future. Some of us wait until the future is here and then deal with it. Others want all the clues so they won't be visited by unannounced nasty surprises (and this sounds like a smart approach).

From a personal perspective, the future is a vision of ourselves, our families, and the world in a time to come. It can be as near as tomorrow or as distant as fifty years from now. Usually, we take a quick flight to yesterday, analyze our current living conditions, and focus on possibilities available to make our dreams come true. The future! It definitely means different things to different people. It means business! And regardless of what your definition of the future is, we are somehow driven to focus more on the distant future: retirement. Hopefully we have a house of our own, and we will live happily for a hundred years. No work, no worries, just lots of fun and leisure. Well, retirement, more often than not, is what we didn't expect. It begins with the need to stay working. What we earn for retirement through social security doesn't cover our needs in retirement. The cost of living will increase, among many other factors that make us work during retirement. On the other hand, robots and automated services have already reduced the importance of human intervention and skills significantly. The older we get, the greater is our chance of losing our jobs, and the harder it'll be to find another job because of age discrimination (Don't believe that age discrimination is unlawful.)

Living the American dream is harder as each day goes by. Our sons and daughters could find themselves renting all the way to the grave. Taking care of us or even giving a handout is out of the question.

Right here and right now, close and personal, we are speeding toward the future. The next day is coming like a couple of hours after now. The next week is coming like the next day. And what they bring is not encouraging. It seems that something isn't right if you check news and don't find that people have been discriminated against, mistreated, abused, stabbed, shot, bombed, or killed. It seems that something isn't right if you don't hear terrible news about school shootouts and stabbings that have left children, youth, and teachers dead—or that police brutality has brought demonstrations to the streets. With this perspective, the future is nothing other than the continuity of the drama and tragedy of the past and present.

But that wouldn't be a fair description of a future that frightens our retirement with impossibilities, stress, frustration, and depression, on top of high blood pressure and a weak heart, lungs, and bones. A fair description of the future would include the projection of both bad and good of today.

The Threats

The government: Despite the fact that we, the people, elect the government, the government stands in the way of our success with its laws, rules, and regulations that in many cases make no sense but must be fully obeyed, or else we face the penalties. If we live in a country with oppressive political regimes, the government controls and quarantines our powers, even when we do our best to obey the laws. We're no more than a servant with little room to breathe. We can dream big and have extraordinary skills and possibilities, yet we're going nowhere fast. Worst of all, our government could be doing a horrible job, where corruption and bureaucracy poison the already small room for us to breathe.

Personality: You could have inherited a learning disability, disease, or bad temperament. You will then face a hard time in school or even not go to school at all. Your temper could land you in jail for a long time, and you might be an outcast after you're out. Your criminal record will fog the road to your success until there's zero visibility. The world's empathy toward the disabled continues to increase, but the reality of life hasn't done the same.

Illiteracy: If you are illiterate, your life is a complete disillusionment, as you're deprived of the means to achieve any significant goals. The internet, in its supersonic speed of globalization, is knocking down all conventional ways of life. If you're illiterate, you are clearly living where the sun never shines, and your bed is made of thorns and dry ice. To make matters worse, illiteracy may be considered to be just about any education below a college degree. Who can afford a college degree nowadays?

Unemployment: There just are not enough jobs to meet the demand. People are working during their retirement. Rich and poor countries are still suffering from the 2008 unemployment crisis triggered by the housing bubble. When you're lucky and have a job, your income barely covers the basic needs—in many cases, it doesn't—because the wages are very low, and raises are insignificant and not mandatory. If you get a raise, inflation and intruders of life will suck it up in a flash. And when you put all your time at your full-time job, there's no time left for a part-time job, or all you do is work. God forbid you get laid off!

Science and technology: Science and technology have been the worst enemies to those earning a living through hard work. They continue reducing the number of people needed to perform any duties outdoors or in the office, and they demand that we stay updated and ahead of the game. Even when we are somewhat secure, our pay could be reduced due to science and technology help.

But their threats to our success don't end there. With our lives entirely online, we can wake up any day to an empty personal or business bank account or in debt by thousands of dollars because of credit card fraud. Our history may vanish entirely as a result of identity theft, and we have no place to go, due to a cyberattack that has shut down the operations of our workplace.

Competition: As population growth continues to rise, so does the number of people ready to replace you, your product, and your service. To that, add competition not only next door but globally. And then there is the threat of big giants like Walmart, Home Depot, and Lowe's forcing the little guys to close the doors.

Poverty: Poverty has been man's worst enemy. It savagely whips us throughout life, depriving us of all means of success. And worst of all is that getting out of poverty happens to be a battle of impossibility. It's quicksand sucking us down unmercifully until we're gone; a twisted mind that ties us down with wire and wraps us with an acid blanket before the whipping with barbed wire. There's nothing like "Floats like a butterfly and stings like a bee." There's only Tyson hitting us like a truck at lightning speed. No place to run, no rope to lean on. Poverty is simply the worst kind of unmerciful serial killer on steroids, loose for the longest time, and no one knows how to tackle him. Every day, more people fall into poverty for the longest time.

Relationship: Something so wonderfully crafted to sparkle an infinity of amazement has been in a rapid decline, thanks to the human quest for self-destruction. No one is interested in tying the knot because the odds aren't good. When the knot gets lucky, it soon will be set on fire by cheating or the frustration of endless stupid arguments. The female is a winner-take-all. If there are children, the mother embraces the nightmare of raising them without the father at home, and the father embarks on a journey to hell.

Health care: We can be the wealthiest people in the world, in possession of all the powers in the universe, and yet live in anguish, pain, and suffering if our health is poor. The killers here happen to be the hundreds of things that can sicken us fast and badly. We continue polluting water, land, and air. We are increasing pathogens and creating the perfect environment for viruses to flourish. The ability to travel anywhere, faster and safer than ever, considerably increased our chances of getting sick and dying quickly. If we dodge death, we will live with hospital bills to hurt our pockets for life. It's like we live in a sickened environment, where diseases and illnesses tie us down, and we let health care costs whip us left right and without mercy.

Ageism: One of the worst problems of ageism is physical decline. Although this decline is a natural process of aging, physically we become weaker. Mentally, we become less sharp. Our bodies and minds perform poorly. Our health is poor as the immune system weakens. We might not get sick more often, but when we do, we'll need stronger medicine and a longer recovery time. We are whipped by our decline of physical power and by sickness. Either one alone takes a big toll on our productivity. When they attack us simultaneously, we are worthless. Say we are suffering from arthritis and disk problems, and a bad cold rushes in to join the party. Ageism hinders our means of survival, and it makes us dependent all around when we need independence the most. The trend will worsen as our elderly get older. This much we know. What we don't know or don't think of is that our lifestyles, combined with our poor diets, smoking, consumption of alcohol, and drug abuse, are accelerating our aging process. The time when we're elderly might arrive at our doorsteps by the time we're forty-five years old—and with it, weakness of all kinds.

The Opportunities

Ageism: The beauty of ageism is reflected in the large amount of experience it has. And experience is a great competitive edge that translates as confidence. We can't ignore the saying "Been there, done that." It's obviously not by chance that we store memories of all kinds. One of the purposes is to help us do better the next time. This is in us. We avoid what gave us trouble in the past and embrace what helped us thrive. The older we are, the greater our scope of experience. Don't be shy about using memories as the powerful tools they are to solve any problem the future dares to throw at you. Use the extra power in you to shine in the future.

Health care: The science of medicine has come a long way. Many diseases and illnesses that robbed people of their power and lives are no longer threats to an individual's means of prosperity. In fact, many diseases are no more. The ones that still prevail are kept under control so we can stand strong to pursue our happiness. A few visits to the hospital can fix any health problems we have. In many cases, a trip to the pharmacy or doctor's office will get us on our feet in no time.

Relationships: The sayings "It takes two" and "Two is better than one" should remind us of the importance of relationships. For a very long time, relationships were a means to raising a family. The husband was in charge of providing for the household. The wife was in charge of raising children and fulfilling her husband's needs. Times have changed, and so have relationships. Now husbands and wives are responsible for the family providence and nurturing. The wife doesn't feel burned out by the responsibility of raising ten or twelve kids because the husband steps in to do his share. A large family, however, is no longer the model. The wife aims for economic independence, and this relieves the husband from financial stress as they work together to make ends meet. They also collaborate on all projects. So playing your cards right, settled down with the right partner, means a double opportunity for success.

You couldn't have asked for better!

Poverty: Of course, poverty stinks. And that gives us the opportunity to bring some deodorant to it. We do that by understanding that we have infinite room to improve. We will move from poverty, to middle class, to upper class. The process brings lots of thrills. Each day is an opportunity to find something new and different because the road ahead is long. There are people with means to help us make use of our talent. The music industry is one example. We know about many rappers who rose from the ashes of drug on dangerous street corners to become millionaires. We know of many who made it to stardom, thanks to the video they posted online, showing their singing talent. There are numerous similar stories. So use the poverty that surrounds you to develop your talent. Then bring your talent to people looking for you, or bring yourself to where you want to be. Any time you look hard, with determination, you'll find sweetness in bitterness, light in the darkness, and strength in weakness.

Competition: As long there's competition, you'll never have a dull life. When you're directly affected—say you're running a business—competition keeps you searching for ideas to beat your competitors. This searching keeps your brain in constant activity. The genes of creativity love it! And it rewards all with the ability to live as young minds in pursuit of new frontiers and, therefore, completely engaged in life. Indirectly we benefit from the competition because it brings us a better quality of products and services for cheaper prices.

Science and technology: We should praise the human curiosity, imagination, and creativity bugs that are always pushing us into breaking-to-fix and creating something new, better, and more powerful. Science and technology continue turning ordinary individuals into extraordinary people. It has made millionaires and billionaires overnight and made life easier and more interesting for everybody. There's not a single dream we may not dream; there's not a single dream we cannot turn into reality. Whatever our dreams are, science and technology will make them a reality. Wherever our destination is, science and technology will take us there fast, safe, and sound. There isn't a place on earth we haven't gone because we couldn't. Our products and services can be seen and purchased worldwide. And from our grandmother's basement or our father's garage, we can ask the world for help with our projects, if online posted videos aren't enough.

Everywhere we've gone, science and technology have stood up right next to us with their smiling faces, telling us that all we need to do is make a wish. We're on a daring mission to colonize other planets and to shake hands, hug, and kiss interplanetary aliens, thanks to science and technology.

Employment: To be unemployed is to have an opportunity to find a job. What a nightmare that is from a negative perspective. On positive notes, we can get the job we want because the branches of employment have increased. We may have to make adjustments to our current situation, but if we need a job, we'll find one. If we play to win, we'll get ourselves a nice reward. Also, the means to start our own businesses continue to expand.

Education: As life marches on its daring journey, dramatic changes follow us each step of the way. Education has taken an important seat in human interaction with the highly technical and industrialized world. Hats off to the governments that have made it mandatory for everyone to get an education. Governments and schools help us earn a higher education through grants and financial aid. Colleges, universities, institutes, technical schools, and free online courses are there for our education. There is not a single field of expertise for which we won't find schools. And we don't need to worry about being unable to understand a course or two because with so much information online, we can go there and get help. (If there's a question, there's an answer online.) Adding a fat diploma to our natural-born skills means becoming an invincible power.

Personality: In the past, if we were born with physical or mental disabilities, or we evolved to be bad-tempered individuals, so many doors would be closed for us. Today, this type of misfortune is an easily manageable obstacle. It sure puts some resistance to our advancements, but it won't make us turn around and go home as sore losers. In fact, we can take a seat at any table, play hard, and take the prize home because we are an opportunity ourselves. Whatever tools we need to achieve excellence, the world has them. As long we're in for the challenges ahead, the sky is the limit, no matter who we are.

The government: With the exception of the countries of oppressive political regimes, the government has security, safety, infrastructure, laws, rules, regulations, and policies as the means for people's prosperity. It cooperates with other nations through policies, treaties, and other forms of cooperation to open doors for our success at home and abroad. Remember globalization? Despite the bad reputation, each day more nations become better friends.

Taking all factors into consideration and projecting their evolution on a threats/opportunities scale, a plate is definitely tilted toward threats. Opportunities are the big winners. The future looks good, but looks could be deceiving. To avoid disappointments, you need to take action and make your dreams come true. Any threat is changeable to opportunities, and any neglected opportunity will become a threat. All the warnings are not enough. Therefore, let's look into some things that can be both threats and opportunities so we can stay ahead of the game.

Back to the future: Whether it is wired in our framework or evolution engraved it in our DNA, memory is a file cabinet where we store our experiences. We go back to it to retrieve whatever file we need. And we don't even need a password—our computer never signs off! This way, we lose no time in accessing the files. Hundreds of reasons lie behind the creation of such files. We needed to be able to recognize faces so we could distinguish our families from strangers, friends from enemies, and threats from nonthreats in the jungle. We also needed to recognize places so we wouldn't get lost. Our file cabinet also allows us to resuscitate great memories that give us satisfaction and boost our desire to store more great experiences. On the other hand, it allows access to bad experience so we can avoid similar experiences as we move on in life. Indeed, we should give far more respect to memory and take better care of ourselves to minimize the chances of any memory lapse or Alzheimer's disease. An individual unable to recognize the past has no present or future.

In our mundane venture, back to the future is usually brought to us by old friends and schoolmates we haven't seen in a long time. This short revival of old times is usually filled with memories of bad behavior, pranks to friends, and traps of boys and girls, especially the ones we didn't like. Then we go on with our lives since we left high school. There's a chance that many of us will fall for the temptation and commit a sin by lying about what we did and didn't do and what we have and don't have. Human nature!

If our current reality doesn't measure up to those of our friends, we are hurt right away. To make the matters worse, we always see our achievements as minuscule compared to those of our friends. Frustration, anger, and a sense of failure can take over to the point that we wish to simply die. But here's the thing: This scenario is a human condition. We all go through it in almost the same way. We could have greater achievements than our friends through the sweat of our brows and our wits, and we'd still see ourselves as the losers of the team. We forget that our friends could have more to show, but it could have been earned through undignified ways. Or it could be that our friends have beautiful houses, but they are going through hell to pay the mortgage. They could have debt to their necks, a relationship in hell, and no life underneath it all. Or she could be the wife sleeping with all rich guys in town.

If you ever find yourself in this situation, remember that not everything you see is genuine and earned with honesty. What's earned through cheating and sneaky ways is a score that doesn't count. But regardless of the circumstances in which your friends have shown a greater achievement than yours, you should stay on the high ground all the time. Don't allow yourself to be victimized. In fact, even if you have been a slacker, keep your head up, and don't show what you don't have or tell false stories to make yourself look good. The best for you lies ahead. Also, don't come up with excuses for your poor performance, and don't allow the dust of "back to the future" fog your road to success. If you want to avoid this back-to-the-future ordeal, stay ahead of the game at all times. Take control of your life all the way. As long you're trying your best, there shouldn't be any reason for a guilty feeling of any kind.

Now, whatever your reasons for going back to the future, it's a trip you make to the past in order for you to understand how much more you can achieve in the future. It shouldn't be a source of frustration and the sense of being the underdog. Many of us have left home in pursuit of a large happiness, and things turned out to be not quite so adventurous. Many of us have taken wrong turns that took us to a lost world. We went through unpleasant experiences and faced outcomes that were undesirable. None of these realities should affect your drive or act as a pushback. They should mean a mandate for your thriving in the future. Refuse to accept the deceptions of back to the future. Find what seems to be a threat, and avoid it. Relive the thrills, reflect on poor performances, and then prepare for a greater achievement in the future.

Building the nicest memories ensures that a trip back to the future will always be pleasant.

Sneaky future: Sneak future is like a magician who shows up unannounced to our doorsteps and then uses its magic to get in the house. It doesn't bother anyone, nor does anyone bother it as it uses magic to keep us unaware of the destructive power already at work.

When you are a young adult who refuses to accept your responsibilities, and instead you fool around and become a parent at age seventeen, or you are a twenty-year-old in a relationship with problems you should be facing twenty years from now, you have been visited by sneaky future. Drugs, alcohol, and cigarettes are some of the sons and daughters of sneaky future in slow motion, giving us initial pleasure and satisfaction. Before we know it, we are addicts at twenty-three, living a messed-up life—for life. At forty-seven, our health complications (physical, biological, and mental) are worse than those of a seventy-year-old. We're ahead of our time in a bad way. The sneaky future has pulled its magic trick on us, and we fell for it.

The opposite side of sneaky future, fortunately, comes with a bag full of treats. It brings a desired future close to us. It puts us ahead of the game. For example, our parents have saved enough to pay for our full college or university tuition, or they have the means to support 100 percent of the cost of our higher education, whatever it is. Or our first ride is a brand-new car of our dreams; at twenty-five we have our own house. The sad part is that, unfortunately, only a few of us are that lucky. The rest of us are left with the responsibility of bringing this side of sneaky future to ourselves. Remember, though, that we have what it takes, and there are plenty of opportunities.

Self-Inflicted Wounds Defeat

When you stand in front of the bathroom mirror and say, "Oh my God, I look just like my father! I can believe how fat I am. I hate my life, hate myself, hate everything … life sucks," you are singing off-key and out of tune. In fact, your song stinks. You will not have a pleasant day when you fill your sunrise with such negative input.

You know that the world is mean and dangerous. You need to act smart to dodge the bullets flying from every direction. How can you dance all day if you wake up in the morning and shoot yourself in the foot? It is not rocket science to understand that if you have a nasty breakfast, you will throw it up in a couple of hours and ruin the chance to venture out that day. You can see the future right in front of you. When you have your favorite breakfast, however, you've filled your soul with joy. Kill the morning gloom and doom with a few punches in the air, shoulder shrugs, or push-ups. And as you get the blood flow going, stretch your legs and lower your back with a few squats, or do whatever lifts your morning spirit. Approach the mirror, look at the guy or girl in front of you, and say, "I am powerful, and I know it. I am beautiful, and I see it."

Those are the kinds of songs you need to sing. They are in the right key with the right notes, and they bring a broad range of listeners because they sound nice to the body, mind, and spirit. You are guaranteed to have a pleasant, fulfilling day, and you'll look forward to doing the same the next day.

Fear Nothing

There are two sides to everything, the good and bad. You must recognize both and stand by the good side. But the future is not just about your selfish view of life in the distance, covered with a blanket of warmth and happiness or tormented by human stupidity. The future is much more than that. And we need to understand it so we can avoid a nasty surprise, and stand on the winner's side. We cannot realistically talk about tomorrow without a trip to yesterday, a reflection of today's reality, and a projection of the trend. If we do that, we will conclude that we are going to have a continuation of calamities and bad things of the past hanging out in the future. That includes corruption, wars, natural disasters, racial discrimination, and other social problems, such as robbery, murder, domestic violence, poverty, obesity, and a health crisis. And the current chaos doesn't inspire any confidence in the future. In fact, catastrophic events today are driving us to a desperate future, where everything is brutally doomed to ashes and is fast approaching a knockout, an overnight invasion of a plague, or a large fireball that makes humankind experience the bad luck of the dinosaurs. But we shouldn't worry about a thing. Chaos, tragedy, human brutality, and uncertainty happen to be part of the phenomenon that has moved with us from one day to another, one generation to another, one millennium to another. Catastrophic events triggered by humankind or an act of God touched base every now and then. We've survived and continue to learn as we go, and we prepare for the next. We've prevented many catastrophes, and we'll do better in the future because good always overtakes bad.

So, if you think the American dream is no more, China is taking over, and the end is near, you are definitely on the pessimistic side, forgetting that as the bad keeps getting worse, the good keeps getting better, leaping to the best, leaving the bad to catch up. You are also forgetting that pessimistic people see impossible obstacles, while optimistic people see endless possibilities.

Regardless of how dark and ugly a reality looks, there is always a light and a beauty to discover. And then there is you. You are the North Star—a winner of greater power by birth. When you combine your greater power with greater opportunities, you become invincible. With invincibility comes endless possibilities! There's not a door you can't kick open. There's not a dream you cannot turn into reality. Sure, the shaken confidence of today jeopardizes the success of tomorrow, and that makes us chose to huddle in a cozy corner instead of venturing out with confidence, but fear nothing— not even fear itself. Conquer the world, enjoy the thrills of life that are meant for you, and match yourself to who you truly are. And remember that the future is what you make of it.

And by the way, while the Chinese and others are building their dreams, we, the Americans, are conquering the universe.

22

The Call of Duty

USUALLY, WE DANCE WITH LIFE, trying to enjoy every moment of it. We go with its awkward twists and turns and spins. We sustain mild cramps and the embarrassment of some flaws and falls. We don't complain because we know that such things are part of the fun. Only when the dance turns sour and the pain becomes unbearable does the questioning begin.

"Why me? What did I do to deserve this? Life sucks" or "Why is my math teacher so gay?"

Yet for some reason, we never ask, "Why was I born? What's my purpose in life?"

From the labs of science, there was the black hole, then the big bang theory, then the universe, and then the single cell or the microorganism, and then the finest product of evolution/ revolution—humans. And from the house of theology, we are God's children, his greatest creation, doing whatever it takes to survive, enjoy life, and reproduce before the game is over for good, for flesh and bones and the soul flies to its eternal life in heaven, paradise, or hell.

On whichever land someone stands, we humans are the special creatures on planet Earth, carrying unique skills that help us accomplish the mission we carry within. And this should answer all the questions we have about why we are who we are. We find ourselves so busy and entangled by life's demands that we forget to reflect on our mission. We have no time to look at the blueprint we carry within for the construction of the castles meant for us to build. We definitely need to be more engaged in our inner selves. But are we really special creatures on a special mission or just ordinary planet Earth occupants, allowed to live, reproduce, get old, and die? Well, let's look into it.

From birth, we are totally dependent on others. We receive the love and care from our parents, relatives, and the world unconditionally. Day and night, our parents and relatives are our closest heroes, and the world is our good friend. As we grow, our independence genes wake up to slowly spice up the party. We begin to crawl, use furniture and house appliances for support in taking our first steps, and demand attention to our wishes and desires. When our wishes and desires are "Access denied," we fight ferociously, using the most powerful weapon we have—crying. And then the big one comes: the fight to feed ourselves by ourselves. In the beginning, this task is very awkward. From the plate to our mouths, only a tiny bit of food will survive the insignificant trip. But we don't care. When the spoon is snapped out of our hands, we definitely care. If crying doesn't do it, we refuse to take the food. Fortunately, someone comes to our rescue, allowing us to make as much mess as we need to, while we try so hard to master this rope of feeding ourselves. Fortunately, we get better with practice. The call of duty has begun to take a stance!

From here we move to touching everything we get our hands on, brushing our teeth, opening the stove, washing dishes, and so on, to only find fierce resistance and tender slaps on the back of the hands as punishment for our disapproved behavior. But we don't stop. The next day we are even more active, more daring. Then we move to building things. First, we copy others, but soon we build our own. Unknowingly, curiosity and "breaking to fix" kicked in as the contributing factors on this road of potential discovery. And it all falls within our uniqueness. We're born with different skills so we can bring different flavors to the world. But there is more.

As soon we're able to ask, the questioning begins. At some point, our question is about our origin. But whatever way the questioning comes, we know that we desperately want to know and understand. And we ask only because we don't find the answers ourselves. The questioning originates from our interaction with the wonder of it all. We don't ask why we have a mom, dad, uncles, aunts, brothers, sisters, cousins, and friends.

We might not ask why there are roads and pathways, trees, rocks, soil, ponds, lakes, rivers, oceans, badlands, forests, meadows, mountains, flatlands, day and night, rain, snow, brutally cold winter, glaring sunshine, and scalding summer days, or why there are clouds and why humans are intelligent and yet so stupid. (At that age we can't realize that humans are intelligent and yet so stupid.) But if Daddy or Grandpa takes us to front porch for a chitchat or for a walk to the barn, around the block, or to the park under a beautiful, clear starry night, we are going to ask why there are so many stars and why they are so small, bright, and far away. And if a shooting star puts on its lightning speed show, we have won the jackpot!

I don't remember asking any of those questions, but my grandpa told me that once I asked how I was born. He answered that a plane flew by and dropped me on top of the tallest and largest tree of the island, about four hundred yards from our house (That answer, as a matter of fact, instilled a flying bug in me.) Everybody probably has a story related to their childhood questions.

On one of my trips to the store with my son Carlos on a clear starry night, when he was about five or six years old, he told me that he knew a lot about stars.

"I am going to be a scientist, Daddy."

"Sure, Carlos!" I said as I cuddled his head briefly in a gesture of support.

A lady who overheard us said in a low, tender tone, almost whispering, "That's good. Encourage him."

While we continue on the quest of knowing the wonders of all wonders, our childhood questions are due to the sense of purpose we're born with. We realize that we're surrounded by mystery and that we need to know as much as we can. No other creature possesses such a gift and responsibility. Yes, we really are special creatures on a special mission, not just ordinary planet Earth occupants who are allowed to live, reproduce, get old, and die. And this is greatly empowering! It gets even better when we internalize our mission and take the first steps toward accomplishments.

The Expectations

The line of expectations begins at insemination and ends after death. Unborn children are expected not to give the pregnant mother a hard time. Children are expected to be angels. Teenagers are expected to be respectful to their parents, siblings, and society, especially the elderly. Adults are expected to be successful, rich, and famous; to help parents, siblings, and family; to respect the culture and the family tradition; and to marry and raise a family by the rules of good citizenship. The elderly are expected to have quiet final years, be as independent as possible, and leave a nice inheritance— cash and assets—for their descendants. The ghosts are expected to leave us alone.

As soon as we have enough brain development to understand life, we expect that the entire world is there for us until the game is over. Therefore, each of us has expectations ingrained in our souls. "What's the big deal?" you may ask.

The big deal is that almost all expectations are big obstacles in our answering the call of duty. We almost always try our best to meet expectations as part of our call of duty, which we dearly want to answer proudly, until we get hit by unfair expectations, the consequences of falling short of expectations, and the above expectations.

Unfair expectations: Unfair expectations are dreams or demands for which we don't have the necessary means to turn them into reality. And what makes unfair expectations so unfair is that regardless of the factors involved, the blame is thrown at the players. Say a signal bulb in your car has just blown out as you're driving in a snowstorm or torrential rain. You get a finger and threatening beeps from other drivers because you turned left without your blinker on. Or maybe your parents expect that you will become a lawyer, doctor, or superstar, even though you're living with them in deep poverty, and you suffer from learning disabilities. Or your boss gives you an impossible forty-eight-hour turnaround on an assignment that requires extensive research for its completion. And there's more: The parents of criminal adults will be blamed for bad parenting, when in reality the crimes committed by their sons and daughters were induced by schizophrenia or other brain imbalances.

On top of all that, unfair expectations are almost always rooted in behavior modifiers where we must act above the standard. We don't always have what it takes to act above the standard. They also drop large sandbags on our shoulders.

Be smart and understand and learn to live with unfair expectations. Most important, make sure they don't fall in short-of-expectations' arms, where the punishment is harsher.

Short of expectations: Short of expectations means a mistake, a failure. Two haunting words everybody wants to dodge—because our culture insinuates that mistakes and failures make us weak—are "shameful loser," a polite name for those who didn't make the cut. No one wants to sit at that table to play with shame, frustration, and disappointment and then face a long line of serial killers carrying improvised torture instruments, ready to chop, slice, and dice.

The boxing fight between Floyd Mayweather and Manny Pacquiao on May 2, 2015, was a long-awaited event, considered to be the fight of the century. It turned out to be an okay fight for some but a very disappointing match for most of the fans. Mayweather did what he had to do to stay undefeated and continue on his journey of beating the world record, which has been held by Rocky Marciano. He thought that scoring another win would be good for him and his fans, only to realize that he came out short of expectations. He even had to respond to those who thought he was scared of Pacquiao. Meanwhile, Pacquiao had to justify his loss. Apparently, his mistake was having confessed that for months, he had been suffering from injuries before the fight, which made those who placed bets even angrier and demanding refunds. It's clear that anyone who makes up to $200 million in less than sixty minutes must show blood, sweat, and tears, which Pacquiao was ready for.

Tiger Woods's adventure outside marriage cost him in sponsorship, sex rehabilitation, scrutiny of fans, and an expensive divorce. Football players, TV hosts, news reporters, and many others have lost their jobs or gone through a hellish period as a result of behaviors considered unacceptable;

To some people, George W. Bush goes down in history as one of the worst US presidents. Barack Obama's election raised the hopes for an unified world, where blacks and whites shared the same table, ate from the same plate, and drank from the same well. The lower end of poverty in the black community envisioned black poverty being lifted up. Ironically, Obama almost lost a second-term election, and racism revived its ugly face in America in many ways, especially in police brutality and killings of black residents.

Famous people take the harsher punishments but everybody's victimized when they come out short of expectations. To avoid the slicing and dicing, we aim to be the best. And that's all good. It brings the best out of us, but let's watch for the side effects. Any time we come out short of expectations, we feel like losers. We drop our chins and walk slowly away from the crowd. Digesting the bitterness of disappointment, we quickly disappear from the area. If frustration and anger don't kill our determination to continue, we vow to prove, by whatever means necessary, that we are not losers. This is a bad move. It flips us from the land of losers to above-expectations' lap. That's like coming out of an oven right into a frying pan.

Above expectations: Whatever definition we give to above expectations, it comes down to a result that exceeded what people had expected of us. In this case, above expectations is a good thing, not a hellish venture—at least it should be. Above expectations is a fast line of delivery, a danger zone, where the flames are hot, high, and intense, and it's almost impossible to go through without getting a severe burn. We have Facebook fake "Likes" for advertisement purposes; corporations showing adjusted performance numbers; job seekers lying on their job applications; and people borrowing their friend's car for a date and making false claims about their finances, education, and employment. At about seventh grade, we tamper with test scores, and we forge signatures. People have gone through a great deal of health complications by using sexual enhancement pills in trying to perform as a sex machine.

In sports, cheating stood strong as an illegal normalcy. Teams, individuals, and countries were accused of doping. Lance Armstrong confessed to his doping but wouldn't consider it cheating. His justification was that everybody was cheating. Russia was accused of government-sponsored doping, prompting President Vladimir Putin to order that his country clean up its act (even though President Putin is, in the eyes of the world, guilty as charged).

It seems that we forget that what makes cheating games stupid, especially in sports, is that sooner or later, the truth comes to light. We lose credibility, and trophies and medals are taken away. And we'll bear the shame and health consequences, or we even might die.

Trying to being above expectations in the automobile industry has robbed us of many souls. The above-expectations tragedy in any area can strike hard and worldwide. In fact, the world continues to suffer the consequences of the 2008 US housing bubble, which pushed the world into recession.

Does any good come from this dangerous territory? Of course! Every time you aim to be above expectations, you gear yourself for a better-than-average performance. This is greatly appreciated but only when our actions are rooted in the strength of our power. Be wise and a pure winner, rather than a hero standing in the shadows of disingenuous glory. And most important, don't kill yourself or change your true nature in trying to meet or go above the expectations of the world. Keep in mind that for your call of duty, your personal dreams, wishes, and freedom won't take center stage alone. You must take the expectations of the world into consideration. In the end, as long as you stay focused on being the best you can be, your call of duty will be the greatest.

Answering the Call

The call of duty is a split road we have to travel simultaneously to get to the merging point victoriously. On one road, we carry our dreams, wishes, and desires. On the other, we carry our obligation to society. Both require our full attention. When we default on one road, we screw ourselves up. When we screw ourselves up, we automatically default on road number two. When we default on both, we have failed to answer the call. When we fail to answer the call, we didn't make the cut. And that sucks. But what's the point, and who cares?

Simply put, call of duty is a responsibility that every creature is born with and bears until death. This planet and the creatures on it make life what life is. And whatever life is, it includes a share of responsibilities among all living creatures, born and created. Sure, there are times that life whips us so hard that we don't want to play anymore, we don't want to count anymore, and we wish we could go back into the womb and stay there forever. Unfortunately, once we leave that dark, wet land, there's no quitting, no deserting, no going back. There's only embracing the mission, the call of duty. Besides, we are all in this—one for all, all for one. And you're not about refusing to live your dreams or allowing yourself to become a dead weight, carried around by others. You're about to shine like a North Star. And you know that action is your costar. You understand that your call of duty—personal and common goods—comes with challenges to face and circumstances to respect. This is a nightmare for the Generation Loser, especially the millennials, but we we're glad to hear that you're well prepared and have understood that and embraced commitment, determination, and perseverance as your strongest tools. You're ready, and we like that!

The start: With the regard to the time you should start answering the call, there are two phases to consider. The first phase begins at insemination and continues until we can be in charge of something. During this period we don't have much of a sense of responsibility, and there's not much expected of us, other than to be a good unborn child and a good kid after birth. Fortunately, we succeed at it, for the most part. Phase two, restrained by many factors such as education, personality, culture, and era, is the real deal. Once we begin high school, our answering the call of duty should start (even better if it's earlier). By now we understand the score: A-plus is excellence. Excellence should be our middle name.

In the meantime, whenever you start answering the call, don't leave the language of power.

Monday to Friday is the same. Monday doesn't suck, and Friday is not the greatest. Every day is equally a challenge that ends at paradise. Make every day count for everything, and everything count every day. Warriors don't pick days to fight or chose days to rest.

This language of power is your empowered voice to warm you up for each next step of your journey, guaranteed to stay ahead of the game in your call of duty. Once you listen to it, you won't ever be a dead weight in someone's backpack, or a fly taking a free ride on a jet headed to China and annoying people throughout the flight. You carry yourself and your backpack on your own wings to wherever you want to go, and you take others with you. That's how you answer the call of duty. Don't fool yourself! Answering the call of duty is not an easy responsibility, but don't fear the challenges. Even if you are a lone soldier, there are enough hands that will reach out to you, offering help.

The Helping Hands

One of the greatest helping hands in call of duty is the head start. Your siblings give you guidance and advice, protect you from danger, and help you find your way around. And if your parents have done a good job, you will not waste time deciding what you're capable of delivering. They will have paved the road for you. Say you are born with sports skills, a great singing voice, or amazing acting ability, and your parents enrolled you in after-school activities in those fields: You've been gifted with a head start. Your foundation is strong already. And if your country has the tools you need for a good experience throughout your life, you've just doubled down on the benefits of the head start.

Another great head start is a legacy, although legacy comes with a side effect—the obligation to protect it. Say you are a son or daughter of a rich and famous family, governed by high standards. To enrich and expand that legacy becomes your responsibility. This could be a troublesome road for you, especially if you want to live without compromises. But if you're in for the challenges, legacy is a truly great head start in your answering the call of duty, and it demands nothing in return. You could turn this head start into one of the greatest helping hands.

Monkey see, monkey do not: We have seen many of our schoolmates spending time in jail for vandalism and other stupid behavior. We have seen many of our friends with their dreams on hold and going through hell because they became mothers and fathers before finishing high school. We have seen actions that prompted people to lose their jobs, get a divorce, or bear the shame. Any of these shadows of death can greatly hurt your potential to answer the call of duty. By simply avoiding any of those actions, you empower yourself.

Inspiration: Exceptional individuals could be born with skills to spring them ahead of the game more than you. Answering the call of duty for them could be as simple as drinking a glass of water. Unfortunately, we all must answer the call of duty. We are going to take the exceptional individuals as our inspiration and use their strategy—obedience to their parents, family members, and good friends; big dreams and a determination to never give up on their quest of becoming the brightest minds—to become an inspiration too.

The one: Helping hands can come from the places we least expect. The world, our country, friends, family, and pets are always there for us. Each one offers distinct support. In the meantime, the greatest helping hand that has ever existed lies where we would never imagine. We get up with it, go everywhere with it, do everything with it, and go to bed with it for a good night's sleep. It is there in sadness, and happiness, in sickness and health, in bad and good times. It's there until the moment we are no more. The one, our greatest helping hand ever, is us. Only we know our true powers and how we want to fulfill our dreams, wishes, and ambitions.

Staying true to yourself at all times is the best way to answer the call of duty at your best.

My grandpa wanted me to be a well-educated, distinguished individual to prove that Arlindo, the priest who rejected the idea of grandparenting, was wrong. Upon my junior high graduation, my father, who wanted me to be a teacher, advised me to think about employment. In 1986 the minister of the Department of Youth offered me a full scholarship in Cuba, Russia, or Yugoslavia in social and/or political science. (I might have accepted the offer if it had been to the USA.) They all hit the wrong note, except for Grandpa.

I am not a distinguished individual, but I have achieved a fair level of education, not by walking the walk someone wanted me to walk, but by walking the walk I chose to walk.

Everywhere you turn, you see individuals delivering their best because they are doing something in an area where they dominate. The opposite happens when we answer the call of duty by the choice of others. This doesn't mean you can only deliver what has been given to you by destiny. "If I am stupid and illiterate, I ought to lay low" is true only if you want it to be. First, we're all winners from the very beginning. Second, if you feel that you're just an ordinary individual, you can use your ordinary powers and transform yourself into an achiever of extraordinary goals. If a first-grader teacher, mechanic, landscaper, carpenter, or burger flipper is all you can be, for example, you can still do what you do like no one else can. And you can empower yourself to enter any field and play like a most valuable player or better. You give yourself whatever destiny didn't give you and achieve excellence. God didn't forbid you from seeking what you don't have, nor does he abandon those who help themselves. He blesses them. This is to say that whoever and wherever you are, you can be what you want to be. In the meantime, never let go of the fact that nothing beats the blooming of your natural-born skills. You are the coach, player, team, and fans. You run your game, you score, and you celebrate your victories. You earn the appreciation of the world because you understand your call of duty, and you respect yourself as the best helping hand of all.

Every generation is criticized for something. The Generation Loser/millennials are criticized for lack of vision, creativity, and self-determination, as well as for being ready to fall for "easy does it." There's a lot of truth to that, but you carry greater power and stronger helping hands than all generations before you. You just need to bring out the warrior in you, and take your greatness to the highest heights and make the world shut up. Then enjoy the outcome. The doors of opportunity will open, one after another, and everything will fall easily into place for you. When you're the best student in your school, for example, you are granted a full scholarship. Schools fight over you. Businesses offer you employment before you even graduate. The best of the best girls and or guys walk your way. Your family, your country, and the world is proud of you. So don't aim to be a good mechanic; be an engineer. Not a teacher but a professor; not an airline pilot but a shuttle pilot. Since the call of duty is something no one can escape, you might as well answer it to the best of your ability, no matter what it takes.

A great success individually is collectively an invincible team.

23

Time

THE COMPLEXITY OF LIFE IS mind-boggling. As smart as we've become, we haven't decoded half of life's mysteries yet. It's good that we've been trying hard. It's also a blessing that we realized that the wonders of life are infinite and that we're determined to discover as much as we possibly can. Time is amazing in the way it drives all creations, especially humankind.

The Bible states that God created everything in six days. The other, from science, states that the big bang, born about fourteen billion years ago, is the origin of everything. Whether only one claim is right or both are, since the beginning time was one of the major factors of our existence and understanding of the past, present, and future.

Approximately 4.6 billion years ago, planet Earth emerged without life. It welcomed the first life (single-cell life) 3.8 billion years ago. About 2.8 million years ago, we were born. We have yet to find out why all the greatness of all lives lie in humans and why it took so long.

Our genes of curiosity allowed us to tamper with time in many realms. We can change crops' harvesting time and speed up the development of birds and animals. Transportation is fast but going faster. In order to have better control of time, we've divided it into a millennium, century, decade, year, month, week, day, hour, minute, and second. Our fascination with time may lie in the fact that time brought us here, and time will take us out. All our actions must respect time; our success and failure are measured by time. Time made us understand all times, so we can live in our time, while we have time. In the end, everything depends on time. We are going to take time to talk about time because Generation Loser couldn't care less about time and Generation Winner seems to have fallen through the cracks of time. All of us ought to understand and better respect time, or we will end up as despicable losers. And so, let's dig in!

On Time

"On time" splits into three parts: (1) to our parents, (2) to the government, and (3) to us. Our success and failure depend on the job done by the trio. Gymnastics, piano lessons, singing classes, and martial arts instructions are beneficial to us at any time we try them out. Starting them on time brings greater benefits throughout our lives, as we have time to explore and exercise our potential thoroughly. Unfortunately, we have no control over this time; our parents do. And how well our parents will do their part depends on how well the government does its part. If the government is a tyranny, where people have no political participation, it could choose to have no gyms in the country and incarcerate anyone who tries to open one. If the government's corruption keeps poverty high, then our parents could have no chance to enroll us in any activities that contribute to our great brain-power development. Education comes to mind as one brain-power development that must begin on time.

Had you waited until you were ten years old to start kindergarten, your learning ability would have been diminished.

Whether or not our parents and government could've done a better job, we must try our best to be on time. We're now in charge of our time management. To be on time for life is wonderful and has many benefits for you. When you leave your house on time to go to school, to work, to church, or to a doctor's appointment, it's almost guaranteed everything will go smoothly. No anger, rage, or frustration in trying to make it on time. You will be at peace with yourself and the world. Any task that awaits is a piece of cake for you. Be on time, all the time.

Late

During my first three years of school, I had a few schoolmates much older than the rest of the class. There was Elias, who was seventeen, in second grade. We would make fun of him until he started hitting us. The adults teased him all the time: "Elias, are you the teacher?"

But starting school late has other consequences. One of them is the difficulty in learning. It's as if our brains punish us for being late. In general, any activity we start late has consequences and drives us to failure. Starting intensive physical activities, such as boxing, martial arts, and gymnastics, after middle age is very hard or impossible for most people. Your heart and lungs, joints, and bones are weak, and your reaction and reflexes are slow. Waiting until you are fifty years old to have your first child is not a wise move either. There could be a severe complication during birth, and you could lack the time and ability to play with your son or daughter.

To be late is to be a loser. Let's get this out of the way and never be late.

To better understand "late," let's marry time to opportunity. The two walk a fine line of a relationship. One sneezes; the other gets the cold. One takes the punch; both feel the pain. Separating them means that you've allowed windows and doors of greatness to close on you.

According to some, you should not sweat over being late because what can't be done today can be done tomorrow. Good things come to those who wait, and arriving late is better than not at all. I support those philosophic principles. They are, after all, empowering. The trick lies in how to use them as empowerment in time. Nowadays, if you lose a great opportunity, you have lost big. If you are thirty years old and working on your GED (general education development, equivalent to a high school diploma), or you're a forty-three-year-old, single, and living with your parents, you are divorced from tons of opportunities. You're also far, far behind the game. Teenagers of Generation Loser can easily be victims of opportunities lost for being late. Here's an example: When you finish high school and take a break for one year, you're walking toward troublesome roads. That break not only has the tendency to prolong itself for few years (in fact, you could end up not going back to school at all) but also makes your mind lazy. Also, you could be very happy with the money you are making and the fun you are having with friends without worries of school assignments. Almost certainly, you'll keep on pushing going back to school farther and farther into the future. Time passes, and your friends are moving up with their higher education while you keep falling behind (and probably don't notice it). In four years they are ready to join the task force of their dreams, while you haven't started your higher education yet. By the time you finish, lots of opportunities will have passed by, and the ones to come could not be as promising.

Now, you could have tried your best to be on time but still be late. You could feel shackled by frustration and disappointments, true symptoms for the condition. That doesn't mean you should curse life, hate yourself, or give up on your dreams. Sure, you have lost opportunities, but opportunities are endless. Weigh your possibilities against your time, make the necessary adjustments to your course of action, and then lace up your boots and tighten your gloves for a rough round; you must win this one. You might not finish strong, but you'll be still a winner. After the victory, change your attitude to never be late in life. Start building good habits and respect the ethics of staying ahead of the game.

Always be ready to seize the opportunity and enjoy the moment.

The Right Time

The government is a master by heart in the game of the right time. It holds or speeds up the work on issues, especially sensitive and/or controversial ones, depending on how the wind is blowing. Immigration issues are not talked about much until crime rates in that group skyrocket. Gun control is not touched until there's a school massacre, mall rampage, or cinema shootouts.

Businesses lie right behind the government. They don't sell winter clothing in summer, nor do they boost ice cream production in winter. Obviously! And last but not least is us.

When we're working on our favorite car that has no air conditioner, we will not put it on the road in summer.

For the most part, we act instinctively at the right time in most aspects of our lives, and as a result, we're successful without struggle. We need to join our preconscious with our consciousness.

Teenage, adulthood, and elderly are some of the human development phases we'd better deal with at the right time. By the way, the right time is the cousin of on time, deserving equal attention.

The Timing of Time

Timing is like a time within right time. So there you are, on the roof, with your target in sight. You don't pull the trigger immediately.

You wait for the perfect moment to do it. Or you are twenty-five years old and holding a good job, engaged for nine months, with the wedding scheduled one year from now. Six months later, your parents get in a bad car accident, and as result, your mother is paralyzed for life. Shortly after the accident, your employer announces layoffs and your name is on the list. You have the right time to get married, but your timing is bad.

The Movement of Time

Time is a self-driven train of one speed for good and bad days, sunny or rainy, hot or cold, day or night, in the United States or Russia, at the bottom of the ocean or up high above Earth. We cannot make it slow down so we can catch up, nor can we stop it so we can be ahead. Understanding its movement helps us plan, organize, implement, and control our movement in order to achieve our goals in the year, month, day, and hour we aimed for. We grew up to be aware of the movement of the time, and we depend on it. Yet we don't seem to be able to synchronize it in a way that we get the best of our time. We definitely need to do better, especially the youngsters. It's important that we understand the wagons pulled by the train and beware of their contents; they could kill us. Here they are:

Lazy time: We are trapped by all kinds of communication and entertainment devices we carry with us to everywhere. Watching television, playing video games, online social interaction, and after-hours outdoor activities are all good in many ways. These activities are fun and relaxing. We can never be sick of fun and relaxing, but we must be aware of the dangers and traps. These powerful, hypnotizing forces of lazy time increase the time we do nothing. The consequences include the neglect to call for a doctor's appointment or an oil change to our car or postponing fixing a faucet leak because they don't seem urgent. These little things may not seem urgent now, but they can turn into big problems later. Embracing laziness can turn us into losers. Generation Loser is all about things that are energetic, fun, and interesting, so they realize very late that lazy time is making them a loser in the game of life.

Wasted time: Wasted time is a shadow of death that comes unannounced in many ways, shapes, and forms, with bags of chocolate bars, cookies, candies, chips, and bottles of sodas. It sits right next to us with a smile and warmth, while it sets a nice trap that kills us softly. Oh yes! It brings pleasure and satisfaction for the moment but it takes away precious time we could be using on better sections of our lives, such as education, fitness, and relationships.

Although defining wasted time is hard, due to its subjectivity, forty-five minutes of gossip about your coworker who's sleeping with her bosses is an example of wasted time. Four hours of video games, three hours of online chat, and wandering around the mall for three hours because you're bored are some examples wasted time. Wandering at the mall is actually expensive wasted time. Define what's wasted time for you and walk away. "Time is money" is philosophical, and we should respect its principles. Generation Loser is definitely not hearing this, which is the main reason for their failures. Would you please listen? Let's enjoy our time as much as we can, making sure that none of it goes to waste.

Time flies: We're surrounded by realities that remind us that action is the main ingredient of any dish we want to cook. In fact, the action in our heads is one of the phenomena that differentiates us from other animals. As soon we understand time, we manage our activities to fit in the time—say, day, week, or month. But suddenly, the agenda is not completed, and we don't see where the time went.

Also, when we reflect on shocking events of the past, we are surprised that it seems like the O. J. Simpson trial, the 9/11 attacks, and death of Michael Jackson were yesterday's news. When our beautiful daughters celebrate their sweet sixteen or our sons celebrate their eighteenth birthday, "time flies" releases its knockout arrows that fly straight to our hearts to fill our souls with the joy of accomplishment, as well as sadness at the realization that our little angels moved way too fast to adulthood. When we're trying to fit a doctor's appointment, picking up the kids after school, a car inspection sticker, making lunch for the kids, and getting ready for the Bible study, time flies (except at the traffic lights; red stays forever). "A minute ago I looked at the clock, and it was 2:45. How in the hell can less than a minute go by but the clock now shows it's 2:57?" you complain. "Time flies" became real and frightening. It could've made you run through red lights, blow a stop sign, or take chances that result in accidents.

And last but not least, when we're engaged in something energetic, fun, and interesting, time flies.

Time flies every day, everywhere, and all the time. We must make our action follow the time in order to have something accomplished in a timely way.

Time of the time: The movement of time is driven by a variety of factors, such as the economy, ecosystem, society, and science and technology. Our ancestors of ten thousand years ago had only a few items on their agenda—probably hunting, fishing, sharpening the hunting tools, and clean up the cave. A small world, a small life, probably rich in happiness, peace, and harmony.

Industrialization and commerce took the main stage of the economy, with money as the main survival tool. We had to chase cash wherever it went. But that reality brought enrichment to our lives, which in turn has its own demand. The head of the household has a lot more on his agenda now and difficult roads to maneuver. Just the normal daily demands create an agenda almost impossible to complete. The exponential population growth, combined with the new way of life, rob our time and redefine life. Let's not even mention the distraction brought to us by technology through smartphones and devices.

We're truly living in a time that's faster than all times of any previous generations. The sad thing is that this fast-paced time gives more trouble that satisfaction. It leaves us frustrated and behind the game, as we find ourselves unable to catch up to time and get things done.

Time and space: Everywhere we go, time is the same; each day is twenty-four hours, each week is seven days, but there's a distinct time movement between an industrialized city and farmlands. In rich industrialized countries, time is faster, in general, and yet slower in the suburbs than in big cities. Rich countries are industrialized nations producing goods and services for the whole world. Massive production is necessary. Speed is an important part of the process. Also, life's demands are greater. You get bills to pay, children to drop off and pick up, gym, yoga classes, and so on.

A lawyer from New York married to a Portuguese woman tried three months' vacation in the Azores as a test for future permanent residence. He didn't last two months—not busy enough. By contrast, farmers hate big cities for being loud and crazy; people and time move at a hundred miles an hour, and stress kills people there.

We are the product of our time and space. Adapting to new time and space always brings a hard challenge, but we must adapt and go on with our projects, or move to someplace else more suitable for our desires and objectives. The quicker we can understand what the movement of time does to us, the better the chances of making adjustments to our course of action.

The Time We Can and Cannot Control

How early we get up and go to work, school, church, or movies; how long we play video games, soccer, basketball, or any other sports; how fast and for how long we drive, eat, or walk in the park are some of the activities in which we are in total control of time. When we are in control of time, we are in control of our destiny. This allows us to move along with our plans without pressure, which gives us the opportunity to perform our duties with less stress, more concentration, and high probability of achievement. We should embrace the time we control to allow our power, grit, and wisdom to shine. On the other hand, being stuck in a traffic jam due to road construction or a fatal accident; waiting for a ride; standing in line at a cash register whose credit card machine stopped working; or lying in a hospital bed after a stroke or heart attack are some frustrating realities of time we can't control. They make us feel trapped, disempowered, and behind the game. Since we are forced to spend a lot of our time with the time we cannot control, it's our responsibility to understand its dynamics and find ways to act smart and dodge the frustration they bring. For example, driving through a busy downtown during rush hour is never a good idea.

The Time You Must Bury Alive

The time we must bury alive is a poisonous, double-edged sword that swings very unmercifully as it slices and dices without reserve, prejudice, or discrimination. And it is color-blind. On one side there's the poison of regrets, and on the other, there's the poison of the trauma of failure. And here's how both sides slice and dice:

Regrets: We curse ourselves because if it wasn't for that party where we got drunk and got involved with those people who later became our spouses and threw us into relationship hell, destroyed our lives, and killed our dreams, we would be rich now. If it wasn't for that stunt in the park that resulted in a detached retina, we would have had the chance to become an astronaut. If it wasn't for that unprotected sex, we wouldn't have been parents so early. If it wasn't for the betrayal of our best friends and the snitching of a coworker we trusted dearly, we would be happily married and hold a job with great pay.

It's fair to say that acts of God, human barbarity, and our stupidity give us tragedies and bitter experiences. And it's quite understandable that we get upset about a catastrophic experience but only to an extent. After all, we stand here as a result of the good and bad events of the past. We can indulge in sorrow and anger brought to us by flaws and the disappointment of a regrettable past and become a loser, or we can focus on our developments and achieve excellence. The second choice is the best.

You see, letting the sentiment of unfortunate actions take you to the land of regrets will simply destroy your life. You'll climb the largest thorn tree and move from one branch to another until frustration brings you to exhaustion, and pain knocks you down. And now you're bleeding to death, inside and out, because you let regrets be a painfully vivid memory instead of a buried dead horse. Reach out to the land of empowerment, where the pictures are not frighteningly depressing, just realistic.

Realistically, there's no guarantee that you would be sipping gold and spitting silver if it wasn't for the wars, greed, and lies of people or the stupid things you've done. It's very easy for your mind to paint ugly pictures or write a distorted narrative of the past. A hereditary phenomenon or not, you must fight this bad behavior. Yesterday has passed. You can't change the past, nor should you mope about its failures. It's unhealthy and has the power to stop you from advancing. Put your imagination to work toward the Disneyland, and remove the self-destruct switch that's installed in your consciousness by regrettable experiences. And since no matter how bad you have it, someone has it worse than you, praise the blessing that you have, and transform it into something impressively satisfying. This is the best way to bury time you must bury alive.

Failures. We evolved by praising and celebrating success and despising, punishing, and trying to erase the failures. This is a good thing, except the way we approach it is not. Also, because failure is disappointing and unforgiving, we put it in the regrettable chapters of our lives. Big mistake! Oh yes, we get busted by this psychological denial all the time. At first, we feel angry, upset, and stressed out when we face a failure. Then we seek places and people to share the blame with. Everybody goes through this cycle in almost the same way, but this is insane! Therefore, when the outcome of your actions is not what you've expected, take it as it is, and accept the outcome of events over which you had no control. The chances are that you used your best knowledge, wisdom, and awareness at the time and acted upon your best behavior. If you didn't, consider the experience a lesson learned.

Because we are raised to be successful, the sense of failure is very painful and destructive. Remember that failure is a step before success, a measure of your determination, a leader of glory.

The time we must bury alive—regrets, failures, mistakes, negative feelings, and everything that can cause harm to our development—is the obnoxious player at every table in the casino of life. This player has powerful cards and is an expert cheater. He is as loud as hell. What he doesn't know is that you have better cards, you know all the tricks, and you're deaf to unpleasant sounds. Use your powers and stay focus on your next move, and don't ever let the time you must bury alive fog your road or bring the storm to your journey.

The Time and You

Time is infinite, but our time is finite. Nowadays our time (longevity) is around ninety years under normal conditions, but it can be shorter or longer, depending on our genes, the environment, and the way we care for ourselves.

From the moment we are born, we begin using our time. Each second that goes by is gone forever. Fortunately, each moment of our existence gives us something new and better, and we move with it to the next moment as we travel through the splits of our true time: child, adult, and elderly. We do not produce in childhood. We spend a great deal of time playing and having fun and learning the ropes. At about twenty-five, we are prepared to be productive as a fully grown adult. Done with school, we are now moving to being what we wanted to be. We have embraced our destiny and started the journey of making our childhood dreams come true. We can still have lots of fun, but we have responsibilities.

Elderly time is retirement. We are not producing much, if at all. We are now reaping what we planted and nurtured for decades. New dreams and projects have slim chances of materialization and shine. And depending on how we care for ourselves, our elderly time could be as early as age fifty-five or decades later. But even when our genes and our care allow us to be active at ninety-five, our best time is about four decades long (twenty to sixty), not birth to death. Between the ages of eighteen and sixty, we're capable of making history. But we can easily fall into the traps of life. Within that period, we see our time moving by fractions of five and tragic events. We relax at twenty years of age, sure that at twenty-five we'll be seriously serious about life. At age twenty-five we embrace the "Life starts at thirty" myth. Then we move the start date of our dreams and projects to when we are thirty-five … and then fifty-five, which got here at lightning speed, bringing a wake-up call. We are too old for many dreams.

We live on borrowed time. We ought to treat it as nicely and carefully as we can, living our lives the best we can because in no time, we are knocking on heaven's door. Appreciate what you have, even if that happens to be just the air you breathe, and then move toward the greatness of life before your time is over.

We grow up to understand that there's a time to get up, shower, eat, go to school, work, or sleep. Our job is hourly waged; our performance is hourly judged. And the more we explore science, the more we understand that scientifically and philosophically speaking, there's not a single reality that escapes time. And our journey fits in our finite time. Time is also the only master instrument for finding the checkpoints of our routes. A bush pilot knows the time she should be over a certain tree or specific landmark. An instrument pilot knows the time he should start receiving the radio signals from a specific beacon. When none of these is correct, the pilots find out what happened. The bush pilot might have missed the checkpoint—still on the flight plan or way off. The instrument pilot might have equipment malfunction—the beacon is out of service for some reason, or he is off the flight plan. For both types of flights, time is the best and crucial reference point. We should use the pilots' strategy on our journey of life, instead of walking blindly.

We know that we have three major checkpoints: childhood, adulthood, and elderly. If we're at twenty-five and find ourselves acting like a child, or at forty-three we're as weak as an eighty-year-old, we are off time. It's time to find out why, and take action.

You see, time doesn't walk, run, fly, speed up, or slow down. It moves at a constant speed by which life moves from one instant to another. The more we understand and respect its movement, the better prepared we will be in making our dreams come true on time—but rather early than late.

It is our hope that Generation Loser understands the time and finds ways to fit in time before it's too late. Don't sit down. Sip on a good wine or smoke a good joint, and fool yourself that you're young, with plenty of time to make all your dreams come true. Remember you're finite, while time and your dreams are infinite. The day we are born, our destiny starts its engine. Our finite journey takes the first step. The checkpoints of life serve us well, as they allow us to measure what we've traveled, what we have to travel, and the speed at which we should be traveling. We're winners at birth to be successful on the journey of life. Since the dreams we turn into reality in our lifetime are the measurement of our success, let's increase our respect for time and double our achievements while we have time.

24

Staying in Touch

WHEN OUR LOVED ONES ARE far away, we are under the disadvantages of distance and time, and we are prone to be victims of "out of sight, out of mind." Keeping frequent contact by phone, emails, texts, Facebook, and video chats, in particular, fuels the flames of communication and keeps the heart warm, no matter how far away and for how long. The success of any business depends on how closely the plan is monitored. Successful individuals (stars from all corners of life) take their secret manuals and rituals as seriously as a skipped heartbeat. They touch base on a strict basis. Any small slip could turn into a deadly fall, which they are to avoid at all costs. Before a shuttle lifts off, the crew knows each other better than they know themselves, and they know the shuttle better than they know their own houses. They also know where all the switches and buttons are as clearly as they know where their fingers, toes, eyes, and all other body parts are. Any new construction plan is revised over and over again to cover all the basics, including the completion date. And yet we go through divorces after wives return pregnant from an overseas vacation that we didn't go on. Reputable businesses close doors and go home. Stars become infamous or broke. Shuttle disasters still happens. And the grand opening is postponed more often than not.

The point is that we would be going through even more devastating calamities if we hadn't devoted great attention to the details of our project developments.

I believe we make good plans, but they are ghostly. Even when they are visible, they soon become ghostly because we fail to stay in touch with them. We get comfortable with keeping plans in our heads and go on with business as usual. When we wake up to a plan A or B that's stagnating or moving too slowly, we promise ourselves to step up and take the game seriously with a written plan that's kept within arm's reach, only to remind ourselves three months later that we believed our own lies. This phenomenon happens in part because we think that writing down plans and watching stuff like a hawk are some things that businesses do, not regular individuals living a mundane life. In fact, when we say that we have a plan to go back to school, look for a better job, or buy a house, we are simply trying to sound smart and decisive.

Now is time to plan, organize, implement, and control your life as big companies do. If a degree, a better job, or a house is the goal you're currently working on, you have to pour all the necessary ingredients in the pot, stay in the kitchen, and cook them until done. Only then will dinner be served. It doesn't matter how many dishes you're making; the process should be the same.

Yes, we know about the difficulties of taking a plan from its birth to the conclusion, but to be a winner, you have to know the game and follow the rules. You can remember the fate of many of your high school classmates who held off on their higher education. Their plan must've been to get a job, save, and then go to college in three years. While they waited, they indulged in the good life—party, strip clubs, nightclubs, drinking—and school now really sucks. The three-year period knocked on the door, and no one answered. Soon after, another three years went by. School is so far away now that it just is not happening because they had a plan in their heads but didn't write it down or follow the other steps closely.

Even a simple project can take forever to take off, and when it does, it moves rather slowly if we don't stick to the plan. This is a wake-up call for commitment, perseverance, and consistency, which are the main tools in every project. Hear this: Everything we do out of the ordinary is a project in itself, and it has our unconscious planning behind it.

Going to the movies next Saturday is a project.

- The plan (layout of the means): We make sure we have enough cash. We decide where to go and when to go, based on our responsibilities on that day, and then we figure out a time to leave home.
- The organization (priority of the steps): If the activities of the day include food shopping, laundry, house cleaning, and taking the kids to a birthday party, we think about ways to get them done in the best order possible. Then we decide on the best way to get to the movie theater.
- The implementation (the plan in motion): Whatever we decide to do, we make sure that we're aware of the time. If cleaning the house is taking too long, we speed up and leave some section of the house for next week. We must be sure to leave at the planned time and take the shortest chosen route.
- The control (taking care of the intruders): If the kids want pizza, we say no because we're going to the movie. If the road we picked is closed, we choose the best detour we know.

And there you have it! A project and a plan organized, implemented, and controlled unconsciously. We have it in us. We just need to take this gift more seriously, and use it on our projects more often. If it qualifies as a project, there should be a plan. Next is staying in touch with it.

Our lives are an assembly line made of many small and large sections, driven by a complex chain reaction. Paying great attention to the signs of trouble, inspecting the whole assembly line ever so often, and having it repaired with premium parts ensures its smooth operation. And the bigger and more complex the assembly line is, the greater the need to stay in touch with it. A low-grade student has a very small responsibility. Yet he or she needs to stay in touch with books and notebooks for a successful school year. The list of responsibilities for the president of United States, Russia, or China can wrap around the world twice. Each president must stay in touch with all government branches, or the nation will fall into chaos.

It is true that due to circumstances out of our control, we find ourselves failing in school, going through relationship nightmares, and losing jobs. There may be nothing we could've done to avoid the tragedy, but more often than not, we're victims of our own negligence. If we're nice to our spouses only once in a blue moon, have intimacy every full moon, almost never show love, respect, and compassion, and—worst of all—let the river take its course, we can't count on happy days until death do us part.

I was asked once, while enduring a ten-year relationship, "How come you never do it like the first time?"

Apparently, I'd fallen into complacency or lost the touch.

We can't stay employed if we call in sick many times, if we lack teamwork drive, or if we perform below standard, nor could we keep our jobs if we are excellent in January and June and suck the rest of the year. We keep our jobs and get raises by defining ways that make us productive at or above standard every day.

Whether it's education, employment, relationships, friendships, or parenting we want to turn into a success, we must stay in touch with the necessary means to take us there. We're living in new times. The stakes are higher than ever. We've reached the fastest stretch of humanity, and we're moving at lightning speed. It can no longer be business as usual that a project is done when is done. The current life's demand is such that we must empower ourselves to move from one project to another with maximum effectiveness and efficiency, while we seek areas of improvement.

A mechanic who learned by monkey see, monkey do, for example, needs to learn the fundamentals of the mechanics and computer basics because cars are being manufactured increasingly more complex, with computers doing many more tasks than before.

It has become mandatory that we separate ourselves from the crowd, breathe a bit, and make a plan to put ourselves ahead of the game, instead of relying only on our confidence that we'll always do fine, no matter what comes our way. We must be more vigilant and trust but verify more often. We must wake up our awareness about the importance of maintaining daily contact with the projects we are working on. The close contact generates interest and motivation, which lead to fulfillment. Don't leave the site of your projects, and keep reminding yourself that the river shall not run its course in this land, and its flow must be under constant surveillance.

25

Game Over

AT THE END OF ALL games, there's an assessment of the performance of the players. The final results fit in one of the three human emotions: happy, sad, or angry. If you played at your best and performed in an outstanding manner, you are surprised that the game has come to end so soon, but you feel good. Obviously, you have enough reasons to feel the way you do—happy and in a mood for celebration. You have done well and can't wait for the next game. If you tried your best but in the end came out as a loser, you're sad. It's understandable. You did, after all, try your best. What else are you supposed to do, right?

On the other hand, if all you did was monkey around and never took the game seriously, even for one day, and you didn't care whether you won or lost the games you played, anger could take over your soul for a long time. Well, that's what you deserve, don't you think? You dug your own grave.

Part of staying ahead of the game is to accept and embrace your losses. It means that you don't kill yourself with self-blame. Find the reasons why you didn't make the cut you wanted, and then instruct yourself to focus on preparation for the next games. Cursing yourself for a poor performance in a game that's over is detrimental to you. Accepting your failure with the understanding that you can do better next time is empowering and deserves your attention.

We are winners, eager for the next game, whether we belong to Generation Loser or a generation of winners. Let's honor this blessing. And honoring the blessings of the winners that we are means to accept the final result of our game, whatever that is. There's always another game to play until the game is over.

Whenever you feel that your game has just a couple of dozen years to live, wipe the slate clean of failures, disappointments, regrets, and anger; color it with happy memories only; enjoy each day; and … let the game be over.

Afterword

GOING TO A SOLITARY PLACE for a moment of reflection is inspiring, soothing, and necessary for the cleansing of our bodies, minds, and spirits. There, we allow our imaginations to marry the inner self, float freely, and take us beyond the wonders. Bonded by inspiration, vision, and enlightenment, the brightest ideas come out of this phenomenal trip, to sparkle a smile on our faces and leave happiness in our hearts. But it also means venturing into turbulent currents that begin with the undeniable conclusion that life is a mild torture for many and a sacrifice for most, day in and day out. And yet such bitter realities can get much worse.

You, the millennials, sons and daughters of Generation Loser, failed by the success of your own generation, wake up every day to face new discoveries that are interesting but carry powerful distractions aimed at keeping you away from your main responsibilities. The players running the games have you in check, close to the checkmate. Your development is quarantined. Your wishes and desires have been carefully studied and recrafted. And your actions toward the achievement of your goals have been watched like a hawk. You are fed, on a daily basis, the sweet, hypnotizing poisonous pills of disempowerment. These pills work to the advantage of the suppliers whose main goals lie in keeping you confined to your comfort zone, instead of pushing you to venture into the wild, to pack experience and widen your perspective of excellence. It's fair to say that everybody has been fed the same pills as you have, but all eyes are on you, for you are the ones carrying the torch of human excellence. This scares some, for if you hold it too strongly, too high, and too wisely, you'll knock the big players—the kings, queens, and sweet princesses—off their comfy chairs, and spill their hidden glasses of a thousand-year-old fine wine, from which they take a big sip every time they fool you or rob you blind.

We, the owners of the generation of vision, dedication, sacrifice, and "whatever it takes" have been trying our best to equip you with the best fighting gear and to train you to face the beast of the kingdom, but the princesses have blinded you with their beauty and hypnotized you with the sweetness of their melodic honey voices. You've literally become the kingdom's adorable slaves.

By many accounts, including the voices of those who sincerely believe that we are moving fast to doomsday without any possibility of reversing what seems to be the curse of all curses, we found you guilty as charged; you are Generation Loser. The voices are supported by the analysis of the way we've been living for the past fifty years, with a particular reference to the last thirty years. And honestly, after a detailed analysis of our current living condition, the voices deserve some credit, except you have no time to listen to them; you're too busy overturning the verdict.

You are going to clear the hypnotizing voices in your head and honor who you are—a generation of the greatness of all greatness. You are powerful and capable of reaching outstanding goals collectively, as much as individually. When the pack slows you down, you become the lone wolf. You walk your walk, think your thoughts, and act your actions, without choosing good days to fight or bad days to rest. You move forward, aware of obstacles and prepared to go around, under, or above them and adjust your course of action, sure of the victory every day. If the shadows of doubt and weakness ever tackle your confidence, you remind yourself that if it was easy, everybody would be a warrior, and then there wouldn't be any warriors at all. You can turn whatever destiny has given you into something extraordinarily better. Kick any elephant—small, big, or giant—out of the room, and have a space to think big and bring your dreams to reality. Any time you feel shadowed by doubts, just look deeper into your soul. You'll find the strength and endurance to go on stronger. Despite the fact that you belong to Generation Loser, your life and the lives of those surrounding you are not a losing adventure. You are, after all, the greater power, and nothing can stop you from embracing your greater responsibility.

We, all of us, are the players of a special game that started billions of years ago, who became, with the evolution, the chosen ones. The special and powerful. We have achieved success in stormy times, and in pleasant weather, we have celebrated outstanding achievements. This trend prevails. We respect it and will pass it on to the new generations with the enhancement we added to it. But it's never easy.

You see—the genes of curiosity and determination pushed us out of the caves and put us onto the path of the pursuit of greatness. We faced uncertainty and increasing danger, but we didn't drop. We knew it was worth it to go on. And thanks to the first warriors, we became the conquerors. We never backed down from our quest, nor did we bow to any beasts. Great power doesn't back down. And you, the greater power, don't even know that backing down is an option, because it isn't. And that's not all. The genes of desire to create something new, better, and different mean that we always improved what we had. We got addicted to the game of excellence. Thankfully, we never let go of that philosophy, and the rewards we have received are the greatest of all. But let's be realistic; the gloom and doom, as well as our carelessness, have tremendous power to suck us down into the abyss and throw us into desperation land. And then we're all losers, except we aren't. We are winners carrying specialties from the very beginning. We are invincible warriors who transform defeat into victory.

To honor that, when you're down and desperate, take cover. Give the storm the time to go by and simultaneously plan your knockout blows. And then get up and go to work. Or when your surroundings are a losing game, and your sentiments are those of a

Generation Loser, just remember who you are and will forever be—a winner by birth—and then reach out to your powers, push the losers out of the way, and claim your trophy. Others have risen from the ashes to become inspirations. You can rise from the dead to become a superhero who defied death.

To those of us walking as fast as we can yet finding ourselves going nowhere, we can easily give in to the pessimistic assumption that our effort is a waste of time and energy, as we slide deeper into frustration and anger. The sirens of despair and cries of desperation seem to be the only songs to our ears. Maybe we should just cross our arms and legs and hope to die, quickly and in peace.

That would be a good thing if we could do it. It's too bad that we can't! We are not the fans of ugly, morbid, and depressing but the members of the invincible warrior team. It's our obligation to get out of the pessimistic corner and reach out to glory. We must continue the celebration of life when there is joy and amusement, as well as when we're in pain and suffering anguish and desperation. The bitter only gives way to sweetness. Generation Loser makes us losers only if we allow it. Let's enjoy life to the full extent, every inch of each phase, with as much love, peace, and brotherhood as possible, in all kinds of generations. Let's be the sole owners of our destiny, the sole architects of our dream castles. Let's be in full charge of our destinies and enjoy life without reservation—because we can.

And so, until we meet again in *Stay Ahead of the Game*, part 3, stay cool. This game is yours. You are alone in a crowd. You walk alone in a crowd. You follow everybody, but you have your path. You can be clear, confusing, and invisible, but you are present and confident. You are the unpredictable but the king of all kings. Prepare yourself for the journey of reading between the lines and filling in the blanks as the ultimate power for you to conquer. Yes, this game is yours!

Author's Note

WITH YOU, I LIVED, AND with you on my mind, I went to bed. In my sleep, I dreamed of you. I loved you, studied you, and concluded that I should reach out to you. About halfway into the first *Stay Ahead of the Game*, a sweet idea landed in my lap: making you the protagonist of *Stay Ahead of the Game: Generation Loser*. After receiving many comments that the original *Stay Ahead of the Game* served youngsters better, it became quite obvious that the sequel must be all about you, the young and powerful.

You are, after all, the continuity of our greatness, the flowers of our revolution, the beacon of our future generations, our caretakers and true representatives. We have made plenty of mistakes that we cannot fix, and as a consequence, we made you the Generation Loser by many measures. We apologize for that. We are afraid that some of those mistakes could weaken your powers. We also fear that you could give in to the distractions attached to the unlimited possibilities you're blessed with and that you cherish now with plenty of passion. Please don't let our pessimistic intuition be right. Keep on making us proud. Fix our mistakes, and surprise us all with the enlightenment of your talent.

For all that, I dedicate *Stay Ahead of the Game: Generation Loser* to all the youngsters, especially my niece Neiva Nadine Fernandes De Brito (Telma).

Thank you all for the inspiration.